The Sands of Windee

D1205176

ARTHUR W. UPFIELD

The Sands of Windee

ETT IMPRINT
Exile Bay

ETT IMPRINT & *www.arthurupfield.com*
PO Box R1906,
Royal Exchange
NSW 1225 Australia

This book is copyright. Apart from any fair dealing for the purposes of private study, research, criticism or review, as permitted under the Copyright Act, no part may be reproduced by any process without written permission. Inquiries should be addressed to the publishers.

First published 1931

This edition published 2017

Copyright William Upfield 2013, 2017

ISBN 978-1-925416-91-6

Chapter One

Mr Napoleon Bonaparte

DETECTIVE-INSPECTOR NAPOLEON BONAPARTE, of the Queensland police, was walking along a bush track on his way to Windee Station. On Windee Station, in the west of New South Wales, had happened something that had awakened his interest. Hence his presence in an Australian State not his own. Hence his garb as an ordinary bush tramp in search of work.

The season was early October, and summer was well begun. From a stockman's point of view it promised to be for the rest of the year as bounteous as the preceding nine months. Spear grass on the plain, knee-high and golden, rippled as a ripe wheatfield. Blue-bush and mulga gleamed with the freshness and fullness of their sap. A flock of newly-shorn sheep which had rumbled away at Bony's approach were in magnificent condition; galahs and cockatoos screamed and screeched, whilst over most of the land the fat and impish rabbit swarmed in astonishing numbers.

It was the third successive good year in New South Wales, and the wonder of it was deeply felt by Mr Bonaparte, who for two years had worked on a succession of more or less sordid cases in drought-bleached Central Queensland. Whilst walking with a bushman's rolled swag of personal necessities within his blankets slung from his right shoulder, and carrying a blackened billy-can half-filled with cold tea, the disguised bush detective hummed the immortal refrain of the "Soldiers' Chorus" in *Faust*.

He walked with the soft tread of the Australian aboriginal. Of medium height, free from impeding flesh, and hard as nails, there was yet in his carriage more of the white man than of the black. By birth he was a composite of the two. His mother had given him the spirit of nomadism, the eyesight of her race, the passion for hunting; from his father he had inherited in overwhelming measure the white man's calm and comprehensive reasoning: but whence came his consuming passion for study was a mystery.

Bony, as he insisted on being called, was the citadel within which warred the native Australian and the pioneering, thrusting Britisher. He could not resist the compelling urge of the *wanderlust* any more than he could resist studying a philosophical treatise, a revealing autobiography, or a ponderous history. He was a modern product of the limitless bush, perhaps a little superior to the general run of men in that in him were combined most of the virtues of both races and extraordinarily few of the vices.

He was seated on his swag fastidiously rolling a cigarette when Sergeant Morris, of the New South Wales police, came into view round a bend of the track. Hearing the hoof-thuds, Bony looked up, saw the sergeant's approach, smiled gently, and then completed his task. When the match that lit the cigarette had been tossed aside, the sergeant was opposite the half-caste, and was examining him from his motionless horse.

"Day!" he snapped.

"Good afternoon, Sergeant!" replied Bony politely.

"Where you heading?" the policeman demanded crisply.

"Windee"—in a pleasant drawl.

It must not be assumed from Sergeant Morris's brusqueness that he was a martinet. He was a dog who growled much and bit seldom, and over his domain, which was half as large as England, he was respected and liked. He questioned Bony, not because he was suspicious of a stranger, but because he had ridden many miles and had fifteen more to ride to his home and office at Mount Lion. Bony presented an excuse for a smoke.

"Name?" he almost snarled.

"Bony," suavely replied the half-caste.

"Bony? Bony what?"

"Baptized by the worthy missionary attached to a northern Queensland mission station with the names of Napoleon Bonaparte. You see, as a very small child, the matron found me eating Abbott's life of that famous man, and she, alas, was a practical joker."

Bony now was not smiling. The sergeant's abruptness vanished. For a second his grey eyes were veiled, and then he was off his horse and standing directly facing the half-caste, who had risen to his feet.

"Am I to understand that you are the detective-inspector of that name?" he asked. Bony nodded. Morris regarded him keenly. He looked into a ruddy-brown face made up of the sharp features of the Saxon; he gazed into the wide-open, fearless blue eyes of the Nordic; and, whilst he looked, the many rumours, and the few authentic cases, which had come to his knowledge of this strange being flashed across his mind. Sergeant Morris shook hands but seldom. He shook with Bony. And Bony smiled. The sergeant knew then that he stood in the presence of a man not only superior in rank, but superior also in mentality.

"I have one or two documents to present to you," Bony explained, "and, if I may make a suggestion, why not fill my billy-can from your water-bag and make tea whilst I hunt for them in the depths of my swag?"

"Agreed, Mr Bonaparte," the sergeant said, turning to his horse, which had been standing with the bridle reins hanging to the ground.

"If you please—Bony," urged the softer voice.

Sergeant Morris turned. Then he smiled quizzically.

"Bony—if you prefer it."

"You see, everyone calls me Bony," the detective explained. "My three children do. So does my chief. Even a State Governor and a British peer have called me Bony. Although I am the greatest detective Australia has ever known, I am unworthy to polish the top-boots of the greatest emperor the world has ever known. I often think, when the humorous matron named me, that she slighted the Little Corporal."

"He was certainly a wonderful man," agreed Morris, lighting the twigs placed around the billy. The sergeant's back was turned towards the other, yet he did not smile, although Bony's simple vanity tempted him. It was by no means empty vanity, if only a fraction of the half-caste's activities which had drifted to him through official channels were true. Then: "Are you here, by any chance, to investigate the disappearance of the man Marks?"

"Precisely. Here are my credentials."

The sergeant stood up, turned, and took from Bony a long blue envelope. It was addressed to him, and, opening it, the enclosure read:

Sydney,

10-10-24.

Sergeant Morris,

    Mount Lion.

After perusing your report on the Marks case Detective-Inspector Napoleon Bonaparte is convinced that it is more serious than a simple bush disappearance. Please render him any assistance for which he may ask. In this matter he will take precedence in authority. Report superintendent.

(Signed) *J. T. TOMLINSON,*

Chief Commissioner, N.S.W.

Placing the document in a pocket of his smart blue tunic, Sergeant Morris produced a tobacco-pouch and papers and made and lit a cigarette before voicing a comment. He was not free from a feeling of annoyance, for he had thought that the mysterious Marks case was satisfactorily disposed of. The whole affair had occasioned him much arduous labour, and if the result had been indefinite it had given satisfaction in that there could have been no other. The feeling of annoyance was engendered by the fact that his conclusion had a loophole called doubt, and that here was a man who had found the loophole and would probably disagree with all that had been done and require the case to be investigated over again. And then annoyance gave way to pleasant anticipation of seeing this noted sleuth at work; for not only was Sergeant Morris an administrator, he was also an enthusiast in the science of crime detection. The tea made, and poured into an enamelled pannikin and the billy-lid in lieu of a second cup, he seated himself opposite Bony, saying:

"Marks disappeared two miles out from the homestead of Windee Station. Rain obliterated tracks, but the surrounding country was well searched. He had a motive for disappearing. What is your theory?"

"I think it quite probable that Marks was murdered," Bony replied seriously. "If eventually I discover he is not murdered, I shall be bitterly disappointed."

Then he laughed at the expression on the sergeant's face, and went on:

"I have taken charge of perhaps two dozen murder cases during my career, and of that number only four were really worthy of my brains. As a general rule, murderers are the most stupid of criminals. Almost invariably they leave a corpse to damn them. A few murderers cut up their victims for the police to discover. Never yet was a perfect murder, but this affair of Marks I am hopeful will come near to it. Consequently I am interested. Nowadays, if there is a corpse in the roadway, or on the doorstep, or lying on the library floor, it fails to interest me. It is too simple—too banal."

Chapter Two

Disappearance of Luke Marks

"I HAPPENED to be at Police Headquarters in Sydney recently on the Cave versus Black cattle-duffing case," Bony explained in his soft, musical, drawling voice. "There I was shown your report and photograph concerning this Marks affair. Although your report was comprehensive, it failed to answer one or two obviously important questions. Your chief was agreeable to my coming, but my chief ordered me to return to Brisbane."

"And you're here?" Sergeant Morris said with faint interrogation.

"I wired my chief saying that I had come across an interesting murder case, and again asked his permission to take it up. Again he ordered me to return. Sometimes, Sergeant, I am annoyed by people thinking that I am a policeman to be ordered about like a private soldier, whereas I am a crime investigator."

Bony chuckled. Morris was frankly perplexed.

"Well?" he urged.

"I wired my immediate resignation, adding that I would demand reinstatement when I had finalized the case to my satisfaction."

As a disciplinarian the sergeant was horrified. He was acquainted, however, with the facts relating to Bony's joining the detective force of Queensland, which he did with no less a rank than that of detective-sergeant. He was badly needed in Queensland, first for his supreme tracking powers, and quickly afterwards for his bush knowledge and reasoning ability. He demanded the high rank, and his terms were granted, and within a very few years he had justified his rank and on special occasions his services were eagerly sought by and loaned to the police chiefs of other States.

One of the half-caste's few vices was a prodigious vanity. Yet this vanity was based on concrete results. His record was something to be vain of. His particular vice, however, was sometimes a source of irritation to his chief, for unless a case possessed unusual features Bony refused to take it up. For this reason his resignation had been demanded and tendered a dozen or more times, invariably to be followed by a request to resume his position when the next baffling bush tragedy took place; whereupon his superiors were only too glad to condone his indifference to authority and red tape for the sake of his unique gifts in the clearing up of crime.

"You think, then, your commissioner will reinstate you?" Sergeant Morris countered.

"Decidedly." Bony laughed gently. "Colonel Spender will turn blue in the face and swear worse than a bullock-driver, but I am what I am because I do not stultify my brains on ordinary policeman's-beat cases. Now detail to me this Marks affair. I will question as you proceed, entirely forgetful of your report."

"Very well," Morris assented. For a few moments he was silent, whilst he drew a rough plan on the red sandy ground with a small stick. Then:

"On August seventeenth a fellow calling himself Luke Marks arrived at Mount Lion in a Chevrolet car, and put up at the only hotel in the place. He gave out that he was a Sydney business-man engaged on a motor holiday trip. He said he was an old friend of Mr Jeffrey Stanton, owner of Windee Station, and would visit Mr Stanton before he went on south to Broken Hill. I saw Marks only once—when I went through the hotel after hours to see that only genuine travellers were on the premises. He was thick-set, about five feet ten, brown hair and eyes, aged about fifty. He stayed at Mount Lion two days before driving off to Windee in the morning. It is only eighteen miles, and he arrived there at twelve-fifteen. He lunched with Mr Stanton, and left at half-past two to go to Broken Hill."

The uniformed man prodded his stick into the ground. "Here is Mount Lion. Here, eighteen miles south-west of the township, is Windee homestead. To go to Broken Hill from Windee it is unnecessary to turn back through Mount Lion. The Broken Hill track branches from the Mount Lion track two miles from the homestead, going direct south-east. The junction of the tracks is ten miles from the south boundary, and about the same distance from the east boundary, of Windee.

"Six days after Marks left the homestead his car was found four chains off the road north of the junction. It was in perfect order. There was no sign of Marks. The country all about is a maze of low sand-ridges on which grow pine trees with a sprinkling of mulga.

"I was notified by telephone and went out at once to the abandoned car. Of tracks there were none, for the ground was sandy and dry, and there'd been two windstorms since Marks was last seen. Nevertheless, I organized Mr Stanton's men on a wide and thorough search, and took two native trackers from a small tribe camped near the homestead in an effort to pick up tracks near the car. The parties were out more than a week. The blacks could pick up no single tracks. In fact they knew, by the nature of the ground, plus the windstorms, that it was a waste of time looking for tracks."

"The trackers' names, please," requested Bony softly.

"Moongalliti, the king, and Ludbi, one of his sons," Morris answered.

"Had you ever had occasion to use them before?"

"Yes. Once a stockman's child was bushed. They found her, but too late. The mite was dead."

"In comparing their activities on the two occasions, would you say that on the second the trackers were loath to work?"

"Well, yes," Sergeant Morris admitted. "You see, they knew when Marks left Windee, knew that six days had passed before his abandoned car was found, and remembered those two windstorms. They wouldn't move and I can't blame them."

"Well, well!" murmured the half-caste, rolling his fifth cigarette with slim, pink-nailed, black hands. "Go on."

"As I stated, the horse parties were out more than a week scouring the country, and they found absolutely no trace of Marks. Considering the nature of the country, ridges of sand a dozen miles all round, excepting in the direction of the homestead, ridges which a windstorm—and there were two of great velocity and of hours' duration—will move several yards, it would really be improbable for them to have found any trace of Marks.

"Although it was not hot weather, Marks would have circled and circled until he dropped, and if he died at the foot of a ridge on its eastward side, the wind would have blown the ridge on him and buried him beneath tons of sand. Circle he doubtless would do, being a city man.

"To me the only mystery is why he drove his car off the track for ninety yards before he abandoned it. But it may be explained by the fact that he looked an habitual drinker, and in fact got drunk one night in Mount Lion."

"What condition was he in when he left Windee?" Bony asked.

"Well—slightly drunk," the sergeant replied disapprovingly. "At lunch Mr Stanton produced a bottle of port, and Marks drank most of it. Drink, I believe, is the foundation of the whole affair. I think he went to sleep in the car, and it ran off the road, just missing two trees, and was eventually stopped by the heavy sand. He probably slept till dark, woke up wondering where he was, and looked about for the track. Forgetting to turn on the headlights in his muddled state, he lost touch with his car and wandered away in a fruitless search for it."

"Humph!" Bony smoked reflectively.

"That was the only solution at which I could arrive," Morris concluded, "and Headquarters were entirely in agreement with me."

"How far from the homestead was the car found?"

"Two miles."

"Only two miles? Generally that distance from a homestead would be within a night- or horse-paddock, where one or more of the hands would be riding almost daily."

"There you are right. The car was abandoned in what is called the South Horse Paddock, which is only three miles square. But Mr Stanton had used it temporarily for sheep during shearing, and it had been eaten bare. So there was no stock of any sort in the paddock at that time."

"Could the car be seen from the track?"

"No. When it left the road it took a wide curve, and stopped close to a large pine-tree. It was discovered by the station bullock-driver and his mate, when they went into that paddock to get pine posts."

"On the face of it, the case is one of simple death by exposure in the bush," Bony said slowly. "That is, from your written report. My attention would not have been drawn to that report had it not recently been disclosed that Marks was a member of the New South Wales police attached to the Licensing Branch. His real name was Green. A week or so after he left Sydney several members of the Licensing Branch were examined by a Royal Commissioner on charges of accepting and demanding bribes. You will have heard of it. Green's name was brought into the examination, and he was missing. The description of your Marks tallies exactly with that of the policeman Green, and the registration particulars of Green's car are identical with those of Marks's car.

"Now the policeman Green had served several years at the station of Wilcannia as a mounted trooper. He was an experienced bushman. The day he left Sydney is known. It was the second day of his annual leave, and it was the day after he had drawn the sum of thirteen hundred and seven pounds from his bank. A week before that he had sold house property to the tune of several thousands. Knowing the crash was imminent, he realized all his assets and cleared off with the cash, and doubtless securities as well.

"You see, Sergeant, we now have a horse of a different colour. It is unlikely that Marks, or Green, would have become bushed, even though drunk. Again, we may almost be sure that he had a lot of money and negotiable securities with him. Here we have a motive for murder. Even without your photograph of the abandoned car the case would be attractive enough to me. The photograph, however, is the crowning point, the basis of my conviction that Marks was murdered, not by the bush, but by some white man."

"And you arrive at that theory from my photo of the car?" exclaimed Morris in amazement.

"Precisely," Bony said slowly. "When you photographed the car you also photographed evidence of murder which to me is almost irrefutable."

8

With obvious delight Bony watched the effect of his bomb. No less than his illustrious prototype did he revel in dramatic situations and startling denouements. His expression then was one of amused satisfaction. He went on:

"This is a case, Sergeant, worthy of my attention. I start my inquiries two months after the crime was committed. Nature has obliterated all tracks, and has had ample time to bury all clues deeply in sand. There is no corpse as a fingerpost to the murderer, as there is in nine hundred and ninety-nine cases in a thousand. Even if I find a corpse, the ants and crows will likely enough have picked the bones nice and clean. There will be no fingerprints; no autopsy is possible; and, because of all this, poor old Bony is going to have a really enjoyable time."

"But the photograph?" interjected Sergeant Morris.

"I have studied all the famous cases of murder," Bony proceeded gaily. "Murders committed in Australia, Great Britain, France and America during the last hundred years. My wife, who like myself is an educated half-caste, reads and enjoys dozens of crime mysteries expounded in modern novels———"

"The photograph———"

"In real life and in fiction as well as in stage plays, there is always a fresh corpse lying around for the detective to work on. All so sordid and all so simple to a man of my intelligence! I shall be shocked and disappointed and disillusioned if Mr Luke Marks is still living."

"Yes, yes. But what of the photograph? What have you learned from it?" demanded the tantalized sergeant.

Bony reached into his unrolled swag and produced a copy of Sergeant Morris's picture taken with a cheap camera, and handed it to his interrogator.

"Look well!" he cried softly. "You see the car. What else?"

"Nothing but the trees in the background," the sergeant admitted.

"Ah! But cannot you see in that near tree a bleached sheep-bone attached to a bundle of sticks arranged like a woman's fan?"

"Yes—I can. By gad!"

"That is a blackfellows' sign which reads: 'Beware of Spirits! A white man was killed here!'"

Chapter Three

The Boss of Windee

JEFFREY STANTON was a squatter of the blunt, downright type that lived and thrived in Australia seventy years ago. At this time, six years after the Great War, he was a living example of what a squatter should be; and, when occasion found him in the presence of our modern squatting aristocrats who reside in one or other of the cities and employ managers, he shocked them by his manners and horrified them by his generosity to his employees. As was his morning custom on weekdays, he left the large "Government House" at half-past seven and walked along a beaten path skirting a deep water-filled hole in a now otherwise dry creek, to reach finally the men's quarters.

Although he would never again see his sixtieth birthday, Mr Stanton's movements were springy, his body was still lithe and supple, and beneath his white pent eyebrows scintillated searching grey eyes. Here was a man raised on the back of a horse, not on a cushioned seat behind a motor steering-wheel.

The men's quarters were situated on the creek-bank, shaded by gnarled box-trees. Outside the weather-boarded, iron-roofed kitchen and dining-room, flanked by the cane-grass meat-house and a huge iron triangle supported by two posts and cross-beam, he found a number of his men awaiting their orders for the day. Seeing him, the men ceased talking, and, seeing them, Mr Stanton paused, scratched his head, and looked vacantly at the cook, the picture of a man trying hard to find jobs for a pack of useless loafers. At last:

"Morning!"

"Morning, Jeff!" several replied in unison.

"How were the sheep doing in the Seven-Mile, Ted?" Mr Stanton asked a stalwart brown-bearded man, dressed in white moleskin trousers, a blue shirt, an exceedingly old felt hat, and elastic-sided riding-boots.

"They're settlin' down—settlin' down," came the drawled reply.

"Well, you settle down into that saddle of yours and look 'em over again. We can't risk them weaner ewes getting hung up in a corner. When you've got 'em broke in properly to find their way to water, you can have a day's drunk in Mount Lion on full pay."

Mr Stanton smiled grimly. Ted looked sheepish, but pleased, and moved away to the horse-yards. The boss glared at another rider, slim, agile and swarthy.

"Better take a ride round Hell's Swamp, Joe," he ordered. "Water should be dried up and swamp probably boggy. Alec can go with you. Engine going good at Stewart's Well, Jack?"

"Not too good. Something wrong with the governors," answered a man who was cursed with an atrocious squint.

"Humph! Archie, you go out to Stewart's Well and overseer that engine. Take the small truck. Bill, Mrs Poulton wants wood. Fetch her in a couple of loads." Mr Stanton turned to a young man of perhaps twenty, fresh-faced, and written all over him the word *Englishman:* "Take the big truck into Mount Lion and bring out a load from Hugo, the storekeeper. When you come back I'll smell your breath, and if I smell whisky you're sacked. Whisky and petrol won't mix."

Four remaining men were given their orders for the day, and although the work set them, as well as the others, would be done easily by two o'clock, they would not dream of asking for fresh orders, since Stanton never gave orders twice on the same day. For perhaps nine months in the year the average daily hours of labour would not exceed six, but during the remaining three they might well average fifteen. Lamb-marking and sheep-shearing are busy seasons. Fires and floods call for incessant labour, and that labour is cheerfully given on the old principle of give and take.

Half-way back to the "Government House"—so-called because a great station is governed from a squatter's home—Mr Stanton met Bony.

"Are you Mr Stanton?" asked the disguised detective. "I am sometimes. The last time I was called 'Mister' Stanton was by a stranger two months ago. My name is Jeff Stanton. Up here we are out of the Mister Country."

Bony's face remained immobile. Stanton's grey eyes examined him keenly from head to foot. Bony said:

"I'm looking for work. Is there any chance of a job?"

"Work!" Stanton suddenly roared, the blood surging up behind the mahogany tint of his skin. "I lay awake half the night thinking out what in hell I'll give my men to do the next day, and you want to keep me awake another half-hour! Things are bad." His voice rose. "What with the politicians and the taxes and the price of wool, I'm that close to the rocks that a cat's hair ain't separating us. What can you do?"

The question was shot suddenly at Bony, who, had he not been prepared by Sergeant Morris, might excusably have been stunned. Entirely respectful, yet inwardly at ease, he replied, "I can paint, drive a truck, put up a fence, and break-in horses."

"Ho! Break-in horses!" Stanton almost snarled. "I never met a nigger yet who could break-in a horse properly. You mesmerizes 'em, and cows 'em, and damns 'em. Anyway, I don't like your looks. I never did like niggers. You're——"

"That's enough!" Bony cut in with assumed anger but secret amusement. "I'm no nigger, and you look like a half-caste Chinaman. Only for your age I'd knock you rotten. Don't think that because you got a few million pounds you can blackguard me. You may think you're Lord Jeffrey, but I'll show you——"

Stanton suddenly threw back his whitened head and roared with laughter. The metamorphosis was astounding—so astounding as to make credible his next words, uttered in clapping Bony on the back: "You'll do! I've got some horses I want broke in, and I'll give you four pounds a head and tucker. Don't mind me! You see, I only employ men with guts in 'em. I can't stand the mistering, hat-raising sort. They get my goat with their bowing and scraping, and when they're sent out to look over sheep they tie their horses to a tree and go to sleep till it's time to come home again."

Over the ruddy features of the half-caste slowly broke his wonderful understanding smile, and from then on the two men, so far apart in birth, brains, and wealth, were attracted to each other. Stanton, rough, clear-sighted, and inclined to call a spade a ruddy spade, glimpsed behind Bony's blue eyes a personality wholly sympathetic and staunch. In Stanton Bony saw a real specimen of the original conquering, pioneering British race.

"When can I start?" he asked.

"Well, I'll have to get them horses in and drafted," Stanton answered, suddenly thoughtful. "That'll take a couple of days. Let me think. Ah, yes! Tomorrow the rabbit-inspector is due to arrive. In the horse-yards is a light-draft gelding with white forefeet. Harness him to one of the poison-carts in the shed and run it all around. Must make out we're doing something." He nodded and passed on.

Bony, chuckling, went over to the horse-yards, cut out the gelding, harnessed him, and took him over to the shed. He had no difficulty in finding the poison-carts. They were light two-wheeled affairs, carrying an iron cylinder to hold the poisoned pollard when it was churned up into small pills and carried by a pipe down to a position behind a disk-wheel and dropped into the furrow the wheel made.

Bony found the pollard in a barrel, and he also found another barrel full of water in which the cakes of phosphorus were kept. There was, however, only a very small piece of phosphorus remaining. It floated on the surface of the water, dirty white in colour, and as soon as he lifted it clear it began to smoke. Obviously it was insufficient to make even one cylinderful of baits.

Unable to discover any further supply of the poison, Bony, calculating that Mr Stanton would have had time to breakfast, sauntered over to the office building adjoining the house. Within he found his new employer.

"We want more phosphorus, Jeff," he drawled. "There's only about a quarter ounce left in the barrel."

"Phosphorus? What do you want phosphorus for?" Stanton demanded.

"Want it for the poison-cart," explained Bony patiently.

"You don't want to worry about poison," came the roared injunction. "All you got to do is to drive the cart about the homestead, so that when the inspector comes to-morrow he'll see plenty of furrow-marks."

"But the law——"

"Law be hanged! I won't poison rabbits and have my horses and cattle poisoned by chewing the bones. 'Sides, I can't afford poison, and it isn't necessary. You drive the blamed cart, and leave the inspector to me."

There was a suspicion of a twinkle in the grey eyes, which was reflected in the blue eyes of the half-caste. He went out and drove the empty poison-cart about until five o'clock, and at eleven next morning he saw the rabbit-inspector arrive, and was near enough to hear and see Mr Stanton shake hands with him and invite him into the office for a drink before lunch.

Chapter Four

The Ants' Nest

THE SUNDAY following Bony's arrival at Windee gave him his first chance to examine the place where the abandoned motorcar belonging to the man calling himself Marks was discovered. Careful to avoid observation, he slipped away after the midday meal and arrived at the junction of the two roads. Under his arm were two strips of sheepskin roughly fashioned as sandals, the wool on the outside. Before leaving the comparatively hard road he put the sheepskin sandals on, and, walking off the track on to the loose sand, observed with satisfaction that the marks he left were very faint, and would be obliterated by the first puff of wind. His feet left no defined footprints, nothing but a faint pattern of minute curves and circles. Even while he stood looking on the first half-dozen marks, the soft south wind wiped them out, whereas marks of his boots or even his naked feet would have remained for days with the wind at its present softness.

Thenceforth he moved about freely, knowing full well that no white man would ever espy his tracks, and knowing, too, that no aboriginal would brave the spirits of the place where, according to the death-sign, violence had been done. In the art of tracking Bony had no equal, and that had led him to become no less expert at covering his own tracks.

The place where Marks's car had been discovered he found without difficulty. There was, however, no faintest indication of wheel-tracks. Standing approximately where the car stood in relation to the black's sign, Bony traced the probable path it had taken when it left the road, and made out the sand ridge which had stopped it. The ridge was not two feet high, and ran due north and south. The wind had shaped it into perfect symmetry. Its northern end was lost amidst a wilderness of sand-hummocks, and its southern end rested against a much higher ridge of sand running due east and west. On the west side of the low ridge which had stopped the car the sand was ankle-deep and fine, but east of it lay a strip of ground three to four yards wide, hard as cement, and known as clay-pan, which ran the length of the low ridge. The car had crossed the clay-pan, and when it stopped its rear wheels would still have rested on it.

Even in sandy country on which grow sturdy pines, these clay-pans are to be found. An exceedingly heavy downpour of rain—probably occurring but once in twenty years—overcomes the sand's power of absorption and collects in pools. The water eventually evaporates, leaving a perfectly level surface of mud which dries to iron hardness, and thereafter the wind is able to sweep it continually free of the omnipresent sand.

In the centre of this particular clay-pan a colony of dark red ants with black legs had excavated their marvellous palace, whilst here and there along the edge of the clay-pan another species of ant, wholly black and about an inch in length, had founded colonies. These latter were not so ferocious as the red ants, nor were they so quick and purposeful in movement. The entrance to each nest was protected against flying sand, and presumably water as well, by a circular rampart, six inches high, which in turn was protected by a mass of pine-needles intricately woven together.

The clay-pan interested Bony. On the soft sand there was but little hope of discovering anything, but the clay-pan might be revealing. He examined its surface with bent back, and sometimes also with bent knees. One particular spot held him for some time. He regarded it from several different angles, and from several varying altitudes, finally convincing himself that two lines almost invisible to him, and quite invisible to a white man, crossed the clay-pan and ended close beside a nest of the larger black ant. Those lines were made by car-wheels two months before. He had discovered the exact position of the abandoned car.

The sign made by the aboriginal—or aboriginals—next claimed his attention. Like all nomads the Australian native is profuse in his sign language, and the sign language is known to a far greater number of people than any one spoken tongue. It is evident that the sign language has been enriched by the coming of the white man, for to-day often the white man's beer-bottles, his discarded motor-tyres, and the bones of the white man's sheep and cattle, are used in conveying a message to be read by a black who possibly cannot understand a word of the sender's spoken language.

The half-caste stood before and a little below the sign that had brought him from Sydney, eight hundred miles to the east. Nine fairly straight sticks, each about one foot in length, were fastened at one end by a piece of old pliable fencing wire, which was so interlaced that each stick was forced away from its neighbours in the form of a fan. He knew that this arrangement was one of five signs of death, and his gaze, moving downward two feet, dwelt on the sheep's thigh-bone suspended from the fan-sticks by the same length of wire.

Now had it been a blackfellow who had died there, the bone would have come from the animal or bird representing the dead man's tribal totem. If his tribal totem had been the emu, then a bone from that bird would have been used. But this bone was a sheep's bone, and the sheep is entirely the white man's animal. Had it been a bullock's bone the meaning would have been the same, and for the same reason.

Bony went back to the clay-pan and seated himself midway between the almost invisible wheel-tracks, with the low bank for a comfortable back-rest, and at his side one of the black ants' nests; and there he rolled a cigarette and settled himself comfortably to enjoy it after he had carefully deposited the used match in a pocket. He had not been there three seconds when a piece of living black and white fluff settled on one of his sheepskin sandals and began an eternal dance. To this fairy bird Bony addressed his thoughts in a low voice:

"Quite a number of people in this very wicked world scoff at luck. They jeer also at coincidence. Yet both luck and coincidence play a most important part in human history. Without a mixture of both, life would be of no interest to me, for the lines of human destiny would be so clearly laid down that there would be no little surprises, no freshness, no—yes, no gamble in life.

"Now it was quite a piece of luck that I saw Sergeant Morris's snapshot, and quite a coincidence that I happened to be in Sydney to see it. Through both luck and coincidence I'm here this warm afternoon engaged on what promises to be an unusual case.

"Mr Marks leaves Windee at two-thirty alone in the car he drives, and is slightly intoxicated. Did he, however, reach the road junction alone in his car? There is a probability that he did not go to sleep at the wheel, that he was stopped between the homestead and the junction, where he was incapacitated and brought to this identical spot to be disposed of. The sign states that he was killed here. If he was killed anywhere else the sign would not be just where it is.

"Presently I must go into the matter of the business about which Marks went to see Mr Stanton—I should have said Jeff Stanton. Everything in its order. Let us first decide, if possible, whether Marks was killed by a white man aided by a blackfellow, or observed by a blackfellow unobserved by him, or if he was killed by a blackfellow or fellows who left that sign to warn their countrymen.

"As it is assumed that Marks had a lot of money on him at the time, we may, I think, dismiss the blacks as the actual murderers. They would have little use for banknotes and no use for negotiable securities. This, of course, Mr Dancing Billy Wagtail, is all conjecture. Somewhere about here Marks was killed. The odds are that he was not killed without a struggle, and wherever that struggle took place, there the ground will have received some evidence of it. By this time the sand will doubtless have buried it, but all the same it will be there—a spot or two of blood, a coin, even a hair or wisp of cloth, or a dozen other things that can be detached from human beings through carelessness or violence.

"I must proceed along two distinct lines. First, to find out what has become of Marks's body, and second, to find what living person benefited by Marks's death. We must go into the history of Marks. Mr Chief Commissioner, that is your job. Anyway, Marks was one of your satellites. In the meantime I must study the Windee people, both black and white—especially black; because the black who put up the sign can tell me what happened here. Now, what ..."

Bony's attention was drawn to the ants' nest at his side. From the corner of his eye he had seen a sparkle of blue light, but when he looked directly at the nest it had vanished. The large circular hole within the rampart was alive with the black ants. Watching them, he observed that they were bringing up out of the nest small stones about half the size of a field pea. These they deposited on the inside slope of the rampart. The man observed that each ant laid down its tiny load on the west side of the hole, where the surrounding rampart cast a shade, thence to hurry round to the east side, which was in full sunlight, and from there pick up another small stone and with it hurry below.

The lesser problem immediately absorbed Bony. Why did the ants bring up out of the nest one stone and take another down? And whence had they collected the small smooth stones in all that great expanse of sand, fine almost as a speck of whirling dust in a sunbeam?

The ants worked on, unheeding him. They all appeared possessed of but one idea. There came to Bony memory of reading of the punishments meted out to prisoners in the old convict days, when a man was compelled to carry a heavy shot up an incline, there to let it roll back, then to return and again carry it up.

But that was all insensate stupidity and cruelty. There is certainly no stupidity of that order among ants. They were not carrying stones up and down for mere exercise, and they were not so developed as to impose such work as a punishment.

"Bony, you read too much," he said aloud. "You read so much that you forget ninety per cent of what you have read. Somewhere, some time, you've read about ants carrying stones." For many minutes he sat, leaning back on his elbow, his mind's eye so active that his physical eyes were without vision. Almost fifteen minutes expired before he sighed with satisfaction. He had remembered. The ants were taking down sun-heated stones to keep the eggs warm, and were bringing up cold stones to be heated by the early rays of the sun when next it rose. "That's it!" he murmured. "They do nothing without a logical cause. Ah! Why, here comes one with a piece of blue glass. Evidently glass does not retain heat as rock will. I must inquire into that."

Up out of the hole an ant carried a piece of blue glass, which reflected the light strongly whilst it was still deep in the shadow. The insect brought it up to the west slope of the rampart and laid it there before hurrying round for a sun-warmed stone. Bony picked it up with the point of his knife and examined it closely on the palm of his hand.

It was flattened on one side, and faceted accurately on the other. It was not glass. It was a cut sapphire.

Chapter Five

An Inspection

WINDEE STATION had grown from quite a small beginning. Many years before the Great War Jeffrey Stanton had bought out a selector holding a Government lease of a hundred thousand acres, of which most was wild hill-country. On that block he ran cattle because his predecessor had run sheep and the dingoes killed most of them. They paid ten shillings a scalp for wild dogs in those days, and Stanton made more money out of the pest than he did from his stock.

The range of hills on which his small property was situated ran almost north and south. The great plain to the west was leased by two brothers and the plain to the east was held chiefly by a pastoral company with offices in Adelaide. Drought and overstocking ruined the brothers on the west of him, and Stanton bought them out with borrowed money. The season changed. He struck several good cattle-markets, and eventually repaid the borrowed money and found himself sole owner of six hundred thousand acres. When the Adelaide company went into liquidation, Stanton again borrowed money and acquired the eastern property, adding a further seven hundred thousand acres to his holding.

At the time of Bony's introduction to Windee, Stanton possessed thirteen hundred thousand acres of land, seventy thousand sheep, and no cattle. He owned, too, a sheep stud-farm in Victoria, an enormous amount of property in Adelaide, and most of the shares in an important shipping line.

Despite his wealth, however, he had never been to any Australian city other than Adelaide, and had taken but one short trip to England, which had occurred after the death of his wife in the Year of the Peace. During this trip he had decided to inaugurate a custom he had practised ever since. On the liner he had been struck by the scrupulous cleanliness enforced by the captain's bi-weekly inspections. It came to him that the captain of a ship must know every little cabin and corner in it, whereas he, Stanton, could not remember how many horse saddles, or how many drays, buggies and buckboards he had on Windee.

Home once more, he placed a man in sole charge of all the plant at the homestead, at the out-station called Nullawil, and in use at the several boundary-riders' huts. The holder of this position, which was anything but a sinecure, had to possess a fair knowledge of the saddlery and carpentering trades. The name of the present holder was Bates.

Every Saturday morning Bates called at the office at about ten o'clock. Jeffrey Stanton, accompanied by his bookkeeper and Bates, then made a round of inspection. This was why Bates entered the office at ten in the morning of the Saturday following Bony's examination of the blackfellows' sign.

"Ready for inspection, Jeff?" he asked casually, leaning back against the open door. Stanton, who had just finished talking over the telephone with his overseer at Nullawil, rose from his private desk and was followed by the bookkeeper, who snatched up notebook and pencil.

A casual examination of these three men would have decided one that Mr Roberts, the bookkeeper, was the owner, Bates a station tradesman, as indeed he was, and Stanton anything. The bookkeeper had been at Windee four years, and immediately Stanton learned that he had held a commission during the war he began the custom he had kept up ever afterwards of invariably addressing him as "Mister" Roberts. Roberts had insisted on returning the courtesy although Stanton had fumed and fussed. However, since Roberts knew all about the office work of a great sheep-station, and Stanton knew nothing of clerical work but all about sheep, they compromised; and, as a battalion well run by a temperamentally balanced commanding officer and adjutant, the work on Windee went ahead smoothly.

The first place to be inspected was the men's kitchen. On their entrance they found the cook examining very carefully a whole carcass of mutton, killed the previous evening. He was a small man, the cook, pale of face, the paleness accentuated by a full black moustache. Taking no notice of the inspecting party, he dragged the carcass along the table nearer the window, where he continued his examination even more carefully.

"What's the matter, Alf?" inquired Jeffrey Stanton.

Alf looked up as though for the first time noticing his employer. He spoke with a trace of the Cockney.

"Oh, nothing much," he said acidly. "I was just wondering whether that there was a dead Goanna or a skinned cat."

"Looks like a sheep to me," Stanton stated.

"A sheep! Not it. That ain't no sheep," Alf snarled. "Think I can't tell a sheep when I see one? A sheep! If them's the sort of sheep we're breeding nowadays, Gawd 'elp Orstralia!"

"It's a sheep all right. But on the poor side," Stanton admitted.

"I should say hit is!" Alf danced with rage, but he went on coolly enough: "Now you don't expect me to cook that for real men with guts, do you?"

"No, damme, I don't!" Stanton suddenly roared. To Mr Roberts he snapped: "Note—inquire into supply of killing-sheep." Then to Alf:

"Heave that out to the dogs. Draw tinned meat from the store. Anything else?"

"Nope. But I ain't chuckin' this art to the dawgs. I'll make stew of it. But it's the second carcass I've 'ad like that this week."

"Yes, yes," Stanton said more softly. "I suppose it's because young Jeff is away. I'll see what I can do."

In the men's quarters they found one of the hands reading a novel on his bunk, his set task for the day having been already accomplished. Stanton gave him a good-natured nod, and glanced over the building before leaving for the cart and harness sheds.

As an object lesson to the general mass of Australian squatters and farmers, Windee Station was probably supreme. Not a piece of harness, not a cart or a machine, was ever found in the open. The saving in general upkeep was treble the wage given to Bates. Every item of harness and saddlery was oiled and clean, the three trucks appeared as though they were seldom used, as also did the two powerful motor-cycles requisitioned when important work in far-off paddocks had to be done quickly. The trade shops, situated in one building, were ever a revelation to the visitor. Everything required on Windee was constructed from raw material brought by motor-truck from Broken Hill, a hundred and fifty miles distant.

On Windee there was plenty but no waste. On most stations and farms the waste and neglect are scandalous. In consequence profits are small and wages are kept down to the minimum demanded by law. Jeffrey Stanton raged and blasphemed if he saw a shovel lying unused in the sun, but he paid his men fifty per cent higher wages than those given by the great mass of station-owners and laid down by law as the minimum. For this he was unpopular in his own class—but he was a millionaire. He expected good service for his high wages, and saw that he got it.

The inspecting party eventually arrived at the blacksmith's shop. Here the blacksmith and two off-siders were welding and fitting dray tyres. It was work that could not be interrupted, and, after nodding to the smith, Stanton looked casually about and was on the point of leaving, when he saw in a corner a heavy cast-iron object that in shape and size was very similar to the case holding a four-point-nine howitzer shell.

It was, he knew, a dolly-pot used by gold miners to pound up samples of ore to dust, then to flood the dust with water and roughly ascertain the gold content.

"Where does that come from, Bates?" he asked, pointing to it.

"Left here for the time by Dot and Dash," was Bates's reply. "They brought it in from Range Hut a month or so back."

A six-nick iron tyre was on the anvil, held by the two off-siders. The part resting on the anvil was white-hot, and the smith's hammer clanged and clanged on it, shooting out white-hot sparks and flakes. Stanton watched for a few seconds, wondering who was the first man to discover that iron would run, and how.

He was reminded of another matter.

"By the way, Bates, we ordered a further supply of nitric acid for that job. It should reach us next week."

"Good!" said Bates. "It's dooced funny where that bottle of acid went to."

"Yes," agreed Stanton; "damned funny! Better lock up the next lot."

Out again in the strong sunshine, where the wind rustled through the leaves of the pepper-tree shading the shop, the clanging of iron on iron behind him, and the screeches of the grey-backed galahs over in the creek trees, Stanton nodded to Bates and walked to the house. The inspection was over.

He paused at the wicket-gate and looked back at the familiar scene. He was facing then to the north, and could see how his home lay on the edge of a great plain. To the east the sand country, whereon grew the pines and mulga, a wide belt of them lying between him and Mount Lion, dark against the brazen sky. To the west all was light—quivering, dancing light. The mirage lay deep over the great plain of salt-bush and spear grass, magically transforming the scattered clumps of trees into towering umbrella-topped masts, and causing the summits of the hills forty miles westward to appear as islands floating on a cadmium sea.

The stern weather-beaten face of Jeffrey Stanton softened. In his heart he felt a great peace. The strife and struggles of youth were over. His boy and his girl were safe from want and neither would ever know the hardships he and the woman who lay in the cemetery close by had known. Not that he allowed them to lead soft lives.

"Why, Dad, you are in a brown study!" exclaimed a voice behind him. "Come along! The morning tea is waiting."

And, turning, Jeffrey Stanton met the eyes of Marion, his daughter, and smiled.

Chapter Six

Bony Educates a Horse

MARION STANTON was dark of hair, with a creamy complexion. The contrast was the most striking thing about her, noticeable long before the features were examined. Then it was that the observer wondered at the wide level forehead, so indicative of calm reason when allied to the beautifully curved chin, tempered by the soft, dainty mouth that made a man think of all that is delightful in womanhood.

In repose her face was not beautiful, but when it was lit by the light of personality shining from her grey eyes it was to glimpse something of wonder and attraction, a richly lovely woman.

She and Stanton sat on the wide fly-netted south veranda with a small tea laden table between them, father and daughter in appearance as opposite as the poles. The man over sixty, the girl not yet twenty-five; the father slight and lithe, the daughter big-boned and active; the one at sixty showing the effects of a hard, tough life spent mostly on a horse, the other at twenty-five revealing womanly gentleness and grace. Yet to observe them together was to know that one begat the other, for when they smiled it was very often with their eyes alone.

"I hope you haven't forgotten that we are to tin-kettle the Fosters to-morrow night," Marion observed, pouring her father his second cup.

"I had forgotten, but I am not going," Stanton said a little grimly. "If you think that I, at my age, intend to travel eighty miles to play the fool round my overseer's house, then you want to think something else."

"That is just what I am doing, Dad."

"Good!"

Stanton drank his tea in silence. His daughter's expression had subtly changed, and he knew that he was in for a battle he would probably lose, because he had lost every battle but one fought between them since the day his daughter was born. He awaited stoically her next broadside.

"Harry Foster has worked for you since he left school in—let me think—yes, in nineteen-seven," she said. "Without counting the years he was away fighting the Germans so that you could make more money, he has been working for you for thirteen years. You have never had one single uneasy thought that he wasn't doing his job with all his heart."

"I've paid him well. I've——"

"He has worked hard for you, not so much because of the money, but because you gave him his chance," went on the inexorable voice. "You gave him his chance because you liked him, far more than because he knew his job. Ethel and he have gone to a lot of trouble for to-morrow night, and if the Big Boss is not there I know they will be ever so disappointed."

Jeffrey Stanton abstracted from his pocket a tin of tobacco, a packet of cigarette papers and a box of matches. From those articles, which he set on the table before him, he looked at his daughter, and said in the voice of a martyr: "May I smoke?"

"Father, you are going?"

"No!"—emphatically.

"Ethel is my best friend, and you will go just to please me, won't you?" Her eyes were twin stars. The appeal in them was a vision of beauty. No living man could have won so unequal a battle. Stanton said:

"Damnation!"

"Dear old Dad!" cried she. "I knew you would say yes. For going I'll make your cigarette for you. I can make them so much better than you can. You always make them with a camel's hump in the middle."

Without speaking, he gave her the materials, and, whilst watching her supple fingers, he thought of his wife and the expression he had seen in her eyes the second before she gave him her first kiss.

"If we leave at half-past seven, we shall get there at ten o'clock," he heard her say when he accepted the cigarette she had made and lit for him. "Mrs Poulton can come with us. You'll let as many of the men go as want to, won't you?"

"Decidedly," Stanton agreed, accepting defeat with quite a good grace. "I'll push 'em off on the trucks before seven, so that we'll all get there together. They'll be fit for nothing on Monday, but what matters work when my lady's whims must be obeyed?"

She laughed at him, and he laughed at and with her—laughed perhaps with a hint of grimness, yet also with a world of affection. The next instant she said:

"And now that is settled, Dad, I want you to let me ride the grey gelding this afternoon. An hour ago I went over to the yards, and Bony was riding him, and assures me he is as good as gold."

Bony's first horse was a grey gelding that had been regarded from birth as Marion Stanton's own. He was a four-year-old, and out of a mare that had once won the Caulfield Cup, the second most important race in Australia. From the top rail of the horse-yards the detective had watched this beauty running ahead of a mob of a hundred wild, unbroken horses flying before the cracking stockwhips of the riders, and his heart had thrilled at the sight of him. To Stanton, who sat beside him, he had pointed out the grey, asking if it were one of the horses desired to be broken, and Stanton had said:

"Yes. I want you to break him first. He belongs to my daughter. If you can't break a horse in properly, I want you to say so now, because if anything should happen to my daughter through your bad breaking, it is quite likely that I'll strangle you."

Bony had been astonished at the feeling in those words, and, looking straight at his employer, had replied gently: "I think I understand."

When told by Marion that Bony had judged the grey gelding fit for her to ride, Jeffrey Stanton's eyes narrowed, not however with opposition. He knew that his girl was probably the best horsewoman in the State, but he knew, too, that ten days is a very short time in which to break in a horse thoroughly. What he said was:

"You must let me talk with Bony first. You see, as yet I've had no sample of the fellow's work. I must be sure before I consent." The grim, hard lines about his mouth faded and vanished, being replaced by lines tender and rare, when he added: "I have sinned a lot in my time, girlie, but if I were to lose you the punishment would be unjustly severe."

"Dear old Dad!" she whispered. "I leave it to you."

Stanton left and went over to the yards where he found the half-caste "mouthing" a pert young miss with a black coat and a white blaze on her forehead. He and the filly had a yard to themselves, and Stanton, looking through the heavy rails, observed with the vision of the expert how light were Bony's hands on the long reins whilst he walked behind the animal.

Seeing Stanton, the breaker called to the filly to stop. Instantly she obeyed, whereupon he went to her and petted her and murmured to her until the slight trembling of her limbs ceased, and she realized that Man was not so terrible as she had always thought.

"Good day, Jeff!" Bony said, strolling towards Stanton when he had removed the gear from the filly.

"Day, Bony! How's the grey gelding?" came from the station-owner.

"Fit, I think. Miss Marion was here a little while since looking him over. I'll try him out for you, if you like."

"Good!"

Bony turned and opened the gate leading to the largest yard of all, wherein were twenty horses, including the gelding. Moving behind the filly, he snapped his fingers, and she trotted out to the mob all facing her way. From a corner of the small yard Bony took up a bridle, and, going to the gate, whistled shrilly with his fingers. Stanton, looking at the grey gelding, saw him hesitate. Again the breaker whistled, commandingly, imperatively. And the gelding trotted right up to him, then stood quite still whilst the bridle was slipped up his face and over his ears.

Stanton admitted to himself that Bony was a marvellously quick worker. With complete satisfaction he watched the horse being saddled. It gave absolutely no trouble. Bony mounted with swift, effortless ease. The horse stood as still as a park statue. Dismounting, he passed to the off-side and again mounted. Stanton was more than satisfied, for very few horses will permit a rider to mount on the off-side.

Now mounted, the half-caste kneed his horse close to Jeffrey Stanton, and asked him to open the outer gate giving egress from the range of yards. Stanton found Marion beside him, and when he opened the great heavy gate, he saw how her eyes were shining with anticipation and delight.

Clear of the yards, Bony walked the horse away over the deep sand for perhaps a hundred yards, then, turning, brought him back at a canter. Close beside father and daughter he dismounted, and began adjusting a stirrup-leather from which they saw hung a leather thong several feet in length fastened to a strangely fashioned buckle.

Bony faced round on the watchers, and lifted his old felt hat when he saw the girl. Stanton was on the verge of passing favourable judgment when the half-caste drawled in his pleasant voice:

"There are two occupations which I love, one of which is handling horses. Knowing that a lady is to ride this one, I have taken a little more trouble. Madam, I stake my reputation that you will find this horse the most amenable to your wishes, the sweetest-tempered, and the very finest animal you have ever ridden, or ever will ride. I wish to show you one thing to prove to you that his education is perfect. Whatever happens, please remember not to cry out."

They saw him vault into the saddle, and then, as though he changed his mind, he slid to the ground and climbed aboard the horse as a sailor heaving himself across a donkey at a seaside resort. Stanton was delighted to see that the animal never moved until his rider spoke. The girl's eyes widened, but she was wondering at Bony's voice and his command of English.

He rode the gelding slowly from them for perhaps a quarter of a mile. Then he swung him round and urged him into a loping gallop. With effortless motion horse and rider swept towards them. Old and hardened in the ways of horseflesh Jeffrey Stanton admitted that he had seen no finer horse, and seldom a finer rider.

Horse and man came on, leaving behind them a cloud of brown dust to rise high in the now windless air. The pride of the horse was arresting. Nearer and nearer he came, effortless, graceful, as though he galloped across a thin red cloud.

And then, when horse and man came abreast of them, they saw Bony sway in the saddle. They saw him deliberately fall sideways.

Puzzled and astonished at first, then alarmed, they saw the rider strike the ground and become enveloped in a cloud of dust. The dust rose and was wafted away. Marion wanted to scream, for Bony's foot was caught in the stirrup-iron. And then, the wonder of it! The horse instantly stopped, swung aside his hindquarters, and stood motionless, looking round and down on the trapped man.

Stanton moved forward to help him extricate his foot from the imprisoning iron, when Bony tugged at the thong and the whole stirrup-leather came away. Dusty and smiling, he rose to his feet to say gravely:

"The only thing poor old Bony cannot do with a horse is to make him speak."

Chapter Seven

Silver and Sapphires

A QUEENSLAND TAXPAYER in partial possession of the facts concerning Bony's activities at this time might have seen reason to complain that in breaking horses he was not working for the State from which he received a salary. The complaint would not have been made, however, had he known everything.

In but few cases had the detective permitted his real avocation to become known to any of the people among whom he was carrying on his investigations, until such times as he chose to reveal it, if at all. His general practice was to drift on the scene of a crime as a swagman, make himself known to the senior police officer of the district, and to him alone, and when his inquiries were complete to lay the result before this senior police officer and unostentatiously depart. ...

When he told Stanton he could break-in horses, he knew from Sergeant Morris that the squatter wanted some horses broken in. He knew also that as a horse-breaker his position could not be bettered on Windee in opportunities for visiting the scene of Marks's disappearance. A station horse-breaker will take in hand several horses at the same time, the horses being at various stages of their training. During the final stage of breaking-in the horse is taken out of the yards and ridden in the open country.

Therefore every day after Bony had got his first horse at the last stage he rode to the junction of the two roads, where he tied the horse to a tree out of sight of anyone passing along the track. In a fork of the tree he kept his sheepskin sandals, and, wearing them, he wandered for an hour or more with apparent aimlessness round and round the clay-pan whereon the abandoned car had stopped. He made that clay-pan the centre of an ever-widening circle.

Bony's reasoning was based entirely on common sense. He had found the exact position of the car when it had stopped. What he knew of Marks's history, in addition to the aboriginal sign that a white man had been killed, compelled his belief that a murder had been committed. Those circumstances pointed to the fact that the crime had been one of violence, and it followed as night follows day that, when one or more human bodies are violently agitated, some particle or object from the clothing on those bodies becomes detached and falls to the ground unnoticed.

It was by an extraordinary piece of luck that the ants had revealed to Bony that cut sapphire, but not an extraordinary thing that the ants had used the sapphire to keep their eggs warm. Sapphires, cut or uncut, do not grow. They are never found in the rough state in the old sand-country of Central Australia. It could be assumed, therefore, that that particular cut sapphire was once set in a ring or a tiepin, that it was one of the objects that fell during the supposed struggle.

It was not luck but downright patience, methodical tireless patience, which added yet further evidence. Bony knew that the Anglo-Saxon race, as well as the Australian aboriginal, instinctively kills at a distance, and not with a weapon retained in the hand. Since in this case the probable weapon used was a gun, the half-caste proceeded to gain evidence of it, if evidence there remained. Standing in the position of the car, it was impossible to fire a bullet horizontally in any direction for more than two hundred yards. Within that distance a tree would stop it, if it did not ricochet from a branch.

Tree by tree, Bony searched for the mark that would indicate the stoppage or passage of a bullet. He examined nearly four hundred trees before he felt obliged to give up the search as fruitless. Yet it was a tree, a pine-tree with branches growing out from low down the trunk, which yielded him a second find. Wedged within a fork he discovered a small disk of silver, very thin and very slightly concave. It proved an object entirely baffling to him as to its use or purpose. Had it been of glass it might have come from the face of a wrist-watch; and if one might guess, which Bony seldom did, that faintly discoloured silver disk might well be the back of the inner case of a small silver watch.

He found the disk precisely nine yards from the centre of the circle, and no more than the cut sapphire could the disk have just grown where he found it. Yet, although the disk could not so far be labelled, it materially strengthened the theory that a violent struggle had taken place where Marks's motor-car had stopped.

Considering all things, the half-caste was well satisfied with the progress of his quest. It was a case absolutely to his liking. Had he discovered the body of Marks, the case would have been so much the less interesting in that a murder would have been definitely established, whereas he first had to establish the fact of murder before he could go on to discover the murderer and his motive for the crime.

He was also well satisfied with the companion fate had given him on the afternoon when the grey gelding was first ridden by Marion Stanton. He rode with Marion along the track to Mount Lion with the unalloyed delight of being in the presence of a lovely woman. The horse was behaving splendidly, a compliment to his breaker; whilst his rider was a compliment to his training.

"Have you given him a name yet?" inquired Bony, seated on a quiet old mare.

"No, I haven't, Mr. Bony," she answered. "Can you suggest one?"

"Do you find his movements easy?" the detective countered with a smile, as unconscious of familiarity as she was unconscious that he was a poor half-caste horse-breaker and she a millionaire's daughter. She said:

"He is the loveliest horse I've ever ridden."

"Then why not call him Grey Cloud?"

"Grey Cloud!" she repeated after him. He saw her lips move whilst she murmured the name several times, watched with his admiration of the beautiful, the contours of her face and her figure. She wore a black riding-habit that permitted her to ride astride, as do all true bush-women.

"Grey Cloud! That will do. Yes, that is a most appropriate name. Why, it is almost poetical. Are you a poet?"

"Alas, no," Bony admitted gravely. "I tried to write poetry once, and its result was almost catastrophic. A certain professor of mathematics had an enlarged proboscis and a shrunken chin. I wrote a verse about him which quite by accident was dropped and picked up by the professor of literature, who saw me drop it. 'Sir,' he said, 'did you write this atrocious drivel?' 'Sir, I did,' said I, and went on to say I was ashamed, and had meant no disrespect to his learned colleague. 'I am not interested in your lack of respect, sir,' was the reply I got; 'I am more than interested, I am stunned, by your utter lack of metre. I shall remember you, sir!'"

Marion laughed deliciously, and Grey Cloud tossed his head and whinnied at the old mare. Then suddenly she became serious, as though remembering something, and asked: "Where was that?"

"Why, at the University, Brisbane."

"And you were there?"

"Yes. I won my way there through a scholarship."

Bony found himself regarded by a pair of steady grey eyes in which was an expression of perplexity.

"And you are breaking-in horses on Windee," she said slowly.

"Why not?"

"But what a waste of a fine education! Why, you could have become a doctor, or an architect, or a—or a ..."

"A policeman," Bony suggested helpfully, and added, seeing a hurt flash in her eyes: "When I left the University I could have become almost anything I chose. I chose to become a student of nature, a master of human psychology, and a teacher of little children. I found in the north of my native State children so far from a school that they were in danger of growing up unable to read and write. I taught many their 'three R's' and gave them some understanding of astronomy and elementary science. In the paper the other day I read that one of those children had gained a Rhodes Scholarship."

Now in her eyes he saw the divine light of enthusiasm, and he went on in his grave, gentle way:

"Of course, I could have used my education purely for my own advancement. I have preferred to use it, when opportunity served, for the advancement of others and for justice."

"I have never thought of education quite like that," Marion admitted, and for a while rode in silence. She could not help thinking how strange it was that for no explainable reason she liked this breaker of horses, her father's servant, a common half-caste, immensely. Was it his steady blue eyes, or the way he smiled, or the tone of his voice, or the silent deference he paid to her good looks?

When they had gone four miles from the homestead, he suggested that they turn for home, to which she objected, saying:

"Oh, not yet! Why, the afternoon is still young."

"But your horse is newly broken," Bony pointed out. "As yet he is not hardened to carrying even your weight over a long distance. There is always to-morrow."

"Then let's gallop."

And before he could say anything she wheeled Grey Cloud, cried to him, and the gelding sprang away. That ride! It was like sitting on a flying feather, and when she reached the stockyards, her face flushed, her eyes sparkling, she leapt to the ground and, turning to Bony, impulsively held out her now ungloved hand whilst thanking him. And he, looking down at the fair hand lying in his black one, saw on the little finger a gold ring set with sapphires, one of which was missing.

Chapter Eight

Dot and Dash

MOUNT LION like a great many bush towns is remarkable for the contrast of its buildings. To-day the court-house, the police quarters, the small gaol, and the post-office are built of bricks faced with cement; whilst the dwellings of the fifty-odd inhabitants are constructed of assorted pieces of corrugated iron, flattened out petrol-tins, and much hessian. As though to soften the contrast, the two general stores, the hotel, and the Catholic convent are built of weatherboard kept in fair repair and roofed with red-painted iron.

At the beginning of the century Mount Lion was four times its present size. During a Saturday evening it was then impossible for any person to run from end to end of its broad main street on account of the crowds on the sidewalks and the horses, buggies, and carts in the road.

At the time Bony first visited Mount Lion it depended on two sources of wealth to stave off utter extinction. Windee Station provided the hotel with "cheque-men" and the stores with trade. The situation of the town made it a junction for mail-cars from Broken Hill in the south, Tibooburra in the north, and Wilcannia in the east. Travellers on these cars were compelled to spend one night at Mount Lion.

The sun rose one Sunday in a sky normally clear of clouds, and by eight o'clock shone fiercely on the iron and tin roofs and glittered on the pepper-trees lining the single thoroughfare, trees planted in the bygone prosperous days. Two cows reposed in the shade of the tree outside the main door of the hotel, and innumerable goats lay beneath other trees or foraged in backyards whose fences had broken down. Across the road from the police-station a number of hens were enjoying dust-baths amid a rubble of broken bricks and mortar, all that remained of a one-time important bank. Of the inhabitants there was no sign.

It was, indeed, a city of silence. At rare intervals a cock crowed, and at still rarer intervals the yellow-crested cockatoo in his petrol-case cage hung from the roof of a store veranda chattered sleepily, or said with great distinctness: "How dry we are!"

And then, as the buzzing of a bee, there came from the direction of Windee Station the roar of a motor-engine. Doubtless the pigeons on the convent roof could see the red dust rising from the south-west road as a smokecloud from a destroyer. Then out of the belt of pine country shot a motor-truck, its headlamps now and then catching and sending back the sunlight, and rushed with increasing roar across the low paraffin bush plain which surrounded the town and which formed the town common.

On the outskirts of the town the driver very wisely slowed to some three miles per hour, out of respect for his truck's springs; for, although he paid the authorities in Sydney a tax of six pounds every year to drive that truck, never a penny of any motorist's money had ever been spent on the streets of Mount Lion.

As a small dinghy in an Atlantic gale, the truck came slowly along the street, and finally into harbour within the shade of the pepper-tree outside the hotel. The cow ceased not to chew her cud, although barely an inch separated her hindquarters from the truck-wheel.

"Oo wouldn't be a cow?" inquired a little, clean-shaven, red-faced man sitting beside the driver.

"I wouldn't," decided the driver. "If I were a cow I could not appreciate beer."

The first speaker alighted nimbly, when a search began for tobacco and papers. Without interest he looked over the town, and then with returning interest at the cow.

"Every time I takes a bird's-eye view of this burg I am reminded of me home town in Arizonee," he remarked to the cow. "Even you has the same markings as Widder Smith's milker. Hey, Dash! Have you got a match?"

The truck-driver, having alighted, searched his clothes. He was almost six feet in height and slim with it, although there was power in the carriage of his body. Scrupulously shaven, his weather-beaten face, his perfect teeth, revealed when he spoke, the crisp curling brown hair, and the cheerful hazel eyes, indicated a man in the prime of life.

"I haven't a match, Dot, my dear friend," he replied in a tone of voice which placed him instantly as from England's upper middle class. "If, however, we arouse the estimable Mr Bumpus, you will be able to purchase a box and buy me a drink with the change."

With one accord they sauntered round the corner and, via the case and barrel-filled yard at the rear, came to Mr Bumpus's bedroom door, which opened on the back veranda. The door they opened without ceremony, then stood in the doorway, which commanded a view of Mr Bumpus's head on one pillow and Mrs Bumpus's head on the other.

"Hu-umph!" growled Dot.

"Pardon me!" murmured Dash.

The lady was first to awake. Her eyes opened to the intruders, and then shut as though she was suffering a nightmare.

"Good afternoon!" Dash remarked pleasantly.

"Nice evening!" added Dot with a chuckle.

"How dare you, Mr Dash and Mr Dot?" squealed Mrs Bumpus. Dash bowed.

"For the fair we dare all, madam," he said. "Awake thy lord, sweet one, for it is near to midday."

"Eh! Wot's marrer?" grumbled Mr Bumpus when an elbow was dug into his well-cushioned ribs.

"Dot and Dash have come to town, Mr Bumpus," explained the tall man at the door. "The day is fast going. Yet if you wish to sleep till night, throw me the keys of the bar and sleep on."

"You'll-fine-'em-on-the-was'-stan'," Mr Bumpus murmured, evidently desiring to sleep until night did fall.

"Pardon, sweetheart!" Dash said deferentially, and walked to the washstand to secure the bunch of keys. When he rejoined Dot at the door he turned and smiled, and wagged his finger reprovingly. "Loveliest, Dot and Dash will take coffee and bacon and eggs for supper. Arise before you have to light the lamps."

"Go away!" ordered Mrs Bumpus with a giggle.

Dash bowed with grace and closed the door, whereupon the oddly assorted pair walked along the passage, paused before a door whilst Dash selected a key and opened it, and entered the bar from behind the counter. Without speech, the little man lifted the layer of many wet sacks from a line of bottles laid as tin soldiers put to bed by a small boy, and placed two of them on the counter. From a stock beneath the counter he replaced the bottles taken, carefully readjusting the bags and pouring water over them from a glass jug. So far away from any source of ice, the evaporation from wet bags was the only cooling agency to hand.

Dash opened the bottles and placed each against a glass on the counter, after which he laid four shillings on a shelf above the cash register and, turning, jumped up backwards beside a glass and bottle. Dot climbed to a similar position via a chair.

"Australia's greatest natural resource, my dear Dot, is its beer," observed Dash.

"Which is why I left Arizonee," Dot said fervently.

"Beer taken in moderate doses on a hot Sunday morning in October is an experience of which to dream whilst one is skinning kangaroos or rabbits."

"You sure brand the right maverick this time, Dash."

"The man who found out that water evaporating from a loosely woven material cools beer was rightly entitled to a peerage," Dash went on sententiously.

"He sure was," Dot agreed, holding his bottle against the light from a small window and sighing to see it empty. Then, as an afterthought, he went on: "Saying, of course, that he was an Englishman. If he was

Amurrican he deserved orl the luck in the White House stakes. What about it?"

There appeared no doubt in the mind of the tall man to what his companion referred, for he said:

"Possibly it would be a wise procedure, my dear friend. As yet I do not hear sizzling bacon or smell the fragrant coffee, therefore let us indulge again in Australia's greatest natural resource. Your turn to serve—and pay."

Dot's button of a nose wrinkled with a smile and his somewhat large blue eyes twinkled with good-humour when he slid down to the floor via the chair.

"If only I was a bartender!" he drawled reflectively, calling forth reproof.

"How your fancy does change! A little while ago you wanted to be a cow. As a bartender you would not appreciate beer to the extent you do as a skin- and fur-getter. Be content to be as you are! Do you ever hear me complain of my position in life? No, sir! I am satisfied, or rather I pretend to be, even to myself. Dot, my greatest respects! Er—did you pay?"

The history of these two men, so far as the people of Windee Station and Mount Lion knew, dated back some five years. Dash's right name was Hugh Trench, and he received a letter precisely five weeks after every quarter-day from a firm of lawyers in London. He came to Windee with a letter of introduction to Jeffrey Stanton, and it was understood that he was to be a jackeroo.

Dot, whose christian name was William, was at that time a dingo-trapper employed on Windee, and between these two, so different in stature, mentality and social position, there sprang up a very close friendship. For a reason that none knew, when Trench had been at Windee some three years he gave up the position he had occupied as jackeroo, with its attendant privilege of living with the squatter, and joined Dot as a trapper and shooter of vermin for profit. Their physical contrast, so accentuated when they were together—and they were rarely apart—won for them the nicknames Dot and Dash.

There was one thing that they kept to themselves in spite of their friendship, which was never clouded by a quarrel or serious difference, and that was their history before they came to Windee. Neither of them knew why the other had migrated to Australia, although Dot was aware that Dash originated in Hampshire, and Dash knew that Dot was reared in Arizona, U.S.A.

When Mr Bumpus entered the bar, each of them was flanked by three empty bottles on the counter, and the sum of twelve shillings reposed on the shelf above the cash register. Mr Bumpus was still in his striped pyjamas and not yet thoroughly awake. He was a large florid man of uncertain temper, and to Dash's polite good morning he grunted. Without smiling, the tall partner said:

"Ah, Mr Bumpus, a faint discoloration on the liver this morning. Trade exceedingly good to a late hour, apparently. Yes, we will have a bottle apiece with you with pleasure. You will find our account settled on the shelf there."

"Why can't you let a man have a little bit of sleep? I can't go night *and* day, and besides, to-day is Sunday."

"A very excellent day for beer," Dash reminded him, still unsmiling. "Did young Jeff have a sporting evening?"

"He'll be thinking so this morning," Mr Bumpus said a little less sleepily, producing a further round of bottles. "The road he's travelling leads to Suicide Corner. It's my business to sell liquor, but I hate to see a young feller like him getting outside so much of it."

"Still hogging the whisky?" questioned Dot.

"Yes, worse luck, and vermouth and gin and rum."

"Quite a mixture," Dash murmured. "What room does he occupy?"

"Number two."

"Well, if you will be so kind as to pour me out a nobbler of whisky in a large glass of soda-water, I will endeavour to persuade him to have breakfast. Presently he must return with us to Windee, as we are due to-night at Nullawil."

"Wa' for?"

"The overseer and his wife, as you know, were recently married. We are to tin-kettle them."

"Well, for heaving's sake take young Jeff with you." Bumpus added two further liquids to the whisky-and-soda. Mixing it well with a glass rod, he gave it to Dash, adding: "If young Jeff keeps going on like this, I'll be falling foul of the old man, and that I can't afford."

"Leave him to me, Mr Bumpus," Dash proclaimed in his grand manner. "Youth and folly go together. We were all young years and years ago."

When he had gone, Dot said:

"We sure are gettin' old, Bumpus. I'll shout this time."

Chapter Nine

Father Ryan Leaves Town

WITHOUT KNOCKING, Dash opened the door of room No. 2 and entered, closed the door, and, going to the bed, stood silently looking down on the occupant. The bed lay lengthwise beneath the wide-open window, through which the intermittent breeze came to belly the lace curtains over the recumbent figure, still dressed in trousers and shirt.

Jeffrey Stanton, junior, was a young man of twenty-two. His robust frame made him bigger than his father, but it lacked the leanness and the wiry muscles still characteristic of the owner of Windee. There was in the face of this young man, whilst he lay breathing strenuously, pride and obstinacy, but no trace of the moral weakness to be expected in one in his condition. His forehead was low and broad as that of his sire, and in regarding the chin and slightly open mouth Dash was reminded of Marion Stanton. Seating himself in a chair at the head of the bed, he put down the tumbler of Mr Bumpus's "reviver" on the washstand and said, in his soft grandiloquent manner:

"The hour is nine o'clock, my very debauched friend. Arise and suffer your ablutions before we break our fast."

No alteration in the sleeper's breathing indicated that he heard. Dash removed his wide-brimmed hat with one hand and ran the fingers of the other through his hair, thereby revealing the sunburn of his features and the rim of white, hat-protected skin at the summit of his forehead. His mouth then was like a spring rat-trap, but when he spoke again the even white teeth softened its grim outlines.

"Your appearance reminds me of a particularly dear old sow on the pater's home farm," he said loudly.

This time the sleeper stirred and, as the porcine mentioned by Dash, grunted.

"I would really like to smoke a cigarette, but I fear, should I strike a match, that your breath would cause an explosion," the tall man observed in yet louder tones.

The response this time was a groan combined with a grunt. Dash sighed, and when the sigh was concluded his mouth was again hinting at a rat-trap. Slowly he turned his body away from the bed, and, stretching out a long arm, took from the washstand an enamelled ewer. It was a large ewer and full of water, but it required no effort for Dash to move it in a circular motion, his arm still outstretched, until it hovered over the sleeper's face. Then from its lip there fell a gentle stream.

Young Jeff moved aside his face as though a fly walked his nose. The stream of water followed. Quite suddenly he opened his eyes. The water fell into them. He opened his mouth and the water filled it. The stream was endless, apparently inexhaustible. The young man guggled and writhed, clawed at the saturated pillows, finally sat up with wildly glaring eyes and waving hands. On the crown of his head fell the stream of water. It splashed as a jet from a garden-hose, washed his hair into his eyes, and streamed down his back and chest, saturating an expensive tussore-silk shirt. And then suddenly the stream subsided to a trickle, from a trickle languished to single drops. The empty ewer was replaced on the washstand, and Dash turned back to find himself regarded with bloodshot grey eyes and a passion-distorted face.

"You—you—you!" he cried, rage making him inarticulate.

"Softly, softly, my dear Jeff!" Dash admonished unsmilingly. He reached for the glass, this time keeping his eyes on the young man. Young Jeff saw a light in the hazel orbs, and from a raging lion became a sulky pup. It was then that Dash smiled and offered him Mr Bumpus's concoction, which he took without thanks and drank. The whisky constituent made him shudder violently, and when the glass had been as violently thrown against the wall he threw himself back again on the pillow.

"I had an uncle," remarked Dash, "who during the two closing years of his life was carried up to bed by two footmen every night at eleven o'clock. My uncle was a gentleman and a man. He drank beer all day long, and eighteen sixty-two port after dinner, yet he arose at six o'clock in the morning and spent an hour galloping round the park."

"Oh—shut up!" cried young Jeff, flinging one wet arm across his eyes to banish the light.

"The trouble, I believe, is that your reading is wrong," continued Dash. "You have been studying the lives of the strong silent men portrayed by romantic ladies, who (the men, not the ladies) invariably order their valets to bring them whiskies-and-sodas. In real life the strong silent man who doesn't say much—myself, for instance—always shuns whiskies-and-sodas and sticks to beer, otherwise he would not be a strong silent man."

"Damn you, Dash! Will you shut up?" demanded young Jeff, jerking up to a sitting posture and throwing his legs over the bedside.

"Gladly," assented Dash, but he added a qualification: "if you will dress and come to breakfast."

"Don't talk to me of breakfast," came the snarl.

"I must, my dear Jeff. A thin slice of unbuttered toast and a cup of strong coffee will make you fit for the drive home. Dot and I have come to town this morning especially to buy a shirt and take you home. If, after breakfast, you still feel unwell, we will then remove the distilled spirit remaining in your—er—inside by driving the truck up and down the main street of this beautifully paved town at five miles an hour."

"I'm not leaving the hotel to-day," Jeff decided, with out-thrust chin. "And you remember that I am the boss's son, and that you are one of the boss's servants."

"I remember only that your father is my friend," Dash said with remarkably altered voice. The indolence, the ambiguity, of his speech was but a mask after all, as was the gently smiling amused expression, replaced now by a brittle hardness. "If you are not off that bed in ten seconds, I'll run you out and kick you round Bumpus's backyard. Spring to it!"

The look and the tone of command utterly astonished young Jeff. It was as though he discovered a complete stranger in a man he had known ever since his return from college. Dash got up and moved his chair to the farther wall, and when he again seated himself and fell to rolling a cigarette young Jeff was stripping off his wet underclothes with shaking hands. The tall man's features relaxed into their habitual lines, and his voice, when he spoke again, was pitched to its usual mildness.

"Of course you must go home, old boy," he said, blowing smoke towards the curtains. "We are giving the Fosters a tin-kettling to-night. The boss and Miss Stanton are going. All hands are going. Dot and Dash are going. You are going. Before we left this morning Miss Stanton asked me to remind you of it."

"Damn the tin-kettling! The silly——"

"The police are lookin' for you, Dash," announced Dot from the suddenly opened door. "An' breakfuss is ready."

"I will submit to be interviewed by the police," agreed Dash, rising elegantly from the rather rickety chair. But before he left he said to young Jeff: "Hurry up and dress, old lad, and we will have a beer before coffee. I really think that beer before coffee is preferable to a liqueur after coffee. But as for getting drunk," he added significantly, "it must not occur again. Your position to-day will not allow of it. Please understand that thoroughly."

"Day, Dash!" snapped Sergeant Morris when he and the tall man met in the passage. "Got a 'phone message just now from Mr Stanton saying that the car is giving trouble. It was to come in for Father Ryan and me. We're headed for Fosters' tin-kettling. Mr Stanton suggested that you would give us a lift."

"Delighted, my dear sir, delighted," Dash murmured without enthusiasm. "I wish to purchase a shirt, and Dot, I believe, desires to don a new pair of gabardine trousers. We'll be ready to start in an hour."

"Good! I'll hunt up Father Ryan. Young Jeff going out?"

"Oh yes! He is dressing now."

The sergeant's eyes narrowed.

"Fat head, I suppose?" he growled.

"A gentleman never has a fat head," replied Dash, in a mildly reproving tone.

"Humph!" And Sergeant Morris was gone.

Five minutes later Dot and Dash and young Jeff sat down to breakfast, of which young Jeff consumed two pieces of toast and two cups of coffee. At the hour of departure Dot and Dash, who had purchased their goods from a storekeeper who made no bones about serving them that day, stood beside the truck awaiting their passengers, one of whom was then settling a stiff liquor-bill with Mr Bumpus.

Father Ryan, who lodged with the sergeant and his wife, toddled along when young Jeff made his appearance, and smiled broadly at each of them in turn. To young Jeff he said, in his faint Irish brogue: "You're fined five pounds, young feller."

"You fined me that amount last time I was in," the young man objected seriously.

"Of course I did, me bhoy. You were drunk last time you came to town. You were drunk last night, for when I looked into the parlour you were trying to play the piano with your feet. The next time it will be ten pounds. I shall expect your cheque," and his reverence dug the young man playfully in the ribs.

Father Ryan was the only representative of God left in Mount Lion. He was known and revered by bushmen as far away as Marble Bar in Western Australia as the greatest little man within the continent. No matter what denomination a man professed, if any, he went to Father Ryan with his income-tax forms or difficult letters that required answering, or to defend him in the police-court—for Father Ryan was a very able advocate when Sergeant Morris prosecuted on the d. and d. charge; whilst the women took to him their babies when they were sick, and their male relatives when they had the toothache.

When a man from Windee or one of the smaller neighbouring stations went into Mount Lion to spend there a week or a fortnight, during which he was nearly always drunk, for there was no other form of amusement, he was known as a "cheque-man". Some there were who spent their money recklessly and cut out their cheques in a state bordering on delirium tremens; others, a minority, were more conservative, more sober, and less helpless when the day came for them to return to the semi-desolation of the bush for a further twelve months.

In the bigness of his heart Father Ryan loved all these lonely men, many of whom were without family or family ties. He knew the stagnancy of their existence and the mental depression with which the bush afflicts them, and he forgave them their lapses into very occasional drunkenness as did his Master. He placed them all in one of two classes, which he called "Gentlemen" and "Drunks".

When a "Gentleman" cheque-man came to town Father Ryan demanded half a sovereign for his benevolent fund, and got it. On the arrival of a "Drunk" cheque-man he bailed him up and demanded three, four, or five pounds for his benevolent fund, according to the degree of doctoring it would require to send the man back to his job or find him another. And the "Drunk" invariably paid up.

When, therefore, a bushman was no longer a cheque-man, when, likely enough, he was a pitiful, palsied wretch, turned out of the hotel "broke", faced with the multi-coloured demons because the booze supply was stopped, Father Ryan was prepared to pick him up, take him to his lodgings in defiance of Sergeant Morris, and, aided and abetted by Mrs Morris, wean him gently from John Barleycorn, build up the food-starved body, finally take him to one of the stores and rig him out with new ready-made clothes and despatch him, per mail-car, back to his job.

No one ever had observed Father Ryan to frown. His face was beaming, as it invariably was, when he fined young Jeff, and it was still beaming when, later in the day, the opportunity occurred to reprove the young man for his folly in a manner wholly distinct from that of the ranting "wowser". Young Jeff found himself addressed and advised by a worldly-wise man, a true sportsman, and a pal.

On the way back to Windee, Dash drove the truck with Father Ryan beside him and the sergeant at the farther end of the seat, whilst young Jeff and Dot sat behind on the floor.

"An' how's the 'roos coming in, Dash?" inquired Father Ryan conversationally.

"Just now, they're a failure, your reverence," the tall man told him. "You will understand, of course, that the kangaroos no longer have their winter coats, and that it's not yet sufficiently warm to get them in paying numbers at the watering-places."

"Ah yes, that is so," admitted the little priest. "What a pity it is that the poor things have to be shot!"

"I agree. Sometimes I regard myself as a murderer. It wouldn't be so bad if there was any sport in getting them, any equality between them and the hunter."

"Sport!" ejaculated Dot from the rear. "There is no real sport in any kinda huntin'. There's gents go a-huntin' elephants with big-bore rifles wot represents hundreds of thousands of dollars in experimenting and plant to make 'em; and there's huntin' in England where thousands of pounds are spent on hossflesh and dorgs to chase a poor little mangy fox.

An' they calls theirselves sportsmen! The feller I calculate is a sportsman is like a cousin of mine. 'Im and some of his pals were sitting over a camp fire one night in ole Arizonee, when a mountain lion shoves 'is head out of a clos't-by bush, and my cousin, 'e says, calm like: 'Hey, Ted, here's a lion. Lend us yer tobacco-knife.'"

Dot raised chuckles all round. The sergeant was interested enough to inquire what happened next.

"Waal, my cousin 'e up and orf after thet lion full of beans; but the lion seed him a-comin', and was so surprised at takin' a bird's-eye view at a human without a gun that 'e skedaddled into Wyoming."

"Your cousin must have been a character," young Jeff laughed. He was recovering rapidly from his liver complaint.

"He was thet, you bet!" Dot admitted, vainly trying to roll a cigarette. "A bit casual like in his ways, though. Killed four fellers in various arguments, and ended by committing suicide."

"Oh! How did he do that?" inquired Father Ryan.

"Waal, yer reverence, it was like this 'ere," Dot explained without blinking an eyelid. "As I said, me cousin was terrible casual. It come on slow like, his casualness. An' then one day 'e was too casual on the draw. He sure was. He was thet casual and thet full of holes thet 'e never even said, 'So long!'"

Chapter Ten

Nature and the Rabbit

OF THE HANDS at Windee, only three did not intend to go to the tin-kettling: Mr Roberts, who was overwhelmed by work; the cook, Alf the Nark (so-called because of his chronic temper); and Bony, who, not having met the Fosters, did not consider himself entitled to be present. The men's quarters during the afternoon were a scene of great preparation, for Harry Foster was a popular overseer, and they intended honouring his bride and him by wearing their best clothes. They borrowed a flat-iron from Mrs Poulton, the "Government House" cook, and Ron, the Englishman, was kept ironing shirts and soft collars for an hour or more.

Sergeant Morris spent the afternoon with Father Ryan and the two Stantons in an easy-chair on the wide veranda of the big house. From where he sat he could see the men's quarters, but throughout the afternoon failed to see Bony, with whom he badly wanted to speak. To preserve the detective's incognito he decided against seeking him out too openly, and waited to see him before making an excuse to leave the house.

Marion and Mrs Poulton brought them tea about three o'clock, and when they arranged the things on a side-table Father Ryan could not but applaud the fact that the snobbery of wealth was entirely absent from the menage. In truth, Mrs Poulton, fat, small, greying, and sixty, was far more a companion-housekeeper than a kitchen cook. She had entered the service of the late Mrs Stanton shortly after Marion was born, and when Mrs Stanton died she undertook the whole of the house-work, the care of the children, and the domestic management of Jeff Stanton. The boss of Windee owed her a debt that he recognized he could never repay.

Mrs Poulton was dressed in her Sunday black, wearing stiff linen cuffs on her wrists and an enormous cameo brooch at the throat of her high-collared bodice. Marion wore a frock of pink charmeuse, and the kindly old priest felt whilst watching her that indescribable glow of content which is felt under such circumstances by a lover of beautiful things after having lived for years in the harsh ugliness of a prison—or a decaying Australian bush town.

As for Sergeant Morris, Mount Lion and a district as large as Wales claimed all his interest as policeman and administrator. In his odd or spare time he was a registrar of births and deaths, and married or buried Protestants if they preferred his unordained services to the ordained services of a Roman Catholic priest. These latter duties, however, were not onerous, since the whole of the people under his jurisdiction could have occupied quite comfortably the Government benches in the House of Commons.

The secret of Father Ryan's wide popularity rested on the fact that first and foremost he was a very human, sympathetic man. His calling never obtruded. A product of Maynooth, Ireland, he shed his political enthusiasms entirely and moulded his religious tenets in conformity with the conditions and the outlook of his parishioners and friends.

Dinner had been served at one o'clock that day, and after tea taken at half-past six he went with Jeff Stanton to watch the men leave for Nullawil. The two-ton trucks were drawn up outside the men's quarters, and when the two men joined the throng of hands arranging their own seating accommodation, Father Ryan was warmly greeted.

"I want you to pile on to Ron's truck," Jeff told them; and then, addressing himself to the driver of the second truck, went on: "Keep behind Ron and pick up the outside men who have centred at Range Hut. Both of you stop at the night-paddock gate this side of Nullawil, and wait for me. Have you got plenty of petrol-tins?"

They assured him with grins that they had, and a few seconds later the trucks pulled out on the eighty-mile journey. They watched the dust rise behind them and listened to the shouts and laughter ever growing fainter in the wonderful still air of early evening.

"They won't be shouting to-morrow," Jeff observed grimly, when he and the padre turned towards the house. "Not one of us will do a hand's turn. I'll be paying out wages for nothing and spending money on seventy gallons of petrol and several gallons of oil."

"'Tis yourself should admit that the smiles and laughter ye've seen and heard this day are sufficient payment."

"Perhaps I should. Father," owned Jeff with twinkling eyes. "They're good lads when treated as men, as I have always treated 'em. You've got to give me credit there."

"Indeed I do, Jeff," the little priest said, giving his companion a sly dig in the ribs with his elbow. "I give you credit, too, with having a little more intelligence than most employers. In that you are one with Mr Henry Ford. You never suffer strikes because you do treat your hands as men, and you are both millionaires. Why, here comes Miss Marion in trouble."

"Dad, why isn't Bony going?" she inquired.

"Not gone? By gad, I don't remember seeing him go on the trucks, now you mention it!"

"No, there he is coming across from the horse-yards. Ask him, Dad! He could come with us. I'm sure he would like to go."

Stanton, turning, saw Bony, and throwing back his head, roared in a voice almost to be heard in Mount Lion.

"Dad!" Marion cried reproachfully.

"Well, you don't expect me to go gallivanting after a nig, do you?" Jeff demanded.

Marion made no comment, but smiled at Father Ryan's smile. The three awaited the approach of the half-caste, and when he had doffed his hat to Marion, Jeff said in his loud gruff voice:

"Why-in-hell ain't you gone to the tin-kettling?"

"Well, as I am not acquainted with the overseer and his bride, I thought it would be presumptuous to go," Bony quietly explained.

Marion, regarding Father Ryan covertly, saw the priest's blue eyes open wide with surprise at Bony's cultivated voice, and was amused. Her father snapped:

"That makes no difference. We have all got to go. Even I have got to go, although I don't want to. Would you like to go?"

Bony remained dubious. Marion suddenly smiled at him and said:

"If you care to go, Bony, you will be quite welcome, I assure you. We can give you a seat in the car, and I wouldn't like to think that you were left behind simply because you have only recently come to Windee."

"In that case, Miss Stanton, I shall be delighted." The brown face was alight, and the gentle smile won Father Ryan as already it had won Marion. Old Jeff nodded agreeably, and Bony withdrew with bared head.

"Rather a remarkable half-caste," murmured the priest.

"He's a remarkable horse-breaker," Stanton said.

"He's one of the nicest men I've met," was Marion's verdict; and then she laughed at the look in Jeff's face, and added: "I really can't marry him, Dad, because he has a wife and three children already."

"That's a good thing!" Jeff growled, leading the way to the veranda.

Twenty minutes later they all got into a car that represented Jeff Stanton's single extravagance, a straight-eight Royal Continental. Young Jeff drove this superb car, and seated next him was Bony, who volunteered to open the many gates. Behind them sat Sergeant Morris with Mrs Poulton as companion, and in the rear Father Ryan sat between Jeff and his daughter.

The sun had set and almost to the zenith the western sky was aflame with crimson, gold and purple. Thousands of galahs wheeled and fluttered about the two tall windmills built beside the great hole in the creek which was Windee's permanent water supply, and their screeches were so vociferous that the excursionists found difficulty in making their own voices heard until they drew away from the homestead and slid on to the great salt-bush plain.

Bathed in the magic fleeting twilight, the great car sped towards the range of hills cutting Windee in halves, and for a little while the members of the party were silent; for, almost as swiftly as they were carried to the couch of King Sol, so the purple and blue shades of the sky sank to the horizon, curved and humped by the ridges of the low hills.

At the wheel young Jeff lounged as though he were handling the steering-wheel of a bath-chair; yet there was no hint of carelessness in the behaviour of the car, and he made it difficult for one to remember that most of his last night had been spent in wild drinking. Two miles out, he pulled up before a gate, and when through that, and Bony again in his seat, they had a run of fifteen miles across to the farther side of the paddock and the next gate.

To anyone used to Australian tracks, to ride in Jeff Stanton's car was an experience to remember. After their recent ride in the ton-truck owned by Dot and Dash, the sergeant and Father Ryan undoubtedly appreciated the difference. The old priest sighed and made himself a little more comfortable.

"I wish," he said with studied seriousness, "I wish I were a millionaire."

"I don't. Why do you wish you were a millionaire?" Jeff inquired with his habitual grimness, which was so often assumed.

"So that I could own a car like this one. May I be forgiven the sin of envy! But why do you not wish I were a millionaire?"

"If you were, Padre, you wouldn't be here," Jeff told him simply. "Anyway I offered to present you with a car and you declined it."

"I know you did, Jeff, but if I had a car I'd have to be after drivin' it, and I couldn't be drivin' it and sittin' back looking at the scenery at the same time."

"Well, if that's all, I'll supply you with a driver."

"It's kind of ye, Jeff, but I'd only be takin' the man from productive work. No, I'll be content just to wish I were a millionaire. There's pleasure in wishing, and less pleasure in having."

Night had come, the warm caressing night of early summer after the fierce heat of the day. The headlights stabbed the darkness lighting up the track for two hundred yards and revealing the startled amazed rabbits. They jumped, crouched down, or raced ahead of the on-coming, whirring monster; and Bony, watching, never for one second saw fewer than fifty of them. Remembering the poison-cart incident, he turned in his seat and remarked to Jeff:

"The rabbits are very thick about here."

"Yes, they're bad this side of the range, and worse on the farther side," Jeff agreed, also remembering the poison-cart incident. "Poison-carts though are useless on big areas of open country. We've had three good years, and during that time they've had splendid chances to breed up. Now we're due for a drought, and King Drought will kill them off. I've seen rabbit plagues so many times, and I've seen so many thousands of pounds wasted in trying to do what nature does for nothing that I no longer worry about them. The work of a thousand poison-carts would be like dipping a bucket of water from the Indian Ocean."

"But it is legally compulsory to use them," interjected Sergeant Morris.

"You're right, Morris, you're right," Jeff admitted, with a mocking sigh. "Someone once said the law was an ass. Whoever he was, he was a wise man. In last week's paper a man serving a sentence for arson was released because it was proved he was innocent. And he received a free pardon from the fool law. I am wondering what he was pardoned for."

"For wrongfully occupying gaol space, I expect," Morris laughed.

Chapter Eleven

Stars and Shadows

THE CAR BEGAN TO CLIMB; the song of the engine was like the low hum of a child's top; and now, when the track twisted round the slopes of the hills boulder-strewn and supporting a growth of stunted wattle and mulga, it seemed to the travellers that constantly they rushed towards a black precipice, and always at the last second, the precipice fled ahead once more, a further intervening stretch of the track being revealed to them. The blackness of the hills at first lay on one side towering above them; and on the other side a lighter shadow was more menacing, for it was the emptiness of a void, and a little later the hill shadows closed on both sides, leaving but a narrow margin of star-studded sky above.

Half an hour later the glare of several fires came into view, and when the headlights swung round in a wide arc in taking the curve the ruddy glow of the fires vanished and there leapt into reality the figures of several scantily clad blackfellows standing facing them, and to one side a huddled collection of squatting gins, outside a few ragged humpies built of tree-boughs and discarded sheets of corrugated iron. Young Jeff stopped the car before a substantial stone house, now occupied by two stockmen, wherein he had first seen the light of day. It was Jeff Stanton's first home, Range Hut.

"Good night, boss!" a voice said, and there standing beside the car was a little wiry white-haired and white-bearded aboriginal.

"Good night, Moongalliti!" Stanton replied affably. "The trucks pass short time ago?"

"Ya-as, boss. Tree—one—two—tree. Gettin' plurry crowd on this track, eh?"

Father Ryan chuckled. Several younger bucks loomed behind the patriarch.

"Only two, Moongalliti," Stanton corrected.

"The two station trucks and Dot and Dash," a young man said in clear English.

"Ya-as. Dot and Dash. Him tree."

"Humph! That you, Ludbi?"

"Yes, boss."

"When are you going back to the homestead? I've work to be done, and I want you and Harry."

"We go bimeby," old Moongalliti said importantly.

"We're going to-morrow, boss," the more civilized Ludbi informed them with greater precision.

"Ya-as, to-morrow, boss," Moongalliti instantly agreed. "'Nother blackfeller come—long—way away. Beeg feller corrob-oree. We go homestead to-morrow. Cook 'em up tucker—marloo—bungarra. Plenty blackfeller—plenty tucker—beeg feller corroboree."

"Sounds cannibalistic," growled Sergeant Morris.

"Well, look here, Moongalliti: you understand you throw-um spear your beeg corroboree, I come and use-um beeg waddy," Stanton said sternly.

"Na-na, boss. Blackfeller all right. Plenty good feller. You gibbit flour, eh?"

"I'll see. On the way in, you keep all them dogs at heel, or I'll be throwing out some poison baits."

The threat raised a squeal from an invisible gin. "We keep orl dogs tied, Mithther Stanton. You no poison 'em. Poor dog—poor dog!"

"Very well, Mary, do as I say. When you get to homestead Mrs Poulton wants your help with the washing."

"And don't you forget, Mary," Mrs Poulton warned her; at which Mary laughed much more soundfully than many a white woman, and the other gins as well as the bucks joined her as though it were a great joke.

Young Jeff, geared in low, let out the clutch, and they slid away amid a chorus of "Good night, boss!" and sped forward over the zigzagging track with the hill shadows continuing to hug them.

"They do mix up the language, for sure," Mrs Poulton confided to the sergeant. "Marloo in their own language means kangaroo, and bungarra is a bushman's word for goanna. There's going to be some cuts and bruises at the end of that corroboree. There always is."

"It wouldn't be a corroboree without a fight," the policeman opined.

"Indeed it wouldn't. And that white-whiskered devil is the worst of the lot. Do you know what he did to Gunda because she ran away with Toff?"

"No. She's Moongalliti's new wife, isn't she?"

"Yes, poor thing! Promised him when she was a baby like I might promise you an unweaned kitten," the lady explained a little indignantly. "Anyway, a young buck from Queensland named Toff came down and she ran away with him. When old Moongalliti discovered it he sent Ludbi and Warn and Watti after them. Ludbi can track, you know. He tracked them nearly to the Queensland border, even though they kept to the high stony tablelands. Toff got away, but they brought back Gunda, who was judged by the old man. And what do you think? He ordered them to hold her down, and then got Ludbi to drive his spear underneath her knee-cap. For weeks she went about with a forked stick for a crutch. She'll never be able to run any more, poor thing."

The sergeant added some condemnatory words to Mrs Poulton's, but Jeff Stanton began to chuckle, and the others were compelled to join in with him.

"The blacks know how to deal with disobedient wives, Mrs Poulton," he said, still chuckling.

"I think it is a shame. Poor thing! You ought to lock up that old devil, Mr Morris."

"I never interfere with 'em unless they go a-murdering," was the sergeant's viewpoint. "Anyway, I'll bet Gunda thinks a lot more now of her husband."

Mrs Poulton sighed with evident perplexity. Then she admitted with a seemingly lighter heart: "Well, yes. She told me when I asked her if she didn't hate Moongalliti that 'ole feller him no good husband, but he good to poor little Gunda. He give me puppy-dog. Me orl right now.'"

When the car slid out on the northern plain of slightly undulating country, with here and there small areas covered thickly with flat, smooth pebbles, Bony was thinking of Ludbi's tracking powers, and wondering why he and the others were so loath to track about Marks's abandoned car. There was something very strange in that, and he decided that after the corroboree he must make friends with them, in a fashion that only his being a half-caste made feasible.

The farther north they proceeded the more numerous became the clusters of trees which the headlights revealed, until the scrub was as thick as that which lay between the homestead of Windee and Mount Lion. Every eight to twelve miles they were stopped by a gate, which Bony got out to open and shut after the car had passed through. Mile after easy flowing mile was indicated by the ivory-faced speedometer until they saw in front a small red light and later the three trucks were revealed drawn up beyond the last gate. A match was struck and held against a cigarette, and for a second the round chubby face of Dot was shown them. And then they were halted behind the third truck, that owned by the strangely assorted partners. The drivers came back and stood near Jeff Stanton, who asked them if there had been any trouble on the road. On being assured that the trip had been uneventful, he said:

"Well, go on and pull up behind the cart-sheds. Tell the fellows to make no noise, for I suppose we must conform to the regulations."

Engines hummed. They saw the first truck get away, and two minutes after—to avoid the dust—the second, and, after a further interval of a minute or so, that driven by Dash. Young Jeff made no start for a full five minutes, since Marion reminded him that Mrs Poulton and she were wearing clothes easily ruined by dust.

Two miles brought them to the out-station named Nullawil. Bony glimpsed a house beyond a line of pepper-trees and several whitewashed huts and outhouses and then he was descending amidst a small crowd of men each of whom bore a glinting petrol-tin and a stick wherewith to beat it. Sensing an eager spirit of joyous expectancy, he felt a tin thrust under his arm and a short bar of iron slid into his hand, and heard Jeff Stanton say:

"Padre, escort Mrs Poulton, please. Marion, your arm! the rest follow on in twos and don't beat your tins until the right moment."

Chapter Twelve

The House of Bliss

THE ORIGIN of tin-kettling is obscure, and to-day it is practised in Australia with more or less ritual—in the farming areas no ritual whatever. In Central Australia, however, where the huge holdings of land are held by city monopolists and oversea shareholders, women and marriages are rare. Tin-kettling a newly-wed pair is an event accompanied by a ceremonial of almost religious inflexibility, whilst with our modern motor transport a distance of eighty miles is but an evening's jaunt. The beating of tinware is merely an adjunct to a house-warming party and the whole affair is often arranged by the bridal couple and the visiting friends beforehand.

On this occasion there followed Stanton and his daughter nearly thirty people. Father and daughter led the procession through the gate in the wicket fence and halted before the main veranda steps, whereupon Jeff called in a loud voice:

"Awake, ye sleepers in the House of Bliss! We are an-hungered and athirst."

No welcome was there. The house remained in complete darkness. The seconds slowly passed before the leading couple started to circle the house. Whereupon terrific din broke out from wildly-beaten tins—din that continued until the procession again halted at the veranda steps, when the echo of it was continued by numerous chained dogs and a great flock of awakened galahs roosting in the all-pervasive scrub.

"Show us a glimpse of the House of Bliss!" Stanton shouted.

Still no light appeared. Still the sleepers slept. Again Stanton led his procession of ear-splitting beaters round the house. The dogs yelped and howled, and the birds rose from their perches and fled. For the third time they came to the veranda steps, and for the third time Stanton called:

"Open, ye dwellers in the House of Bliss!"

And then a light sprang up in one of the rooms. A window was thrown open, and a voice raised in pretended anger came to them:

"Enough! Who are you who should disturb the slumbers of those within the House of Bliss?"

"We are friends of the bride and friends of the groom. We are in need of refreshment and desire to rest," was Stanton's reply.

"Gladly then will you all be admitted."

The window was closed. Light after light sprang up in room after room, until there was not a dark room in the house. Suddenly the main door was thrown open. A brilliant petrol lamp was brought out and suspended from the veranda roof, and then the veranda fly-netted door was flung back and a man and a woman, both dressed in white, stood looking down on them.

"Enter, friends of the bride!" entreated the woman.

"And of the groom!" cried the man.

"Enter our House of Bliss!" they invited together, and stood back whilst Stanton and Marion mounted the three steps. On the veranda a young man not yet thirty, slim, wiry, fair and good-looking, the born horseman indicated in his stance, and a young woman, small and dark and vivaciously pretty, waited to receive them. The men shook the hands of both with genuine good-fellowship, and the two ladies kissed and petted the bride with real affection.

Bony was the last to be greeted. Dressed in a well-fitting grey suit and wearing spotless linen, his European cast of face and blue eyes expressed understanding sympathy when he bowed to host and hostess with infinite grace.

"This is Bony," Stanton said by way of introduction. "Meet Harry and Edith Foster."

Bony found himself being regarded by the keen appraising eyes of Foster, and then the overseer's hand was thrust towards him, and Foster said:

"I'm glad to meet you, Bony. I've heard how you trained the grey gelding, and I'm always glad to make a friend of a good horseman."

"And will you train a horse for me like you trained the grey gelding, Bony?" inquired the bride.

"It would please me much, if a horse can be found as teachable as Grey Cloud," was Bony's smiling consent. The girl's big brown eyes were unsmiling, although her mouth smiled. Her looks and bright chatter doubtless would make a strong appeal to many men. Bony, however, was unaffected. There was absent from Edith Foster that inward light that made of Marion Stanton a lovely woman.

She and her husband led their guests into the house. The petrol-tins were stacked on the veranda. The ladies disappeared with the bride, and the groom conducted the gentlemen to the long dining-room, at whose farther end several adjoining tables supported great dishes of sandwiches, buttered scones, cakes and rank on rank of bottles and glasses.

"Say, Harry, wot's it like to be tied up?" asked Ted, the tall, bearded, sun-blackened stockman.

"Great, man! You should try it."

"Have to be callin' you Mister now, Harry. Like they would down in the Mister Country," drawled Jack Withers, and from long experience Foster knew that Jack was looking at him and not out of the window.

"Better not let the boss hear you," he was advised, which raised a general laugh.

The ladies came in, and Father Ryan drew the bride's arm through his and beamed at her with his twinkling eyes, and, taking her to where the groom was, he slipped his other arm through Foster's and with them faced the company.

"People, look upon the most wonderful and beautiful thing in the world," he said with softened voice. "Behold love, which is God!" And then, squeezing the arms he held, he said to the newly wed: "Neither of you is of my faith, but please accept the good wishes and blessing of an old man."

Whereupon young Jeff started up the ageless refrain:

"For they are jolly good fellows!"

Listening, Bony was thrilled by the universal affection expressed by Marion's sweet voice, Mrs Poulton's lighter notes, old Stanton's deep tones, and the roar of other voices, a few tuneful, most of them raucous. There was here none of the ridiculous and childish caste feeling of the cities. It was a gathering of simple human beings, united by sympathy and happiness, together inside a house, set many, many miles from the next human habitation.

Harry Foster's eyes were bright with unshed tears and his voice trembled whilst he thanked them in unstudied homely phrases. The bride's eyes remained bright and proud, and Bony decided that here was a hard, well-controlled woman, who undoubtedly would be the ruler. And he smiled at the thought of Gunda and of Moongalliti, her indomitable husband.

Father Ryan was escorted to the refreshment table, and the company were invited to "wade in and help yourselves". The big room resounded to loud voices and laughter. Corks flew and bottle-tops fell to the table with tinkling thuds. The ladies were served by their escorts, and the feast went on merrily for half an hour, and the bride went to the door and called for Mary.

And Mary, a great fat gin wearing a scarlet one-piece muslin dress, white silk stockings, and blue carpet slippers, ambled into the room with a huge tray, and ambled out again with a pile of used plates and glasses over the top of which she had difficulty in seeing her way.

For five minutes the talk was gradually becoming desultory, when Jeff Stanton asked Marion to play something. Smiling radiantly, she arose and crossed to the brand-new piano her father had given the newly wed; where, seeing her intention, Dash, dressed now as a London club man, opened the instrument and arranged her seat.

"Shall I turn over the music?" he asked softly, his eyes alight with the wonder and beauty of her.

"No. Not now, please. I'll play a few pieces I know by heart. I wonder if Ted has brought his accordion."

"I'll ask him, if you wish."

She nodded, her fingers fell on the notes, and she began to play a piece from "Lilac Time". Presently the big stockman, with an exceedingly old but perfectly kept accordion under his arm, stood beside her, and, looking up at him, she smiled and saw the answering boyish grin with a tiny thrill of happiness.

The piece she was playing was brought to a close. The accordion player then seated himself near the piano, and when Marion began to play "Annie Laurie" he joined in with truly exquisite skill.

Listening raptly, the company found interest in Bony, who joined the accordion player and from his pocket took a long green box-leaf, and, holding it lengthwise between his fingers, began to blow on it. The high full tones he produced from the leaf, now as a hurricane wind through kangaroo grass, now as the hiss of rain on water, softened and beautified the coarser tones of the accordion, and when the tune was ended the applause was uproarious.

Bony whispered to his partners and they agreed to what he was proposing. Marion played a few preliminary notes and then the accordion broke into "The Prisoner's Song". Bony did not join in for several minutes and when eventually he did it was a little while before his leaf music was heard. The stockman began to play ever more softly. The leaf wailed ever more loudly. Now the accordion was silent, and presently the piano became silent, too, and for a while Bony played alone. The company sat with half-closed eyes, enthralled by the weird tones, haunting, repining notes that cried for light and freedom, the wailing voice of a hopeless prisoner.

And when he finished he rose smilingly and bowed to their applause, and Ted swung round and grasped his hand and squeezed it as mangle-rollers would do.

"Now, someone, sing a song!" called out Marion gaily.

Bony retired to a corner and carelessly dropped into a seat beside Sergeant Morris. Men were urging someone else to sing or recite. Marion was again playing the piano softly, and to Bony the sergeant said in a low voice: "I have two letters for you, Bony, and we must make an opportunity for me to give them to you."

"Letters? Official?"

"One official, one private, both with the Brisbane postmark."

"Oh, the chief writes wanting to know what the devil this, that, and the rest of it; and my wife writes that the children are well and that she still loves me," Bony predicted with a smile. "What do you think of the bride?" he asked.

"What do you?" was the guarded response.

"Nice sort of a girl. Who is she?"

"Daughter of old MacKennie. Owns a run called Willoughby. Comfortable, but not rich. Willoughby is east of Mount Lion."

"And that tall, well-dressed man—Dash, they call him?"

"He's a mystery."

"Good! I like mysteries. What do you know of him?"

"Precious little," Morris admitted. "Came in nineteen-nineteen. Receives a remittance from London four times a year. Was a jackeroo on Windee for three years, and suddenly threw that up and joined Dot. Quite a retrograde social step, but they get on well together and make money."

"H'm! Any vices?"

"None chronic. Drinks no more nor less than I do," the sergeant went on. "Yet no one knows his people, or what part of England he comes from inside Hampshire, unless Jeff Stanton does. People must be big bugs, because Dash is a gentleman in the commonplace acceptance of the word. He gives one the impression he was once in the British Army."

"No doubt of that by the way he carries himself. Now about the nigs, Morris. Do you know why they are at Range Hut?"

"Oh, just on a walkabout, I think. Have you made any discoveries?"

"Nothing of importance," was Bony's evasive reply. "By the way, do you know who gave Miss Marion her ring set with sapphires?"

"Lord, no! Never noticed it. Why?"

"I was just wondering. It is rather a unique ring. The setting is entirely old-fashioned. You see, I know a little about jewellery. Have you sent for Marks's or Green's record?"

"Yes. Last week. I'll let you have it as soon as I get it. But have you discovered nothing as yet?"

"One or two little things."

"What are they?" pressed the sergeant.

"I have found out that there was a struggle, a fierce struggle, when Marks's car came to a stop, which was where it was found. When I receive the man's history I may be able to say how he was killed, as well as prove indubitably that he was killed."

"And you found no trace of the body?"

"No. I rather think there is no trace to find."

"No trace? But the body or portions of the body must exist. To totally destroy a body is the most difficult thing in the world."

"One would think so, to read the newspapers and novels of to-day, wouldn't one?" Bony said naively.

Chapter Thirteen

"And so to Bed"

THAT THE tin-kettling of the Fosters was a huge success was agreed with complete unanimity. It was five in the morning when Jeff Stanton, in conference with Father Ryan, decided that the hour of departure had arrived.

Stanton's party was the same, and they left ahead of the trucks on account of their greater average speed. The false dawn tinted the eastern sky, which now they faced. The air was cool enough for the women to need their wraps, but not for the men to wish they had brought overcoats.

For a while conversation among them was general, and then gradually silence fell and the silky hum of the giant engine was the only sound. Marion sat with Mrs Poulton in the rear, and she nestled against her father and was promptly asleep with his arm around her. Mrs Poulton slept lying back in her corner quite comfortably. Father Ryan smoked a cigar, happy and content; the sergeant wished he was at home and in bed.

As for Bony, his mind was busy. There were several points in regard to this case which wanted clearing up, points that it should have been easy to clear up. There was the question of the object of Marks's visit to Windee. He had arrived at Mount Lion with the full intention of interviewing Jeff Stanton. At the time of the search for Marks Sergeant Morris had asked casually the business that brought Marks to Windee. He was told that Marks was a one-time friend, and was satisfied with that because so far there was no suspicion of foul play.

Bony felt that to get Morris to ask Stanton bluntly what business Marks had with him would not yet be politic. He had no proof, or even leaning in thought, that Stanton had had anything to do with Marks's death or knew the manner of it. Time was on Bony's side. Marks's history might disclose valuable aids to putting a theory on a practical basis. Then, again, the aboriginal tribe was about to return to Windee after a "walkabout" that had hindered his questioning them. Once he became friends, especially with old Moongalliti, he could work to find out who was responsible for making that warning sign. For whoever made that sign witnessed the murder. Yes, a great deal lay in the womb of time.

The most astonishing feature to date was the fact that the sapphire which the ants had brought up from their nest had originally been set in the ring now worn by Marion Stanton. That she had been implicated in any struggle with Marks seemed very remote, yet skilful questioning of Mrs Poulton had elicited the fact that Marion had habitually worn the ring given her by her mother. And that night, whilst playing on the leaf, he had been able to make certain that the missing stone had been replaced by another when the pianist's hands had rested idly on the keys. He had not boasted when he said he knew something about jewellery.

There was yet another mystery which, however, was entirely distinct from that of the disappearance of Marks. To most men this second mystery would have appeared trivial. It was the singular fact that Dash had left the "Government House" to become a vermin-destroyer and fur-getter.

To meet Dash even casually was to place him immediately in the squatter class. It required no brain fag to decide that he was a gentleman. The fact of his being a remittance man was peculiar, but not necessarily discreditable; and certainly his habits since he had been at Windee had been above reproach.

He had brought a letter of introduction to Jeff Stanton, and had been offered the position of jackeroo, or pastoralist's apprentice. This position entitled him to a room in the "Government House" and to be treated as one of the family—a position quite in accordance with his upbringing.

Then suddenly he left all that to become the partner of an illiterate American, and to carry on work which the least fastidious gentleman would not undertake because of the exceedingly rough living and the necessity of constantly handling dead animals. Why did he make that sudden change? Why suddenly give up a life of comparative comfort among his near equals at least for the rough, uncouth existence of a fur-getter? Money was not the object. At least it did not appear so, for Dash was not extravagant, neither did he drink to excess. Something had happened a few years back which had never become public property.

This, as well as the greater problem, occupied most of Bony's wakeful thoughts. He had arrived on the scene of a crime of violence two months after its commission, when the sand had overwhelmed all traces of it. Before he could prove who committed that murder he must prove that the murder itself had been committed, for the blackfellow's sign was not definite proof. Whilst this sign pointed to the fact of murder, whilst it entirely satisfied the half-caste, it would not weigh a featherweight in itself with a judge and jury. As Morris had hinted, the judge and jury would want nothing less than proof of the existence of Marks's body, or identifiable portions of it, to satisfy them that murder had been done.

As a case, it delighted Bony. From the fallen sands of time he had to reconstruct the crime, as from the sands of the bush he had to recover clues and definite proof. Here was no corpse on the library carpet silently crying for vengeance, and giving the investigator a dozen important clues with which to start his tracking. Yes, Bony was absorbed. His belief was becoming strengthened that at last he had found the perfect murder—had stumbled by chance on a problem worthy of his exceptional intelligence. ...

Entering the homestead was like coming into harbour, and the sense of limitless space vanished, to be replaced by one of protection from the sleeping elements. Alf the Nark was in the kitchen of the "Government House", and Mr Roberts had done his best to set the breakfast-table. The trucks arrived whilst they were eating and discussing the tin-kettling, and Alf the Nark was then in his own kitchen, grousing as was his habit.

An hour later the homestead was as still as the grave. Father Ryan and Sergeant Morris had gone, driven to Mount Lion by young Jeff. Mr Roberts sat at his desk in the office. Alf the Nark punched dough for the next batch of. bread, and everyone else was sound asleep.

Young Jeff pulled up before the police-station, adjoining which was the house occupied by Sergeant and Mrs Morris, with Father Ryan as their lodger. Mr Bumpus was standing in his door, and, seeing him, Sergeant Morris suggested a reviver. Father Ryan hesitated for the fraction of a second, and young Jeff seemed to understand why, for he said: "It will be all right, Father; I am driving the dad's car."

"Of course it will be all right, my son," chuckled the little priest. "We will partake of some refreshment, 'and so to bed', as the immortal Pepys used to put it."

Within Mr Bumpus's private parlour they were served with a glass of bottled beer, and it was young Jeff who was the first to leave. Again at the car, he detained Father Ryan and handed him a cheque for five pounds.

"My fine, Father," he said, smiling.

"Thanks, son! Remember, next time it will be ten pounds."

Chapter Fourteen

The Passing of a Cook

ALF THE NARK aroused the men at five-thirty that evening by beating an iron bar on the enormous triangle outside the kitchen. The gleam in his black eyes indicated that he was in a towering rage.

Cooking on an Australian station does not induce placidity of mind. In the first place it is a seven-day-a-week job; in the second it very often happens that one or more of the men are late to meals having been delayed by sheep-work in a paddock; and in the third place the hours are long, and the cement or wooden floor of a kitchen is particularly hard on a cook's feet.

On account of these drawbacks cooks are scarce, good cooks are priceless, and all cooks are martinets. A cook's uncertain temper is, therefore, regarded with the indulgence given to lumbago, or gout, the sufferer receiving all consideration and sympathy.

When Alf the Nark started work in a kitchen his temperament was well-nigh angelic; but when the first month had passed—and Alf had a ten-pound cheque behind him—the small worries of life began increasingly to annoy him. At the expiration of three months a man accidentally spilling his pannikin of tea on the table, or not removing his eating utensils to the wash-up table when passing out, was quite sufficient to cause the speechless Alf to remove his apron with dramatic gestures, go roll his swag, and almost run to the office for his cheque.'

This indecent haste to quit a job invariably caused great inconvenience to his employer and to the men, who were compelled to cook their own food the best way they could until another cook was procured. That did not worry Alf the Nark unduly. He walked, if he could not get a lift, into Mount Lion, and made straight for Mr Bumpus's hotel but before he became quite drunk was "bailed up" by Father Ryan and persuaded to hand to the jovial little priest five pounds. Left in peace then to drink his fill whilst the balance of his cheque lasted, Alf passed a gorgeous week or ten days, leaning against the bar for sixteen hours and intermittently sleeping on the hotel wood-heap for the remaining eight.

The culminating brawl that preceded his escorted stroll to the one-cell gaol at the rear of Sergeant Morris's house was never remembered. When finally he regained consciousness his limbs trembled as with palsy, and his companions were reptiles and insects seen elsewhere only on the planet Mars.

Then came his appearance in the small court where the storekeeper, who was a Justice of the Peace, regarded him with judicial sternness. The sergeant or one of his troopers gave evidence after Alf had, as usual, pleaded "not guilty", and the J.P. sentenced him to seven days without the option of a fine, as he had been advised to do by the sergeant before the court day.

Again in the cell, dishevelled, unwashed, tormented by dreadful multi-coloured creatures, Alf was presently visited by Father Ryan bearing the orthodox prescription of a stiff whisky-and-soda. Since Alf had eaten nothing solid during the whole of the debauch, the restorative doses of alcohol were given on the strict understanding that the prisoner drank a bowl of Mrs Morris's soup.

By the time Alf the Nark was due for release Father Ryan had obtained for him another job. The grand old man never had any difficulty in getting Alf the Nark a job, for Alf the Nark was a most excellent cook—for three months. When the day of release came, Father Ryan escorted him to one of the stores, and there paid out the cash for what clothes and necessaries the man required, thereafter to lead him to the hotel, buy him one drink, and from the hotel escort him to the mail-car, pay his fare, and stand by him talking in his merry way till the car pulled out.

Alf the Nark, with many such another, worshipped Father Ryan. It mattered little to any one of them what religion Father Ryan represented. They respected him for his cloth as they would any other minister, but they loved him—well, because he was Father Ryan.

And when he had seen them go out of the township the little priest sighed, entered his book-filled study, and made up his accounts. Every penny that he so jovially demanded in "fines" was accounted for, and every penny expended in "doctoring his patients" and fitting them out for the jobs he found for them was also entered up. At the end of every month the sergeant and the J.P. were invited to audit his accounts, and they invariably did so, for Father Ryan was insistent.

After beating his triangle calling the men to dinner, Alf the Nark began to cut up two roast legs of mutton. Usually the first man entered the kitchen-dining-room precisely ten seconds after the triangle was struck, but this day the men were in bed and asleep, and it was fully ten minutes before the first of them arrived, having had to wash and dress.

"Soup?" snarled Alf.

"Please," came the sleepy answer.

"Soup?" snarled Alf to the next man, and so on until all were seated and occupied. Then: "I've 'ad enough of this. If yous think I'm going to be on deck orl the blasted day and 'ang about 'ere 'arf the night waiting for yous to grease yer 'air, you're mistaken. There's yer tucker. Eat it or chuck it art. I'm finished."

With a superb gesture he ripped off his white apron and threw it on the floor. One of the men impolitely laughed. Alf became speechless and danced on the apron, and, still speechless, rushed out to his room, where feverishly he rolled his few belongings in his blankets, and almost ran to the office. Half an hour later, with his cheque in his pocket, he set out on the eighteen-mile tramp to Mount Lion, visions of whisky-bottles drawing him on, memory of fits of trembling, of awful depression, of frightful creepy tormenting things obliterated.

That night the men washed up their own utensils and cleaned out the kitchen-dining-room, and when Bony had performed his share he sauntered down the winding empty creek until he came to a fallen tree. There he sat and gazed out over the great plain whilst the sun went down, and marvelled at the stupidity of men and the sinister influence of the bush which so greatly augments their stupidity.

Quite suddenly he remembered the two letters slyly given to him by Sergeant Morris, and these he took from a pocket and examined the superscriptions. That addressed to him in his wife's handwriting he opened first, and read:

> *Banyo,*
>
> > *nr. Brisbane.*
>
> *Dearest Bony,*
>
> *Detective Holland came out from town yesterday especially to tell me that you had left Sydney for the Western Division N.S. Wales, on another case. He says that Colonel Spender is very angry, because you went to Sydney only to finalize a case and have gone off without authority, especially when there is a murder case giving them trouble out of Longreach.*
>
> *We are all disappointed, too, because we were looking forward to a walkabout beyond Winton. When are you coming back? We haven't had a walkabout now for nearly nine months, and you know how it is with us. Little Ed is going to the Banyo school next week. Bob wants to go west and get a job on a station, and I know you won't like that. You had better come home and stop him. …*
>
> *Do come home, dear Bony. But there, I know you won't until your present case is finalized. Charles is going up for his University entrance exam the week after next. He is going to be like you, but like you and me and all of us the bush will get him in the end. It's in our blood and can't be resisted.*
>
> *We send our love, dearest Bony. All are well.*
>
> > *Marie.*

The handwriting was neat, the spelling faultless. The writer was a half-caste like Bony, and in her way an equally satisfactory product of mission station education. Bony was smiling gently when he replaced the sheet in its dainty mauve envelope and thought of the pride of his life, his eldest son Charles, to whom he had bequeathed most of his mental gifts, and then of the lad who was always unhappy at school, always pining for the bush. The call of the bush was knocking at Bob's heart almost as soon as he could walk, whilst the call came to his wife and himself much later in life, but nevertheless was equally insistent, equally compelling.

Once more he smiled, this time a little more broadly, when he ripped open the official envelope from Headquarters, Brisbane. The typed part was terse and to the point. Below his name and rank it read: *You are hereby notified that you are allowed six weeks' leave of absence without pay, as from October 1st, 1924. Should you fail to report at the expiration of this period your appointment will automatically cease.*

It was signed by Colonel Spender, Chief Commissioner, Queensland Police, and under the signature a vicious ink-splashing pen had inscribed three further words: *You are sacked.*

Whilst returning this communication to its envelope Bony chuckled, for he could so easily visualize the colonel's purple face when he dashed down these three words with final impulsiveness. As in the past, he would, when the Marks case was finalized, report for duty. He would be shown into the Chief Commissioner's office, there to receive a lecture on discipline and asked pointedly how the devil and what the devil he thought the service would be without it ... "and for heaven's sake go and help that fool to find out who stole the Toowoomba Bank cash and bonds!" or "assist that ass on the Cairns murder case!"

Presently he rose and in the soft warm darkness walked back to the men's quarters, where he accompanied the accordion-player on a succession of box-tree leaves.

At six o'clock he was up cooking the men's breakfast; and the men, who thought they would have had to cook their own meals, were highly gratified. To Jeff Stanton, who came into the kitchen after he had given out his orders, he said in his calm manner:

"I do not like cooking, but I will carry on until you can get a cook. I hope that will be soon."

"I telephoned to Father Ryan last night, Bony. There is no cook in Mount Lion wanting a job just now. I'll do all I can to get one. How much have you been making on your breaking-in contract?"

"Somewhere about seven pounds a week."

"Well, that's a stiff price to pay a cook. But I'll pay you that in wages as a cook. The men must have a cook, and it is unfair that you should receive less wages as a cook than you were making breaking-in horses."

"But for the money I would rather break-in horses," Bony said, yet was pleased that Alf had left hurriedly.

Chapter Fifteen

The New Cook

THE IDEAL STATION-HAND is the man who can do any job required to be done on a station. Most men follow up a particular line of work—horse work, rough repairing, cooking, fencing and well-sinking, team driving, or truck management. There are many men, however, who can do any or all these things creditably, and Bony was one of them.

The vacancy in the men's kitchen made by the dramatic departure of Alf the Nark presented to Bony a sure avenue of winning his way to the hearts, via the stomachs, of Moongalliti and his tribe. To these natives, whose habitat was a hundred-mile radius of Windee, Bony was quite an outsider. Had he been a full-blooded aboriginal they would never have accepted him as one of themselves, because his totem would not have been their own. As a half-caste, and a strange half-caste, he would at all times be regarded with suspicion; but as a station cook, with somewhat of their racial blood in him, he could successfully bribe them and win a measure of friendship with food, for food and the getting of food occupies far more of the native mind than any other subject.

To have approached them abruptly and casually asked which of them had put up the sign near Marks's abandoned car would have produced looks of blank astonishment and protestations of complete ignorance, not for any reason to fear they had infringed the white man's law, of which they knew very little, but because the meaning of their signs is kept but little less secret than the ceremonies accompanying the initiation to full adulthood of their young men and women.

Bony got on with his job well satisfied, and that morning baked the bread from the dough made by Alf the Nark. At nine-thirty he struck the triangle for morning lunch, at twelve for midday lunch, and at three for afternoon lunch, and was towards four o'clock "putting on the dinner", when a step behind him caused him to look around and see Marion Stanton regarding him with amused but friendly eyes.

"You know you are a surprising person, Bony," she said laughingly, and seated herself on the only chair in the place—the cook's chair. Bony's face lit with that inward flame which was as the slow turning up of a lamp-wick.

"Why should you think that, Miss Stanton?"

"Well, in the first place you are a university graduate, yet you break-in horses most expertly; secondly, you play divinely on an ordinary tree-leaf; and now I find you cooking, having been told that you really can cook. What else can you do?"

"What I can do, you know. Is it not enough? I can very easily enumerate what I cannot do: I cannot manage a station; I cannot preach a sermon; I cannot dance; and, alas, I cannot compose poetry."

"Do you want to be able to do those things?"

"I should like the gift of composing poetry," he said gravely.

"Why?"

"That I might write a poem about you!" was the bland reply.

Marion's face flushed, and the smile gave place to a look of haughty surprise. Bony went on unperturbed. "Yesterday when I looked back and saw the hills riding on the mirage sea I felt sad that I could not fix the beauty of it with words as a great painter with his brushes. To make an immortal copy of beauty, either with brush or pen, would, I believe, be a most satisfying accomplishment."

"I think I begin to understand you," Marion told him. By this time the freezing look had melted away.

"I am glad of that. Permit me to attend to this custard for one moment."

Watching him at work over the big range, Marion recognized that she was strongly attracted by this man's personality. He was so natural, so utterly without affectation, and so perfectly free from the slightest taint of coarseness. No other men of her acquaintance, and they ranged from an Irish peer down to a horse-boy, possessed the likeable personality of this half-caste. Dear old Father Ryan was splendid, of course, and he came very close.

"Have you been doing station work ever since you left the university, Bony?" she asked softly.

"Mostly station work, yes," he replied, turning. "You see, had I been a half-caste Chinaman, or a half-caste anything else, I should not have felt the call of the bush as I did and do. A lot of white people, even in the Australian cities, know very little about the Australian native, and nothing whatever of the cause of his being the happy nomad that he is. White people, some of whom are quite intelligent, imagine it to be possible to throw the mantle of the white man's civilization about a native or a half-native and keep it there. I have never known a half-caste, even with the educational attainments I possess, remain all his life in a city among white people."

"Nor I either, Bony."

"From the mission where I was reared I graduated to a high school and from there to the university. Mastering the arts and sciences came to me with extraordinary ease. Many people who knew me foretold for me a brilliant future. 'Observe the white man's culture in Bony,' they said. For a little while I believed them, and then one day I began to want something that I couldn't define or name. You yourself, having been born in the bush, might be able to name my want."

"Well, it is hard to describe it, Bony, unless we name it the Call of the Bush. I have felt that call when I was at college and during the time I was in England with Dad."

"That is it, Miss Stanton. You were born in the bush, and have felt the call. How much more plainly must I have heard that call with the blood of countless nomadic ancestors in my veins! I left Sydney when I was twenty-two and went back to North Queensland, where I first saw the light. And my body craved for complete freedom from the white man's clothes. I wanted to go ahunting as my mother's father had hunted, and I wanted to eat flesh, raw flesh, and feast on tree grubs, and then lie down in the shade and go to sleep, fed full and feeling the wind play over my naked skin.

"That is what I wanted to do; but reason, the trained white man's reason in me, caused me to behave a little less primitively, and in the end the white and the black blood in me called a truce; and behold the result to-day—Bony!

"I have worked on stations. I have taught children their 'three R's'. I go to Sydney to study psychology occasionally, and to Brisbane to supervise the education of my three children. Marie, my wife, also a half-caste, stays there because of them, but neither she nor my children nor myself can resist the call of the bush. You understand and sympathize; but how can the white fool understand who has never been farther than a few miles from a city? It is like caging a full-grown galah and expecting it to be happy."

"And are you happy?"

"Quite, although for many years I was very unhappy. Now I have come to balance accurately the white man's impulses against those of the black man."

"Tell me about your wife and children," she said. He did so, the while making a bread-pudding for the men. He told her of his firstborn, who was following so decidedly in his footsteps, of Bob being tortured by the call of the bush, and of baby Ed, who was adventuring to his first school. He watched the changing expressions on her face and glimpsed the purity of her in her eyes, and he came to know that in spite of the ring she wore she knew nothing of what lay behind the blackfellow's sign of the sheep's leg and the sticks fashioned as a fan. To know that was why he had conducted their conversation as he had done. In the art of guiding conversation, and establishing scientific conclusions from it, Bony had few, if any, superiors.

He was, however, in several respects not unlike the great man whose names he bore. In conducting a case he knew how to make his dispositions, and when and how to force his opponents into inextricable situations. Within rigid bounds he was unscrupulous. If he wanted an object as proof of a contention, and that object was in the pocket of another person, he would not hesitate to obtain it through sleight of hand with a dexterity that many expert pickpockets would have envied. Nor would he scruple to employ the gentle art of "pumping" to extract information from unsuspicious people. He proceeded to "pump" Marion.

"The bush always had a very strange fascination for me," he remarked in his gentle way. "Birds and insects and animals always interest me. The honey ants, those peculiar ants who live in a tiny cavern deep in the earth, and are fed with honey by the other ants until they become so full they are unable to move; and the black ants, who heat small stones by laying them in the sun to take down to keep their eggs warm. I know a man who, watching a nest of those ants, actually saw one bring up a tiny nugget of gold. The nugget had dropped off someone's watch-chain, for it was quite evident that it had had a fastener of some sort."

"How strange!" Marion said, her face alive with interest. "It reminds me of the sapphire I lost from this ring months ago. I lost it, however, in the house somewhere, so the ants hadn't a chance. I am positive about that, because all the stones were in my ring when I had breakfast one morning, and I hadn't been out of the house when I missed it."

"That was very unfortunate." Bony was watching her.

"Indeed, yes. The ring was my mother's engagement ring, and she willed it to me before she died. I was obliged to send it to Adelaide to get the stone replaced."

"Perhaps I may be able to track it." Bony smiled. "They say I am rather good at tracking. Once in Queensland I tracked a lost man when the aboriginals gave it up."

"Indeed! That's another thing you can do! It is a pity you weren't here a month or two back. There was a man lost not two miles from here. I expect you've heard all about that?"

"Yes. The affair appears most peculiar."

"It was. All the men and even Dad and I, rode out day after day and never found a trace of him. No one ever saw him after he left the house, having taken lunch with us. Dot and Dash were kangarooing in the next paddock south, and never came across his tracks. Of course, it was some time after he went away that his car was found and the search was made."

"Were there no trackers among the blacks here?" inquired Bony innocently.

"Yes. There were Ludbi and old Moongalliti, and the day we took them to the car you would think they couldn't track a horse after rain. They were almost useless. Said too many days past when Marks walked away from the car."

"Very sad. Most sad. I suppose Mr Marks was a friend of your family?"

"Oh, no. Dad had had some business with him years ago, and he called on Dad to persuade him to make some investment or other. If he had been a friend it would have been dreadful. … Why, just look at the time! I've been here an hour. You are to be complimented, Bony."

"And you, madam, to be heartily thanked."

Marion rose, but at the door paused to say:

"Do you think I could ride Grey Cloud this evening?"

"Decidedly, but permit someone to ride with you until Grey Cloud has proved himself."

"Thank you! I will." Marion smiled and was gone.

Chapter Sixteen

Bony Goes Courting

A CONVERSATION conducted by Bony was seldom without result to him. The conversation he had had with Marion pleased him immensely.

There was certainly a good deal of the mystic in Bony, although he seldom admitted it. Of all the great world religions he was sceptical, but where several religions agreed he agreed also. Which is to say he believed in the fundamental existence of God. Of all things spiritually beautiful Bony was a worshipper. A beautiful view, a glorious sunset, and a lovely woman—not necessarily a beautifully featured woman—always won homage from him. Seeing and sensing the spiritual beauty of Marion Stanton, the soul of this strange man thrilled, and he was made positively happy to be once and for all convinced that she had nothing whatever to do with the disappearance of Marks.

He now awaited two things: the arrival of the aboriginal tribe and the receipt of Marks's or Green's official history. If a certain happening was mentioned in the history, it would justify his referring to an eminent authority the small thin silver disk, with the details regarding Marks, for positive identification. Should his own theory as to that silver disk be substantiated, then the death of the man Marks was proved.

On the evening of the third day of his cooking activities one of the riders informed him that the blacks would reach their main camping-ground, half a mile down the creek, where there was another deep water-hole, that night. Bony smiled and waited patiently. And the following evening, while he was washing up, a guttural voice spoke to him from the doorway, and there he saw Moongalliti's cunning old face.

"Goo'-day-ee, Cook!" greeted the chief, with a broad happy grin as though welcoming a lifelong friend.

"Good day!" drawled Bony, carrying on with his work.

"Alf, 'e bin gone Mount Lion for pop-eye?" came the friendly inquiry.

"That so. Full up with grog by this time."

Moongalliti laughed heartily, seating himself on the doorstep. Then: "You'm the new cook, eh?"

"Yes."

"What say? Bimeby you gibbit tucker, eh?"

"Perhaps."

"You come long way? You no Windee feller, eh?"

"No. I come from North Queensland."

"Um! Nor' Queensland—long way, eh? Wot 'em your totem?"

It was a question Bony had been expecting. The sergeant had told him that the totem of those people was the emu; and, to make him akin to them, he said: "My totem—emu. My lubra mother she emu totem."

Moongalliti beamed, and regarded Bony with fresh interest. "Good, eh?" he exclaimed with seeming enthusiasm. Then he said something in his native dialect which Bony could not understand; and the half-caste told him in a North Queensland native dialect that Moongalliti was a spirit-slaying, bone-pointing old scoundrel, which that important personage likewise did not understand. He reverted to his broken English.

"You young feller bin—bin ... You young feller bin made—bin made buck?" he inquired casually.

That was another question Bony had been waiting for. Laying aside the plate he was drying, he removed his white apron, and pulled up his shirt about his neck, and old Moongalliti saw welts made by a sharp flint on Bony's chest, and chuckled with satisfaction.

"You orl ri', eh?" was his judgment.

Bony turned about and showed Moongalliti his back. Across his shoulders was cut a rough square and in its centre a circle, and when Moongalliti saw these his black eyes bulged and he crept closer to Bony, the better to examine the brand.

"My!" he said, almost in a sigh. "You beeg feller chief, Nor' Queensland, eh?"

Turning, Bony nodded, set his shirt in order, then resumed the apron of his calling. Moongalliti's attitude towards the stranger half-caste had become almost deferential. He now was convinced that Bony had been through the initiation ceremony making of him a man, but he was astounded to see that Bony was very high in the mysterious cult, little known even among the blacks, which may be compared in many respects to the craft called Freemasonry.

Inwardly Bony was delighted to find that the old fellow recognized that sign. It would smooth away many difficulties of access to the heart and the mind of the chief or king of this small tribe.

Moongalliti left presently with as much waste and unused food as he could carry. Bony watched him across to the creek-bed, where he was met by an old white-haired gin and a much younger one who limped badly. With a lordly air Moongalliti gave them the food to carry, and himself walked on before them. The next evening, and in the future, it would be the women who would come begging for food. The reason the chief had come himself that night was to "place" the strange half-caste, the new cook.

Thenceforward every morning two young lubras passed the kitchen on their way to work at the "Government House", and repassed on their way back to their camp every evening. At Bony they cast curious shy glances, and since he doubted not that both he and they were watched by Moongalliti or Ludbi, or others of the bucks, he made no overtures to them whatever. Regularly, when the men had finished dinner and he was cleaning up, two and sometimes three of the oldest gins came along asking for tucker, and to these Bony made himself particularly pleasant.

To several of the young bucks Jeff Stanton offered employment at white man's wages, but this they declined until such time as the corroboree was past. Judicious questioning of the hands, particularly of Jack Withers, elicited the fact that Moongalliti's tribe consisted of forty-three adults, of whom eighteen were women, and an unknown number of children of all ages. The stockman, the man of the atrocious squint, was at all times exceedingly interested in the blacks, and was chaffed unmercifully by the others, who professed to consider him in danger of becoming a "combo", or a white man who is married—more or less—to a lubra.

In any case, to Bony, who comforted his romantic heart with the salve of sympathy, Jack Withers related details regarding prominent members of the tribe which were useful to Bony, as well as obviating the necessity of too much questioning of Moongalliti. For Bony wanted that gentleman to think he was uninterested in the tribe just then.

And now nearly every day there arrived a strange aboriginal and sometimes a three-quarter or a half-caste. These, Withers explained, were relatives and members of the tribe come in from neighbouring stations for the corroboree. Going about their work in the paddocks, they had come across a sign informing them of the coming corroboree, and there and then asked for their pay and left their employment. Some came in buckboards, others on horseback, and one arrived on a resplendently new bicycle.

The majority of these late-comers were youths and quite young men. It was common knowledge among the whites and the adult blacks what they were facing. The young fellows themselves made shrewd guesses but appeared resigned. Singly they were induced to go hunting by several of the bucks and Moongalliti, and when purposely drawn near a certain place, which was a singular knob of ironstone twenty feet in height, the young man was suddenly seized by his companions and thrown to the ground. Quite heedless of his yells in their own excitement, they held him fast whilst Moongalliti proceeded to use a stone with a razor edge in such fashion that the yells became shrieks. After various cuts had been made the open gashes were plugged with a compound of mud and healing herbs and bound with rag—it used at one time to be grass-rope—whereupon the now adult buck was taken to an out-camp and kept there until it was time to remove the mud plugging, when the flesh would never again close over the cuts.

That went on for several days, till every uninitiated youth was made a buck, and then one day the whole of the male population came into the main camp triumphantly escorting the graduates, on whose heads was set a cone of dried mud and grass and their own hair. The gins acclaimed them and the smaller children regarded them with envy. Around the fire that night they felt themselves to be heroes, as indeed they must have been, remembering Moongalliti's stone knife.

The stage now was set for the corroboree.

Jack Withers reported great activity in the black camp. From five to seven gins visited Bony every evening, and one of them, very ugly and fat, to whom no buck at the time was married, regarded Bony wtih favourable eyes. Deliberately and openly the unscrupulous Bony courted her. Besides her portion of scraps and old bread, he made for her delectable peach pies and crowned her happiness one evening with a great slab of toffee. After the others had gone she lingered and assisted in the clean-up for the day, and little by little Bony obtained—at least in part—the information he desired without giving her the faintest suspicion of what lay behind a few leading questions put to her at long intervals.

Runta was ignorant of some things but cognizant of others. It appeared that Ludbi was out hunting. He carried a rifle. He was north of the junction of the two roads when he heard a car coming from the direction of the homestead. He heard the car almost stop and move on again, and then suddenly he saw the car coming through the bush and two men fighting in the front seat.

Runta said that Ludbi saw one of them killed, but how he was killed, by whom, and what happened after she did not know, for Ludbi had held long confab with Moongalliti, and Moongalliti had threatened him—or any one else—with the pointing-bone if he, or she, spoke a word to a living soul of what Ludbi had seen.

Poor Runta never realized that she had told Bony all this, for the threat of the pointing-bone was tantamount to a sentence of death. What the detective had learned through her was both much and little. It was corroboration of his conviction that Marks had been killed, but did not give him the name of the killer. The only additional confirmatory fact he had obtained was that the killer was a white man, not indicated by the fan-stick sign.

This single fact deepened rather than lightened the mystery. The act being a murder of a white man committed by a white man, what was behind Moongalliti's sudden failure of tracking powers and his threat of the pointing-bone against any of his tribe who told the little they knew? How came the blacks to be mixed up in an affair entirely white?

The more he delved into the sand of this case the greater became the quantity of sand which fell in to smother his excavations. To the main issue the mystery of the sapphire and the mystery of Moongalliti's orders were added. Bony was delighted. He went about his work singing in a cracked voice, and sometimes playing quick jazz tunes on a box-leaf. He smiled on Runta and playfully poked the rolls of fat beneath which somewhere were her ribs. He saw several of the bucks and Moongalliti talking with Stanton one afternoon, saw them take a station hand-cart and proceed with it to the store. Later they dragged it past the kitchen loaded with two bags of flour and a case of jam. The corroboree would be held the next night.

Chapter Seventeen

The Corroboree

AT NOON on the day of the corroboree a bunch of half-naked aboriginal children clustered in the shade cast by a solitary box-tree growing well away from the main avenue bordering the creek. Several of the older boys were sitting in the branches, and children on the ground constantly called out an ever-repeated question.

All these children had an uninterrupted view of the plain, and the direction of their searching looks was north-east. At all times they could see ten to a dozen thin columns of grey and red dust staggering slowly across the vast expanse from west to east; for the miniature whirlwinds twisted up dust and debris at times as high as two hundred feet.

And then suddenly one of the boys in the tree gave a shout, and the others became silent. Far out on the plain dust rose and slanted eastward—dust not caused by a whirlwind, a flock of sheep, or a mob of racing horses, but slowly and steadily rising dust from human feet. It arose from one point and remained there steadily, for the marchers were making straight for the outpost tree.

At five Moongalliti, with his bucks marshalled on either side of him and the women and children behind them, waited at the edge of the timber belt to welcome their adjoining tribe. The strangers came forward slowly, obviously tired, yet excited as well. In numbers they equalled Moongalliti's people, the chief leading, behind him his bucks, carrying spears and war murrawirries, and behind them the women, loaded as Egyptian donkeys, with their own belongings as well as those of their lords.

Fifty yards from the home tribe the strangers halted, and the strange chief, Mertee, and Moongalliti, walked forward to meet each other, weaponless. What each of them said at the same time was something like:

"Oo-la-oo-la-um-yum-oo-la-oo-la!" spoken very rapidly without pause or cessation. They flung their arms about each other's naked bodies, hugged and danced on their big-footed, thin, spindly legs, and grunted.

"Oo-la-oo-la-um-yum-oo-la-oo-la!"

The official wording of the welcoming ceremony was double Dutch to Bony, standing with some of the men nearby—they having agreed to postpone their dinner for one hour; and it was double Dutch to Jeff Stanton and Marion, who, seated in the big car, watched from a greater distance. The meeting of the two head-men was one of extravagant affection, and after about five minutes' hugging and "oo-la-ing" Moongalliti and Mertee walked towards the former's people, with Mertee's tribe hurrying after them, no longer in ordered array, but a couple of mobs.

The two mobs intermingled with happy yells and shrieks of laughter, whilst children eyed stranger children gravely, considering whether to fight or be friends. And then, like a slow-moving "whirlie" of black sand carrying in its swirl the flecks of white and blue and red gaudy feminine raiment, the whole rolled towards the creek, flowed down into its bed, surged up on the farther bank, skirted the water-hole, and ranged itself about a mound of glowing embers before settling into comparative stillness—and silence.

At a short distance from the fire the banquet was set out on sheets of bark, flattened petrol-tins, and disused saucepans and colanders rescued from the station rubbish-heap, arranged in a circle. Jeff Stanton's flour, mixed with water, had been baked in the likeness of rocky slabs, doubtless of rocklike hardness as well. Quartered kangaroo, sheep's offal, goannas, yabbies from the water-holes, bush yams, and enormous emu legs, lay in mixed profusion, piping hot, around the rock-bread.

Forming a circle outside the food circle, the bucks sat cross-legged. Behind each buck sat his woman or women, and again behind them the children. The widows and spinsters—there were remarkably few, for a reason that shall be mentioned—crept to the side of their more fortunate sisters who shared with none the love and thrashings of their lords.

No toastmasters or other makers of ceremony being present, no time was lost in useless civilities. The bucks seized those items of the menu which tempted most their individual palates, and for a while those behind them listened with ill-concealed impatience to smacking lips and crunching teeth. And then from the inner circle there appeared to slide yard-long bones with great lumps of meat still adhering to them, whereupon shrill feminine cries raised in argument and the yells of clamouring children on the outermost human circle competed with the yelps and barks of a hundred dogs of all sizes and mixed pedigrees which hemmed in the diners with a cloud of stifling dust.

It will now be understood that the spinsters and widows experienced a lean time, since what they got had to be snatched from the hands of wives who had babies and children to feed from what they left.

At the chiefs' table was shown a little more decorum. They ate from one dish a mixture of Bony's bread, two legs of mutton, a great quantity of white, slug-like tree-grubs called bardees, two small piles of honey ants swollen to the size of peas with the native bee honey showing through their transparent bodies, yams, and one enormous goanna some six feet in length. Behind them sat their respective wives and families.

One by one the bucks stretched themselves and sighed. One by one they lit most evil-smelling pipes or roughly made cigarettes, and at a gutturally spoken command the remains of the banquet—and the remains were by no means small in quantity if lacking in quality—were passed to the women, who broke up into groups and fed. One by one the women stretched and sighed, and lit old pipes and cigarettes—charged chiefly with cow-dung—and, a little while after, one by one the children sighed and stretched and rolled over on their backs. All hands slept torpidly, whilst the countless dogs scratched among them for scraps and bones.

That night none of the gins sought Bony for food and a little "bacco"; even Runta's love had failed, weighed down by the lead of an enormous meal; and Bony, seated on a petrol-case at the kitchen door, sighed and smoked innumerable cigarettes.

The sigh was not inspired by the absence of Runta, nor by relief at her absence. He sighed because it was one of those times when within him war was waged between the spirit of his father and the spirit of his mother. During these times of spiritual strife his black ancestry invariably almost won. The one influence that decided the battle in favour of the spirit of his father was his love for things beautiful and his loathing for things ugly, an influence passed to him by both his parents. Although his base complex urged him towards native savagery, he could find in it nothing of real beauty, nothing of the beauty he had discovered in the white man's art, in the white man's striving towards ideals of cleanliness and purity and achievement.

This night Fate offered a salve for his spiritual wounds. He was reading at a late hour Mendel's treatise on Heredity in Flowers, when at the door of his room appeared the almost naked form of Moongalliti.

"Goo' day-ee, Bony!" he said cheerfully. "Gibbit bacco."

Laying down the book, the half-caste examined his tin, and, finding it less than half-full, gave it to the chief and from a box obtained a full tin. He was wondering what lay behind this visit. Then:

"Mine fren', Mertee," Moongalliti mumbled, and there beside him stood the visiting chief. For a while all three were silent, when suddenly Moongalliti said: "Mertee, he tell-um me plurry liar. You let um see sign, Bony."

Bony understood, and, rising to his feet, pulled up his shirt and allowed them to see the initiation cuts on his chest. Mertee, apparently satisfied, grunted; then Bony turned round, and the ensuing silence was at last broken by Moongalliti's triumph.

"Plurry liar, eh?" he said cheerfully.

Again Mertee grunted. Bony rearranged his shirt and, sitting back on the bed, slowly began to remove the tin-foil from the airtight tobacco-tin. Moongalliti took a huge pinch of tobacco from his tin and began to chew. Mertee obtained the tin with determination, and presently he also was chewing. After a little while Moongalliti said:

"Wot you say, Bony?" He pointed first at himself, then at Mertee, and finally at Bony. "Orl same. You come alonga sign stone? You'm tak' place sun get-up. Mak' Ludbi an' Warn an' Quinambie orl same us?"

Bony slowly smiled, his blue eyes alight. Why not? Why not for one hour be as they were? Why not ease his soul-hunger of the craving to dive deep into the mysteries of their cult? Still smiling, he left with them. The moon was almost at its zenith. They walked along the creek-bank beneath the leafy box-trees, as their gods always walked in the fairy world of silver and shining dewdrops. At the camp three youths joined them, and the party went on along the creek for half a mile, then turned out on the plain for a further half-mile, reaching then the hummock of ironstone.

Bony and the chiefs scrambled to the summit—the three young men stayed below. On the summit the three began to remove a thick layer of weather-corroded stones and rock rubbish, and after nearly twenty minutes' labour uncovered a level floor of rock squares approximately four yards each way. The rock squares were much broken and chipped, bearing witness to the centuries that had elapsed since they had been laid. Yet on the eastern side was still to be seen, chipped deeply on the squares, a perfect circle, large enough to enclose a standing man's feet. The preliminary labour completed, old Moongalliti pointed to the circle; and Bony, thrilled to the core, bathed in the glorious moonlight, threw aside his white man's clothes, and naked stood within the circle. He faced to the east and held up his arms in a sign.

The precise ceremony that followed cannot be described. No white man knows, and no black man yet has been a traitor. An observer on the ground below might have seen the three young bucks join the three on the summit. He might have seen those six figures moving about, and assumed, when three figures only could be seen, that three laid themselves on the square of squares. He would have seen naught else, nor heard a single cry, yet in the morning three young bucks wore on their backs a plaster of mud and herbs kept in place by swathes of old rag.

How came that cult, with a resemblance to Freemasonry, to Australia? Who and what kind of a man was he who brought it? Did the cult date from times when the Lemurian continent joined Australia to India? It was a mystery too deep for even Bony to penetrate.

He fed his men on time the next morning, debonair, shaved, and cheerful. He cut up sheep's carcasses with a glittering butcher's knife as expertly as probably he had cut human flesh with a sharp stone but a few hours before. The battle of influences for the mastery of his soul was ended, and he knew once again, within as well as without, the blessed tranquillity of peace.

And indeed, it was a day of peace. The blacks lay in the shade, gorged and slothful. Even the children were less exuberant, and the dogs yelped only in their nightmares.

It was long after midnight when uproar broke out in the blacks' camp. It awoke Bony, who, standing at his door, listened and smiled and felt glad that he was Bony after all. He guessed shrewdly that in the blacks' camp one of the bucks had been flagrantly caught in the act of making love to another buck's gin, belonging to a tribe not his own.

Chapter Eighteen

Aftermath

DURING THE NIGHT the uproar down the creek broke out sporadically, and when dawn lightened the sky Bony, with Jack Withers, who was as much interested as the half-caste, made their way to the scene of the commotion. They found the two tribes on opposite banks of the creek, the women and children behind the men, the women screaming shrilly and their lords howling guttural threats.

"Wonder wot's stung 'em," said the man with the awful squint.

"Woman! Woman undoubtedly is the cause of it," Bony opined. "Ninety per cent of murders, riots, and private fights are caused by woman—peace-loving woman."

"I wouldn't be surprised if you ain't right," Withers said in his slow drawl, as though Bony's statement conveyed an entirely new idea. "Ole Moongalliti looks terrible narked, and Mertee ain't lookin' too cheerful."

The chiefs occupied front places. Moongalliti, attired only in a loincloth, clutched a heavy murrawirrie in his left hand, and three or four wooden spears, with iron-hard, needle-pointed tips, in the other. Mertee was similarly armed. The bucks behind each were armed likewise with spears and murrawirries. Of the opposing armies only Moongalliti was really angry. The bucks' faces were sullen, and appearances indicated that the majority of them would much prefer peace with honour, and a few more hours' sleep to recompense them for the time lost during the night.

Moongalliti was walking up and down before his bucks, his face continually turned towards Mertee, his white hair and beard matted, his long thin legs looking like jointed ebony rulers. From his wide mouth flowed a stream of unintelligible jargon, which a child could have seen expressed insults, invective, and lurid curses.

"My! Ain't he going some?" chuckled Withers.

"It will end in a brawl," said Bony.

"Hope so. Ain't seen a dog-fight for years."

"Nor I. It will amuse me," agreed Bony calmly. "In a few minutes the spears will begin to fly. I suggest we climb this tree to gain a better view."

"I'm on"—and in thirty seconds Withers was on a comfortable branch, which gave him a grand-stand seat. Bony climbed up beside him.

The exultation of his warrior ancestors lifted him entirely out of his ordinary existence. Everything was forgotten in the fierce expectation consuming him. His cooking job, the necessity to prepare breakfast on time, was simply wiped from his mind.

"Look, Bony! Mertee's warmin' up at last!"

"He had to. No self-respecting aboriginal could for long stand Moongalliti's unpleasant language."

Moongalliti suddenly slithered down the steep bank to the dry sandy bottom of the creek. He dropped his murrawirrie, and with his left hand took from his right all the spears but one. White foam was on his lips, and his face was terrible in its passion. His body, bearing a score of battle-scars, shook and trembled whilst he defied Mertee, cursed him and his father and his mother, and implored him to become a man and come down to him and fight.

"Ah!" Withers sighed long and with great content when Mertee, with an answering yell, sprang down to the creek-bottom, where the opponents were but twenty yards apart.

"Oo-um—oo-um—oo-um—oo-um—oo-um!" yelled Moongalliti.

"Yulm-yulm—yulm-yulm—yulm-yulm!" responded Mertee.

With the swiftness of light Moongalliti's arm was flung back, for a fraction of a second the spear became horizontal, and then the weapon was flying towards Mertee with deadly precision.

"Got him!" shouted Withers.

"No!" cried Bony.

To the watchers it appeared that the spear had reached Mertee, but in that last second he stepped smartly aside, and the spear passed to touch the ground yards behind him and slither over it for yet further yards. To a new-chum his agility was nothing less than amazing. In comparison a Spanish bullfighter would have seemed as slow as a turtle on land.

Mertee used a spear-thrower, a perfectly balanced piece of flat wood with a socket at its extremity to hold the butt of the spear. He bent over sideways as an athlete putting the weight, straightened as a length of clock-spring, and his spear described an arc. It rose much higher than Moongalliti's head, and then rushed down on him. As briskly as Mertee he stepped aside, and the spear quivered in the ground close behind him.

"'Ot stuff, Bony, old lad!" Withers cried.

"It will become hotter," Bony told him gleefully.

Again the two combatants each threw a spear, and again each stepped aside. A third and a fourth time spears were exchanged without a hit. It was then that Moongalliti's cunning became apparent; for, when at last neither he nor his opponent had a spear left in hand, Mertee was forced to run back to pick up Moongalliti's hand-thrown spears, whereas his own stick-thrown spears stuck up out of the ground close behind

Moongalliti. Not for nothing had the white-headed chief fought his hundred fights.

His hands reached out and swept up two of Mertee's spears, and then he rushed on Mertee, who was running back to retrieve a spear many yards to his rear. He reached one. Moongalliti stopped. Mertee crouched to pick it up. Moongalliti threw. Mertee seized the desired spear, sprang upward and to one side. But when he leapt aside Moongalliti's spear was hanging from his left thigh.

The bucks roared, the gins screamed, the children on one side yelled insults to the children on the other. Withers clapped his hands and yelled: "Encore, encore!"—almost falling off the bough. Bony's eyes were twin points of blazing blue light.

The concert of all these sounds utterly drowned the barks and yelps of the numberless dogs. Momentarily, even Moongalliti was stunned. He appeared transfixed with astonishment to observe Mertee dancing on his right leg and holding the spear in his left thigh with both hands. Mertee shrieked more with humiliation than with pain. He continued to shriek until his ebony chest was flecked with foam, when it appeared that he became insensible to pain, for he suddenly plucked out the spear and, still shrieking, dashed for his murrawirrie and rushed madly on Moongalliti. Seeing him coming, the heavy awkward weapon, used as a sword, whirling about his head, Moongalliti made haste to retrieve his murrawirrie and rushed to meet him.

"Scrum! Scrum! Get to it! Get to it!" yelled Withers when the bucks of both sides leapt down to the creek-bed. Spears began to fly in all directions. Everyone yelled or screamed, and Withers, to keep his end up, added to the uproar.

"Let 'em alone! Damn it, let 'em alone! Boo-hoo! You'll spoil it! Let 'em alone ... let 'em alone!"

The women were now jumping and slithering down the creek-banks, and, utterly regardless of the vicious spears, sprang on those which fell near them and broke them into half a dozen pieces. Bony and Withers saw one of the three young men whose backs were caked with mud stagger with a spear right through his chest and collapse. Another buck dropped like a pole-axed bullock when a murrawirrie was brought down on his head from behind. After that it was difficult to follow the actions of any unit, because the men were bunched as in a Rugby scrum, and the women clawed at them from the rear in vain efforts to pull them away.

Excitement made Bony speechless. His blood was aflame with ecstasy, and he was moving back along the branch to reach the main stem by which to get down to join the fray, when from almost below them the reports of a double-barrelled shot-gun very nearly caused both him and Withers to fall to the ground.

The effect of these reports was astounding. There followed instant silence, instant cessation of all movement. It was as though what had gone before was a rapidly screened talking picture, when the machinery had broken down and the scene on the sheet had become a fixture. And then, precisely as though the operator had adjusted his machine and set the picture again in motion, the crowd broke and fled the instant two further shots roared up and down the creek.

"Go it, Moongalliti!" Withers yelled with a resumption of enthusiasm. "Even money on Moongalliti! Ten to one on Noonee! Hop it, Noonee, hop it! By cripes, you'll beat him at the post!"

Mertee painfully but manfully followed his fast-disappearing tribe into the belt of timber dividing the creek from the plain. A mob of "home blacks" rushed down along the creek-bed, helter-skelter towards their camp, followed in the rear by old Moongalliti, with Noonee, his first wife, almost as old and six times his weight, close on his heels.

"Let's 'ave a look at the dead 'uns, Bony," the irrepressible Withers suggested gaily, and, without bothering to climb down the tree, he lowered himself from the branch and dropped the nine or ten feet. Bony followed him, and when he stood on the creek-bank he came face to face with Jeff Stanton.

"Why-in-hell didn't you try and stop 'em?" Jeff demanded.

"Stop 'em?" Withers echoed, a look of utter astonishment causing his eyes to cross still more. "Stop 'em? Why, I wouldn't 'ave stopped 'em for a hundred quid! It's the best bleedin' dog-fight I seen for years."

"I am glad you enjoyed yourself, Jack," Jeff said with biting sarcasm. Then: "We had better examine the corpses."

Together with Bony, Withers, and most of the homestead hands, Stanton gained the creek-bed, and at that moment one of the corpses sat up, gazed round blankly, uttered a yell and, springing to his feet, raced up the farther bank as quickly as a dog-chased squirrel runs up a tree. Stanton fired two more cartridges into the air to hurry him, but further haste appeared impossible.

The buck with the spear sticking out between his shoulder blades was quite dead. He was Moongalliti's son, Ludbi. A third casualty was alive and seemed merely stunned.

"The biter bitten," murmured Bony.

"Moongalliti urged them on to fight when they were by no means inclined, and the only one killed of them all is Moongalliti's son, whom he loved."

"Humph! What's this?"

Up the creek came a small flock of women, led by Noonee and Moongalliti. The old man walked proudly erect, his white head thrown back, his beard matted with blood from a cheek wound. Stanton and his men drew back. Moongalliti came and looked down on the face of his son. His lips twitched. The women raised their arms and wailed. Noonee, Ludbi's mother, cried aloud and fell on the body.

And Moongalliti, erect as a soldier, arms hanging stiffly at his sides, turned towards the east, silent, his face immobile save for his trembling lips.

Bony touched his bare shoulder, and the old man's eyes came slowly to rest on him.

"Moongalliti," Bony said softly, "Ludbi was a man. Beneath the moon last night he faced its cradle."

Bony raised his right arm as a sign.

Slowly the old man's right arm went up too, and when it rose the fierce face softened and tears fell down his scarred and wounded cheeks.

Chapter Nineteen

Bony Instructs Headquarters

SERGEANT MORRIS arrived during the afternoon, the fight and its tragic result having been reported to him over the telephone by Jeff Stanton. He walked into the kitchen about four o'clock after he had been given tea and scones by Marion on the big house veranda. Bony was preparing the dinner, and neither he nor the sergeant spoke until both were assured that no one was by to see or hear.

"Good day, Bony," the policeman said in greeting, with far less than the habitual gruffness he used to people whom he considered his social inferiors. "Cooking, eh?"

"I shall be glad when Jeff gets a cook, for I am becoming tired of cooking."

"The cooking didn't prevent your attendance at the dog-fight this morning, I am told."

"Alas! Man, after all, is a brute beast," sighed Bony. "Nevertheless, I was entertained and thrilled."

"Humph!" Sergeant Morris looked as though he did not quite approve. "Anyway, as you were a witness, tell me all about it."

"I believe I saw you talking to Jack Withers," Bony remarked blandly.

"Yes. I got his statement."

"Then why in the world, my dear Morris, do you attempt to waste my time?"

"Well, I want a corroborative statement from you. You and Withers appear to be the only witnesses of the affair from first to last."

"In that case, send me a copy of Withers's statement, and I'll sign it as my own. Yes, yes! I know you are a senior police official, and stuffed full of red tape, but Ludbi's death was the result of a tribal affray, and not murder, and therefore nothing for us to worry about. Have you got the report concerning Marks?"

"Yes. How is the case going?"

"According to plan, Morris. It proceeds unhurriedly to its destined end."

"And you still believe it was murder?"

"Decidedly. I know it was murder."

"You do? Who did it?"

Bony smiled provokingly, and said: "As yet I do not know the identity of the killer. When I do, it will be a most difficult matter to prove."

"Why?"

"I will explain," Bony answered, rolling out a slab of dough with which to cover a large meat pie. "As I once told you, nine hundred and ninety-nine cases of murder out of every thousand are affairs of the utmost simplicity. The body of a human being is discovered, either whole, as was the body of the victim of Milsom and Fowler and kindred cases, or in pieces, as were the victims of the romantic Crippen, the money-loving Mahon, and the atrocious Landru. It has been said by people of great intelligence that the human body is one of the most difficult objects to destroy completely. Landru, the French bluebeard, came very near to success. Deeming utterly failed.

"Why it should be considered that a human body is difficult to destroy, and why murderers, who in their normal state are thinking, reasoning beings, should make such blundering failures of their attempts, has, to me, always been a source of amazement."

"You, then, could succeed in completely destroying a body?" Morris said, with sceptically raised brows.

"Man, I could completely destroy a body in six quite different ways. It is really simple."

"How? Describe the methods."

"How can you, my dear Sergeant?" Bony evaded, with gentle reproof.

"All right! If you won't tell, don't."

"If I did tell you, Morris, you might start at once removing your enemies," the detective laughed.

The half-caste finished his pie-making by decorating the edges of the pastry crust with a fearsome butcher's knife. Observing Morris watching the knife, Bony smiled queerly and turned back to place the pie in the oven. Then he added wood to the fire, pushed in a damper, examined the contents of several pots, and finally filled two tin pint pannikins with tea, and put them on the table.

"Have a sip of real China tea," he urged Morris.

"China tea?"

"Yes, China tea! Made by the Chinamen in our great cities. They collect the tea-leaves from the hotels and restaurants, take them home, dry them over a stove, and sell them to those provision merchants who supply squatters with rations for the poor station-hands. I believe the wholesale price is somewhere about one pound per ton. The profit must be enormous. Now, please, the report." Morris handed it to him, and sipped in silence whilst Bony read.

"William Green, born 10 February, 1878, at Louth, River Darling, N.S.W. Educated State schools, Louth and Parkes. Passed into N.S.W. Police Force 9 Oct., 1907. First station, Wilcannia. Second, Sydney Central. ..." And so on, until: *"Resigned to join A.I.F. Served with A.F.A. at Anzac and 5th Division in France. Decorated M.M. 2 June, 1916. Promoted commission rank 19 June, 1917. Received head wound about 22 September, 1917. Discharged A.I.F. 17 January, 1919. Rejoined N.S.W. Police Force 18 November, 1919. Transferred Licensing Branch May 1923."*

Then followed an amazing mass of detail relating to Green, alias Marks. As a dossier it was creditably complete, and Bony expressed his satisfaction by seizing his pannikin of tea and drinking the health of the N.S.W. Police Force.

"The report seems to please you," observed Morris.

"It does, Sergeant! It does!" smiled the gratified Bony. "Now I want you to make dossiers of some other people."

He rose, and for some little time was absent in his room. On his return he carried several letters and a package, as well as some loose sheets of paper.

"Post these letters and register this package for me, please," he requested. "You see, I cannot post anything at the office here, excepting letters to my wife. Now here is a list of every white person known to have been within a radius of ten miles of Marks's abandoned car the day he left Windee homestead. All these people are as fish in my net. Among them is the sting-ray for which I am looking. By my peculiar method of inductive reasoning I have identified all but seven as harmless fish. Among the remaining seven, therefore, is the sting-ray. I wish you to render me a comprehensive report of everything you know and can ascertain of these seven people. Here are their names."

With quickening interest Sergeant Morris read the list: *Jeff Stanton, Young Jeff Stanton, Mr. Roberts, Jack Withers, Ned Swallow, Dot, Dash.*

"But I think I've told you the history of most of these people," Morris objected.

"No matter. Get it down in chronological order. One of these seven men killed Marks or Green—we'll stick to Marks—and one or more of these seven disposed of Marks's body. If I possess the pasts of these unidentifiable fish, I may dig out of the cemetery of the past one little bone which will ally itself with the sting-ray. Do you think that Headquarters would bring here from North Queensland a very old friend of mine?"

"I don't know. What do you want him to be brought here for?"

"Not to kiss him," said the bland Bony. "I want to introduce him to friend Moongalliti."

"What the deuce for?"

"Because I am sure he will like Moongalliti." Then Bony became serious: "I intend trying to obtain certain information from Moongalliti," he explained, in his way of imparting what seemed much but which amounted to little. "My efforts, however, will, I think, be without result. My friend's method will, I am positive, be more successful. He is a charming person, although I believe he has not washed for sixty-seven years, which is his age. I want you to instruct Headquarters in Sydney to send a man to Burke, in North Queensland, there to get in touch with a tribe chiefed by Illawalli. He is to tell this chief that Bony wants him, and is to bring him to me as fast as aeroplanes, trains, and motors can bring him."

"Instruct Headquarters?" Sergeant Morris gasped.

"No less. If you prefer a request it will be delayed. They'll want to know why I want Illawalli. Tell them what I have said as though you were the Great Corsican himself. Tell them that if they refuse or delay granting my request I shall throw up the case."

"Do you often instruct your own Headquarters?" Sergeant Morris asked with forced calmness, although his worship of discipline writhed under this irreverent handling.

"I have found during my career as an investigator of crime that if one wants a thing one has to issue a demand and not seek a favour," Bony explained calmly. Then with superb vanity he added impressively: "My Headquarters know that I have never failed in a case, and that I am the only detective who has not failed and failed repeatedly. They also know my views about delaying and wasting time."

Sergeant Morris burst into hearty laughter. He really could not help it. "I will forward your instructions," he promised, with a purple face.

Chapter Twenty

Fire Salvage

Ludbi's death quickly drifted into the limbo of things forgotten. Sergeant Morris discovered that no one among Moongalliti's tribe knew or could remember the buck on Mertee's side who had driven the fatal spear. It was more than probable that no one belonging to Mertee's tribe, save the thrower of the spear himself, could have named the slayer. The details of tribal battles are lost in the excitement of the participants, which is extreme, and, since it was not deliberately planned murder, the law passed it over. Ludbi was buried in due course with the usual tribal honours.

At the end of the first week in November Bony was still cooking in the men's kitchen. By then he was utterly bored, and he was more pleased even than Jeff Stanton when Father Ryan telephoned to say that Alf the Nark was recuperating in the Mount Lion gaol, and would be ready for work at the end of a further two days.

Hearing this, Bony sighed relief, and the men sighed for the opposite reason. Runta, who came regularly at sundown to obtain food and roll her big black eyes at the handsome cook, began to wail when Bony informed her of the approaching return of Alf the Nark. She spoke fair English.

"You come camp with me, Bony," she said with delightful naiveté. "You marry me and you'm work no more for old man Jeff, eh? I get plenty tucker for you."

"Bimeby," replied the unabashed Bony, prevaricating. He spoke in her vernacular. "You'm no like Bony for long; Bony very bad man. He'm got awful temper. He'm beat two lubras with a waddy, so hard that they die."

"Oh! Oh, Bony, you fool me!" gasped Runta.

Very solemnly Bony shook his head. Then, placing the tip of his forefinger against the middle of his forehead, he said significantly: "Sometime now, sometime presently, Bony bad fellow. Killum quick. Debil-debil in here."

Runta faded out. Bony knew that he had frightened her temporarily, but that next evening her courage would permit her to gaze again on the adored one. His reading was correct. Watching for her, he espied her coming up along the creek, and, when she finally reached the kitchen and poked her head in through the doorway, she became as a rough-hewn block of black marble.

Bony was seated on the floor. His fine straight hair was fiercely ruffled. His face was smeared with flour. Before him stood a statuette fashioned from dough, and he was menacing this statuette with a very businesslike waddy or club. And then Runta saw herself being examined by wild, terrible eyes, and she saw her hero move forward on his knees and one hand, the waddy in the other. He was creeping towards her. Quite evidently it was one of the periods of "sometime now, sometime presently". Poor disillusioned Runta fled screaming.

From the doorway Bony watched her flight and experienced a qualm of remorse. Playing Don Juan was not a weapon he used often, but in this instance he considered the end justified the means. From Runta he had discovered an important fact, whilst through Runta he had broken the ice of suspicion and was now well received by Moongalliti.

Alf the Nark came back in triumph. He entered the kitchen and resumed his duties with not a particle of grit on his poor liver. Bony went back to his horses, and in five days had his first post-cooking horse in the last stage of its training. Thenceforth on every afternoon he rode by devious ways to the junction of the two roads, and for several hours walked about in his sheepskin sandals, or over-shoes.

On previous occasions he had found where the skinned carcass of a kangaroo had been burned. A charred piece of wood, a bone or the long tail of the animal, invariably not skinned, charred and blackened, always indicated where the carcass had been burned, in spite of the ever-encroaching sand. There was nothing unduly startling in this, since, on many stations, the single condition laid down by the squatter in giving his permission to skin- and fur-getters to operate on his holding is that all carcasses must be burned. Rotting carcasses are breeding-grounds for the blow-fly, and this fly is the sheep's greatest enemy.

Walking in ever larger circles, with the spot where the abandoned car was found as a centre, Bony had carefully examined almost half a thousand acres. On that area he had found the remains of almost a hundred fires, and these fires had been lit between eight and twelve weeks previously, or, to be more precise, some had been lit before the disappearance of Marks, and some after.

It was no mean feat to establish the approximate dates of those fires. Yet it had been done to Bony's complete satisfaction by observing the quantity of sand swept over them, and the condition of a bone here and there, which had been partially cleaned of flesh by the ants where it had not been so cleaned by the fire.

After this point of date had been decided, he learned in his roundabout way that the kangaroos shot and burned there were the work of Dot and Dash, who at that time were camped near a well, situated a mile south of the road junction in what was called South Paddock. He determined to examine that camp-site after he had re-examined all those hundred fire-sites.

The re-examination of the fire-sites occupied the afternoons of more than a week, and at the conclusion of this second scrutiny Bony decided that one particular site might be well worth examining for a third time. With no little difficulty he smuggled away from the homestead a short-handled shovel and a small-meshed sieve, and took these tools one night to a fire-site about four hundred yards north of the road junction and three hundred yards north of the abandoned car site.

The following morning he made pretext to require more particular instructions about a certain horse of Jeff Stanton's, and heard his individual orders to the men. During that afternoon no one of them would, in their work, be riding near the fire-site he proposed to sift with his sieve. At three o'clock he started work.

Of the hundred-and-odd fires that Bony had superficially examined, this particular site had one peculiarity. It had been a large fire, and the reason of that might have been that more than one carcass had been burned there. On the other hand, Bony did not exclude the possibility that the charred remains of a human body might lie below the charred remains of a kangaroo. A second fire might have been lit over the site of the first.

Very carefully he removed the sand that had drifted round and over this fire-site, proclaimed by a kangaroo's hind-foot. One by one he removed a quantity of bones by feeling for them in the loose combination of sand and ash. Satisfied that he had recovered all that the fire had not consumed—and ordinary fire consumes very few bones—he carefully sorted them and eventually obtained proof that all belonged to the bodies of three kangaroos.

A further fact he discovered was that the wood which burned the carcasses had not been just thrown on them and fired. Jeff Stanton's condition had been carried out conscientiously, for Dot and Dash had laid a bed of wood to make the burn more thorough.

Now with great care Bony began to put the ash and sand mixture through his sieve. The residue remaining from each sieve-load he emptied on a chaff-bag, and when he was satisfied that the whole of the fire-site had passed through the sieve or lay on the bag, he paused in his labours and began making and rolling a cigarette.

With the most interesting section of the examination before him, Bony smoked complacently and visualized the scene of the killing of Marks. The act committed, it was at once urgently necessary to dispose of the body. Fire was the easiest and most practicable method. There were no disused mine-shafts down which to throw a body and then explode over it a few tons of earth and rocks. There was no steam power on Windee, no big steam boiler to drive the shearing machinery, no big boiler furnace to incinerate a human body. All Windee power plants were petrol-driven.

There was to be taken into consideration, however, the probability that the murderer or murderers of Marks might have scooped a hole anywhere in that vast region of sand and simply buried the victim, certain that the first windstorm would wipe out all tracks. That method of disposing of the body would naturally occur to the average mind, especially the mind of a killer who was a new-chum to the bush.

This theory, however, was discounted by two facts. Not one of the fish in Bony's net was a new-chum, and not one fish was there who did not know that, although the first windstorm would obliterate all tracks, there was the certainty that a future windstorm would blow the sand from the body and expose it. To obviate this danger the murderer might have taken the body by truck or car from the scene of the crime and buried it in hard ground on the great plain, or somewhere near the hills.

If that were so, Bony's task would be infinitely greater, but the hangman's rope for the murderer would be infinitely more sure. He was not safe whilst the body existed in whole or in part, and, whilst Bony had so far nothing tangible on which to base his belief, he did believe that the body no longer existed, in whole at least. Ludbi had known, and Moongalliti knew, the killer of Marks. The killer, therefore, was absolutely in their hands. They would blackmail him for even a pound of tea, and, knowing that their demands would inevitably increase, the killer would have vanished before then if he were not absolutely secure from blackmail, even secure from their accusation, in the knowledge that no body existed. No one had left Windee since Marks had disappeared. Neither Moongalliti nor Ludbi had come into any coveted possession, such as good clothes or any of the hundred-and-one trinkets of which a blackfellow dreams. And, given the chance, the aboriginal becomes a front-rank expert at blackmailing.

Bony extinguished the cigarette and put it in a pocket before drawing the bag of sieve residue to him. Every piece of matter he examined with his keen eyes, finally to lay it down on his other side. Most of the material was plain charcoal. There was a quantity of blackened pieces of furred skin and five small bones that he decided were knuckle-bones. Since a kangaroo's paw is five-fingered and similar in shape to the human hand, and since many kangaroos have paws almost as large as the human hand, Bony considered that these bones came from kangaroos' paws. To be sure on that point he pocketed them with the intention of sending them to the Research Department at Headquarters.

The pile of seeming rubbish on the bag was growing appreciably less. Still, there might yet be evidence that something more than kangaroos had been burned. Marks's teeth had been gold-filled, and, although the fire would have sundered the gold from its setting of bone, its temperature would not have been high enough to melt the gold. And then he came on melted metal, and his knife proved it lead. It had run into irregular flat cakes. He found three such cakes of lead, and knew them once to have formed bullets that had killed the burned kangaroos. From that he knew it was Dot who had shot those animals, for Dot used a .44 Winchester carbine firing a lead bullet, and Dash always used a .22 Savage firing a soft-nosed nickel-plated bullet.

The refuse not yet examined was becoming a very small collection, but to the very end Bony persevered. He had concluded that his work was fruitless, yet he felt no disappointment, for there were other avenues to be explored, when he came upon a single blackened boot-sprig, a boot-nail less than half an inch in length. Hurriedly he went through the remainder. It gave him nothing of significance. His reward for all his labour that afternoon was a single little boot-nail.

The nail proved that something in addition to kangaroo carcasses had been burned there.

Quite slowly, smiling radiance came to Bony's face.

Chapter Twenty-one

At the Source of Life

SUMMER'S FIRST heat-wave found Dot and Dash at Carr's Tank, twenty-two miles south of Range Hut, and lying at the west foot of the ranges. The tank was a great square earth excavation from which thirty-thousand cubic yards of mullock had been taken by bullock-drawn scoops. The mullock formed a rampart, and through this rampart cement pipes conducted the water from a shallow creek—when water flowed in it—beginning in the hills.

Wholly enclosing tank and banks was a six-wire fence, but so numerous were the kangaroos that hardly one strand of wire remained taut. With no difficulty whatsoever they climbed through the fence to drink at the dam in preference to drinking at the man-made sheep-trough a hundreds yards out, and kept filled by a windmill.

Still farther away was an erection of corrugated iron, hessian bags, and flattened petrol-tins, which served as a kind of house for two stockmen. This sort of house substitute was less in evidence on Windee than on the great majority of Australian stations. There exists an Act that requires the squatter to house his men in enlarged iron boxes, also an Act requiring him to use poison-carts to destroy rabbits. However, since no one lives in the bush with the intention of settling there, but rather to make a cheque and then settle elsewhere, the want of any degree of comfort is a matter of indifference.

The two stockmen and the partners were having an early dinner, since the latter had to be at their places at the dam before sundown. In spite of the terrific heat in the interior of the hut the four men appeared to enjoy eating, seeming hardly conscious of the perspiration that ran from them, brought out by the scalding hot tea drunk from tin pint pannikins. The wind, gusty and hot, rattled the iron sheets nailed to the framework of the structure, and sometimes thickened the atmosphere with fine red dust. Countless flies hummed and settled in eyes and on bare necks and arms. That day the temperature in the shade at Windee was from 102° to 112°. At Carr's Tank there was no shade much for a distance of fully a mile in any direction.

"Feeling a bit warm, Dot?" queried Ned Swallow, a youthful, lank, red-headed rider.

"Not exactly," Dot rejoined, helping himself to what purported to be plum duff. "I was jest wonderin' whar the draught was coming from. Say, Tom!"—to the second rider—"you sure can make plum duff!"

"That's a better pudding than general," Tom growled.

"Well, it's fillin', anyway. Try some, Dash?"

"I think not," Dash said, eyeing it suspiciously.

"Seems as though the outside third of it kinda got stuck on the cloth when you heaved her out, Tom," Dot observed.

"Yus. I forgot to wet the cloth afore I put her in. Still, it'll go better cold. She'll have lost that slummicky look. Don't you blokes wait to wash up. Me and Ned'll do that."

"You are very decent, Tom. I'll roll a cigarette, and Dot and I will adjourn." Dash went outside and dried his face, neck and arms with a towel. The sun was getting low, and already thousands of galahs whirled about the tank, or strutted on the banks looking like tiny grey-coated soldiers. Around the tank lay a plain covered with fine red dust. One mile away the scrub began. Before the tank was sunk, all that plain bore scrub-trees, but by now the stock converging there daily had eaten or killed them. Across this arid desert drifted an occasional low cloud of red dust, whilst at a point far to the north-west a huge towering red column denoted that the sheep were coming in to drink.

Dash settled himself at the summit of the rampart at that angle which commanded the iron reservoir tanks, windmill, and troughs giving water to two paddocks, with a great sweep of the plain beyond; whilst Dot, at the opposite angle, commanded the shorter stretch of plain bounded by the range.

As a slowly oncoming destroyer sending up a red smoke-screen, a long line of sheep moved across the plain to the dam. Shadows of tank and windmill lengthened with magical rapidity, and the wind became merely a fitful zephyr.

The red dust-screen came ever nearer. Dash could observe the faint white figures of the leaders of the flock of three thousand sheep. On his side Dot could see a similar flock of sheep coming from the other paddock to drink. A mile away three black pin-heads behaved as well-drilled jumping fleas, and between each jump a spurt of dust arose. They were the vanguard of the kangaroos coming leisurely to the dam in fifteen-foot jumps, tireless, wonderfully speedy, infinitely more graceful in action than a racing horse or whippet-dog. At the edge of the scrub numbers of these animals, who had slept and drowsed away the day, were sitting bolt upright watching their leaders, and in twos and threes and fours they bounded out on the plain, so that a few minutes after Dash had seen the first three pinheads he could easily count thirty.

Water! The Spring of Life!

The nearest water lay eighteen miles to the north; the next nearest thirty miles to the west. Between these places the only moisture to be found was in the sap of the trees. In a week or so, when the last of the tiny grass roots were dead, twenty to fifty thousand rabbits would come to water every night with unfailing regularity. Numbers of them even then were drinking at the edges of the square sheet of water in the dam. Others were converging on it in easy stages of a few yards' run, with pauses to sit up and look around with alert suspicion.

When the sun, still fiercely hot and flaming red, was but four fingers above the horizon, the dust-cloud was within a quarter of a mile of the troughs. Fifty sheep were to be seen moving at its base. Tens of hundreds walked in the cloud in several parallel lines. Dash could hear their plaintive baaing above the scream of the birds, and he observed with never-slackening interest how but one sheep of all that great flock constituted itself the leader. It was an old yet robust ewe. When but a hundred yards from the troughs she broke into a quick amble, followed by those immediately behind her. That seemed to be the point when every following sheep broke from a walk into a run.

A white flood of wool rolled over the ground to the water. The galahs rose from the troughs with a thunderous roar of wings to fly a short distance away and settle like a grey blanket on the expanse of plain. The white flood, reaching the trough, poured around both sides of it and rolled outward as from a centre when the main body of the sheep swelled its volume.

A vast milling, dust-raising, baaing, struggling mass of animals! The level of water in the reservoir tank feeding the trough began gradually to fall. Then from the surging mass one sheep became detached. It was the old ewe leader. She ran back over the way she had come, followed by several others, and then stopped when two hundred yards from the tank, looking back with cunning placidity. In twos and threes, their bellies distended with water, sheep left the mob and joined her, then, with her, to stand a while looking back. Not one ran ahead. And not before all but a few lingerers had drunk their fill did she lead them out across the plain to the scrub and dry grass, the red mounting dust, now rising straight and to a great height, marking their passage.

The army corps of galahs was retreating by battalions to roosting-places in the mulga-trees on the hills. A thunder of hoofs caused Dash to look to his left and observe the second flock of sheep—also led by a single animal—charge in and around the second trough. When they also had gone the sun was set and Dash lay with his .22 Savage resting in his arms. There were seven kangaroos within point-blank range of his rifle, namely, three hundred yards.

Dash settled down to careful shooting whilst the light held. The cartridges he used cost fourpence each, so that he could not afford to miss often. Dot, firing from his .44 Winchester his own loading cartridges, the cost of which he had carefully worked out at five shillings per hundred, could well afford to take chances; but his weapon was far less deadly beyond two hundred yards than the Savage.

His partner heard him shooting, and sometimes cursing. A quite friendly rivalry existed between them when in the morning they counted their respective bags, after which the merits of their rifles would be argued. The light began to go rapidly, and presently Dash missed for the first time that evening. His following shot also was a miss; and, slipping down behind the rampart, he walked to where a single blanket was folded in its length. Beside it lay a double-barrelled shot-gun of beautiful workmanship, several boxes of BB size cartridges, a billy-can of cold tea, and a hurricane-lamp.

It was his night position. It was situated in a right-angle on the narrow strip of level ground between the bank of the dam and the rampart of mullock. In a similar position in the opposite angle lay Dot. Each of them commanded two sides of the square-shaped tank, and to shoot each other was impossible unless one fired diagonally across the water.

Lighting a cigarette, Dash lay back on the blanket resting his head on his hands. To regard him then was to wonder what form of madness had exiled him from home and country. There was no trace of dissipation on the strong sunburned face, no hint of weakness about the straight mouth and square chin.

His cigarette finished, he sat up and sipped from the blackened billy-can. Above him the sky was blue-black and the stars did not twinkle with so-called tropical brilliance, despite the fact that it was cloudless. The features of the mullock marking his zone of operations were blurred by the general shadow, but those angles of the rampart commanded by Dot still revealed the crevices among the rubble in a soft amber glow. The level summit of Dash's rampart was clear-cut against the dull pink sheen of the western sky. That skyline would be visible all night long, hence his then position.

A form, soundless in movement, grotesque, almost monstrous, slowly pushed up on that skyline. Dash reached for his shot-gun. The form became still for a moment, then slowly changed from the grotesque to the beautiful, from the monstrous to the lovely, when the kangaroo sat up, his tail resting on the ground balancing him like a third leg, his small but noble head and lifted stiffened ears outlined as a clear-cut silhouette against the darkening sky.

A sharp flash, a roar, and the 'roo lay thrashing in its death agonies.

"Poor devil!" sighed Dash.

From beyond the bank a succession of twin thuds went out as warning to the converging kangaroos, when one or more gave the signal by jumping and bringing their tails down on the earth with a sound like that of a stick beating a dusty carpet.

Dot fired, and Dash heard the wounded 'roo "queex-queex" with pain and anger. Then his attention was taken by the rising figures of two 'roos directly opposite him and less than twenty yards distant. He fired twice rapidly, and both animals fell dead. Dash was thankful.

At about eleven o'clock the shooting became less frequent, and Dot at last called out for an armistice. Dash agreed, and lit his lamp. Whereupon each man dispatched his wounded animals with his hunting-knife.

"How many?" Dot asked when the lights revealed both at their respective camps.

"Twenty-nine," replied Dash without enthusiasm. "What is your tally?"

"Thirty-three," came the triumphant answer.

After that silence fell once more. The tall partner lay on his side, smoking and thinking. The air was still heated by the roasted earth. The silence became oppressive, more oppressive than the sounds of continuous thunder.

Presently the armistice was called off and hostilities were resumed till dawn.

•　　　•　　　•　　　•　　　•

"Thank heaving, to-day's the last day of me week's cooking!" Tom said during breakfast, with tremendous fervour in his drawling voice. "Yours starts to-morrow, Ned. An' then you can show us yous can cook better'n Bony."

"He wants a lot of beating, does Bony," the young rider conceded. "I've met that bloke before somewheres, but I can't place 'im. When 'e smiles I nearly get 'im, but not quite. Anyways, 'e can cook, and 'e can break-in 'orses, and 'e can play on a box-leaf. Not a bad sort of a bloke, Bony."

"Naw. Quiet-like," Dot agreed.

"Deep," rumbled Tom.

"Deep as 'ell," chimed in Ned. "I'll place 'im one of these days. I know I runned across 'im somewheres. Maybe in Queensland; maybe up in the Territory."

Dash rose from the table and wiped his lips with a handkerchief. Dot rose immediately after, and wiped his with a bare forearm.

"We'll do the washin'-up," he said to the stockman.

"Good-oh!"

When the washing-up had been done and they went outside to smoke cigarettes in the long shade cast by the hut, they watched the two riders set out in their respective paddocks on jogging horses. The army corps of galahs was mobilizing in continuous battalions about the dam. The crows were strutting suspiciously around the dead kangaroos, whilst high above them several eagles circled with wings as still as those of aeroplanes.

The cigarettes smoked, Dash went over to the ton truck, whilst Pot procured the skinning-knives and steels. Into the truck presently they loaded a dozen 'roos and took them a mile away towards the hills, where they were dumped and Dot fell to skinning them. Dash brought the others to Dot in similar loads, and when all were thus removed from the vicinity of the dam he also fell to with his skinning-knife.

It was not work that an English gentleman would do voluntarily.

By ten o'clock the animals were skinned, for both were practised workers. Back again at the hut, they drank cold tea and smoked another cigarette; after which Dot set to work pegging out the wet skins on a hard clay-pan with short pieces of wire used as nails, whilst his partner mixed and baked a damper and a brownie, and peeled the potatoes in readiness for that evening's dinner.

For lunch they had cold mutton, bread and jam, and tea. The merciless sun beat down on the iron roof above them, and set all the plain outside dancing in the mirage. The stillness of noonday settled on the world, and the only things that moved were the heat-defying crows and the eagles settled on the heap of carcasses one mile nearer the hills.

Having lunched, they smoked, and slept until four o'clock, when Dash put the leg of mutton in the camp oven and prepared the simple dinner, and Dot went out to take up skins pegged out the day before, and now as hard and dry as boards. Ned came riding home, and, pausing beside Dot, announced triumphantly:

"I remember Bony now. He was a police-tracker at Cunnamulla in 'twenty-one. Got his man, too."

"You don't say!" Dot calmly observed.

Chapter Twenty-two

The Great Will-o'-the-Wisp

DECEMBER WAS BORN in a temperature of 100°. When it was twelve hours old the mercury of the thermometer on the homestead veranda recorded 115°.

Every well on the Windee holding was in requisition, for three of the great open dams were dry, and the water-level in others was rapidly sinking. The early summer thunderstorms that year were extraordinarily erratic in their courses and afforded no measurable rain. It was now more than three months since the last rain fell.

Over all that vast extent of country owned by one man there was not to be found a single green shoot of grass or herbage. East of the range of hills the hot and rainless period had no apparent effect on the sturdy salt-bush; but the salt in this tiny shrub, plus summer heat, caused the sheep to linger round the troughs at the watering-places and consume much more water than those on the range itself and on that vast stretch of country west of the range. Here the winter grasses raised by a plenitude of rain to the height of a tall man's knee were wheat-coloured. Mile after mile of yellow grass, like an illimitable wheatfield just before harvest, lay encircling the ever-widening areas of bare land in the neighbourhood of the dams and wells.

Bony was out, riding the last horse of his breaking-in contract—a contract he had extended as long as possible. His horses were a credit to him, and Stanton was pleased, as well he might be. He offered the half-caste the contract of erecting a set of sheep-yards a mile above the homestead on the creek, and the versatile Bony accepted, exceedingly glad that his open stay at Windee was to be prolonged.

He was riding a gay young filly, all black without a single white blemish, and, whilst riding with his habitual care, he was considering a point that required explanation. Within the last week he had definitely felt a change in Marion Stanton's attitude towards him.

Her pleasing democratic bonhomie, pleasing because bonhomie was the natural expression of her sunny nature, had vanished, and had become replaced by an unaccountable coldness. Instead of personally asking Bony to saddle Grey Cloud for her evening ride, when he almost always accompanied her, she had instructed the station groom to perform the office on three consecutive evenings. Once she and Bony almost met on the office side of the house; but, seeing him, Marion had deliberately turned in through a wicket-gate.

Not only was Bony perplexed. He was saddened also by this inexplicable change of front, because he had delighted in her beauty as well as in her personality. Going back over the rides they had taken together, he could find not one that indicated how he had offended.

Her coldness apparently affected Jeff Stanton as well. During the last few days when he had met the squatter Stanton was subtly changed from the bluff, downright man of his reputation. When Jeff looked at him Bony felt that he was being rejudged, and by a man carefully adjusting the scales. His changed attitude was not the result of bad work on Bony's part. Of that Bony was quite sure.

Both these people accepted him for what he was. The colour-bar in him was no bar to them. He pleased the squatter by the thoroughness of his work, and he pleased the girl by his intellectual gifts and attainments and his sympathetic personality. And now suddenly he sensed that he displeased them both. This displeasure he could not understand. He had no clue to it.

Reaching the road junction, he guided the filly off the track more by his knees than with the reins, and eventually tied her to the tree in whose fork he kept his sheepskin sandals. It was a very still day, and before leaving the horse he watched her for a few seconds, and then, seeing that she was neither suspicious nor suspected the proximity of any other horse and rider, Bony moved away on yet another examination of the scene of Marks's disappearance. He had covered twenty-five yards when he came on the tracks of a single horse, a horse that had walked.

At once Bony was interested. There were, he knew, no horses in that paddock. The tracks indicated that it was not a loose horse broken into that paddock from another, for the trail was too straight to have been made by a riderless animal. He threw himself into a quick ambling stride, as that of a man wearing snow-shoes, and back-tracked the strange horse till he found that it had left the main road about four hundred yards Windee side of the road junction. Turning about, he followed the tracks back to where he had picked them up, and continued to follow them, his mind going over recent weather conditions to ascertain their age. They were between seventy and seventy-seven hours old—approximately three days—and the horse that had made them was either Grey Cloud or Doll, Jack Withers's mare. Of that Bony was naturally very sure, for the shape and size of the hoofs of every animal he had broken and every animal in work at Windee had been carefully inspected and memorized in his ordinary routine.

The strange tracks led Bony direct to the clay-pan and sand-ridge where Marks's car had been found, and where he had been presented with a sapphire by the industrious ants. They led north from that place, and, coming to the fire-site he had so meticulously examined, they circled twice before going on again for nearly half a mile, when they began to take a wide curve that eventually ended in a straight line going back to Windee.

Why had the rider made an obviously special visit to that fatal locality? Was it because he, Bony, was suddenly held in suspicion? If so, had the suspecting person made that visit to look for proof that Bony also had visited that place? The purpose of the rider was all too obvious. Walking slowly to his tethered horse, Bony smiled. The unknown rider had found no proof that Bony had ever visited the place; but he, Bony, had found proof that a strange rider knew precisely where Marks's car had been found, and also knew where three kangaroos and a human boot at least had been consumed by fire.

Had the unknown rider ridden over that maze of sand-ridges to find proof of Bony's activities? It was the outstanding question. If so, Bony was suspect by someone. Was that someone Jeff Stanton, or his daughter, or both; and were the coldness of the one and the curious weighing of the other the outward signs of their suspicion? Their altered attitude seemed to indicate suspicion of him, and that in turn indicated that they knew something about Marks's disappearance after all.

Since the afternoon was yet young, Bony took the Mount Lion road for no other purpose than to quieten his mount, his mind concentrated on the tangle of this Windee skein, which appeared to be becoming increasingly tangled. So absorbed was he in this mental effort that he was startled when Sergeant Morris spoke to him and he saw the policeman sitting his horse at the edge of the track.

"Day, Bony!"

"Good day, Sergeant! We are well met."

"I was on my way to Windee on the chance of speaking to you," Morris said in his grim way. "We are fortunate to meet here."

"Indeed we are." Bony gazed about with an abstracted look. Then: "I see there a fine pine-tree throwing a most inviting shade. For at least thirty minutes I have not smoked a cigarette."

"Good enough," Morris agreed softly, smiling at the perfect accent and studiously correct grammar.

Their horses standing in the shade of another pine-tree, the two men threw themselves on the soft red sand cooled by the shade, and set about rolling each a cigarette. Then: "Have you any news, Sergeant?"

"Yes. Headquarters have consented to send for your dear friend, Mister Illawalli. You appear to have the power of charming even a police chief."

"Your chief commissioner is a man of perspicacity," Bony murmured. "However, in common with my own chief, he is a man of fixed ideas, at least in regard to myself."

"In what way?"

"They will persist in regarding me as a policeman, one who arrests petty thieves and ordinary inebriates; whereas I am a crime investigator. On the other hand, they know how useless it is to hurry me, or direct me, for they know that when I want a thing done I have most excellent reasons for having it done."

"Won't you tell me why you have persuaded Headquarters to fetch your friend from North Queensland at an expense of something like two hundred pounds?"

There was a note of pleading in Sergeant Morris's voice, and for a little while Bony studied the strong face cast in the military mould. He asked a somewhat surprising question: "Do you believe in spiritualism?"

"I think there is more in it than the sceptics will admit. Why?"

"Do you think that if you take a half-caste baby, rear it, educate it, and finally teach the grown man a profession, that he will follow the profession most of his life and remain a lifelong unit of the white man's civilization?"

"I'm damned sure he wouldn't. The black blood in him would pull him back into the bush. Every bushman knows that. It's happened too often."

Bony sighed. "Yet there are intelligent Australian people who will not believe it. However, as you appear to be a man with an open, reasoning mind, I will take you a little into my confidence."

"Good! I'm all attention."

"Very well. There is a very great number of people who regard the Australian aboriginal as standing on the lowest rung of the human ladder. Because they have found no traces of a previous aboriginal civilization, no settlements, no buildings, no industry, they say that he always has been a man of a very low type. Yet, for all that, he has possessed for many centuries that which the white race is constantly striving to obtain, and which its striving brings no nearer. The blessed possession I refer to is Contented Happiness, the only human possession worth having. ...

"The despised black man, ignorant, without wisdom, is contentedly happy. He desires nothing but life's essentials. In his profound ignorance and unwisdom he ruthlessly practises birth control. He makes sure that the very occasional mental degenerate and the physical weakling will not reproduce their like, and he keeps the population down well below a point which the country's natural food supply will support by the same method of birth control.

"The blackfellow thus is the world's greatest statesman. Every race, every nation, has something to learn from him. True, he has none of the white man's monuments to boast of or to point to as evidence of a supreme culture. Such monuments he would regard as millstones about his single ethereal monument of happiness.

"Because the blackfellow is so lacking in that boastfulness which is the white man's prerogative, the white man looks on him with contempt. Yet the blackfellow possessed culture when the white man ate raw flesh because he did not know how to make a fire. He did not inscribe his culture on tablets, nor did he force it on the general community. His secrets are well kept, and his powers well restrained. Old Moongalliti can kill a man or woman by merely willing it. A love of ceremony demands the pointing of a bone at the doomed man. It is not the pointing-bone that kills, but will-power.

"I have known instances where a white man has died because a contemptible Australian black has willed it. Old Illawalli can project his mind into the brain of another man and read that man's thoughts throughout his whole life as easily as you or I would read a book by turning its pages. I am glad to see you are not laughing."

"I am a bushman," Morris said simply.

"Good! Now Moongalliti and I belong to the same cult or craft. He knows who killed Marks and how the killing was done. Wait—do not interrupt. In my own way I have questioned him, but without any result. I could obtain what I want to learn through the craft which unites us; but to pass on or make use of the knowledge would be to break my oaths and stain my honour. Illawalli will get the knowledge by a different method. He will hypnotize Moongalliti without Moongalliti's knowledge."

"Ah, I see the drift now."

For a little while Bony fell silent. He was making yet another cigarette. Then: "Even when we know who killed Marks, I am afraid we shall only have disposed of the preliminaries of the case. We shall have to prove that Marks is dead and was murdered, for Illawalli's testimony will not be admitted. Again, so far we have no glimmering of the motive for the crime. Have you those records for which I asked?"

Chapter Twenty-three

Circumstantial Evidence

THERE WERE NOW four questions that Bony badly wanted to answer but found he could not. What had become of the money it was believed Marks carried with him, amounting to about thirteen hundred pounds? The cashier at the bank had issued one-pound treasury notes to that amount, and the numbers of these notes were not ascertainable. Did Marks carry the money the day he was killed? If he did, how was it that the murderer had not left Windee to spend it, especially when the case seemed to be officially forgotten?

Circumstances seemed to indicate that the man or men responsible for the removal of Marks was or were too clever or too cautious to permit even that moderate amount of money to remain in existence. In all probability it had been burned with the body, if the body had been burned.

What had been the precise nature of the business on which Marks had visited Jeff Stanton? Stanton's explanation of it to Sergeant Morris was exceedingly vague. It might—Bony considered it tentatively—be the real motive actuating the killing. Supposing Jeff Stanton to be the murderer? As a supposition it would account for the non-appearance of Marks's money, or for the absence of any result of its being put into general circulation. Yet, if Stanton committed the crime, and supposing Marks's body had been incinerated beneath where lay the charred remains of three kangaroos, how came it that those animals had been shot by Dot?

Bony was constrained to believe that the secret lay hidden in the business discussed by Stanton and Marks in conference. The finger was inclined to point to Jeff Stanton, if it could be assumed that the money existed. Neither Ned Swallow not Jack Withers was a man who would continue at work when possessed of thirteen hundred pounds. Both men were normally intelligent. Withers was extremely excitable, as was shown when he witnessed the corroboree fight; whilst Ned Swallow was by no means a quick thinker, or able to act instantly with circumspection.

These two men Bony crossed off the list of seven suspected fish, leaving five—one of which was the sting-ray. The two deletions were effected because Bony was justifiably sure that Marks's killer was a man of strong will, a clear mind, and ruthlessly determined. This character fitted Jeff Stanton to perfection. In many respects it also fitted the bookkeeper, Mr Roberts; and what characteristics were lacked by Dot were supplied by Dash, so that together they also would fit.

The third question was what lay behind the altered attitude towards him of Marion Stanton and the faint suspicion behind the eyes of her father? It was a clear question and demanded a clear answer. It did not raise nor could it be answered by other questions.

The fourth question was what lay behind Moongalliti's threat to point the bone at any of his tribe who breathed a word of what Ludbi had seen, be it little or much, and this question could only be answered by old Illawalli, then being hurried to Windee.

They were the four principal questions among a larger number. Bony would have liked to obtain answers to the mystery of the sapphire in the ants' nest, the mystery of Dash leaving the "Government House" to become a fur-getter, and the mystery of Jeff Stanton's earlier life before he took up the land on the range.

The reports furnished by Sergeant Morris were fairly informative. The dossiers of Dot and Dash started from their arrival in Australia. Their overseas history was not important to the case. The lives of both Marion and young Jeff were easily traced, and but little more difficulty was experienced in dealing with Ned Swallow, who came from Queensland, and Jack Withers, a Victorian. Mr Roberts was born in Adelaide, came of a well-known business family, and for years was employed by a stock and station agency. About all those everything was fairly clear. But nothing could be found regarding the birthplace or the first twenty-two years of Jeff Stanton's life. It was quite a minor point, but it added to the collection of mysteries.

Thinking about these several matters, Bony paid a visit on foot one Sunday afternoon to the tree in the fork of which were concealed his sheepskin sandals. With these on his feet he swung south by west for two miles, when he came in sight of a windmill and well, and the inevitable water-troughing. A hundred yards or so from the mill he came upon a camp-site, the one occupied by Dot and Dash when Marks disappeared.

There remained still the poles with which the partners' tent had been erected, whilst a dozen yards from these was the site of the camp-fire. A litter of empty tins revealed that the two men liked peach and melon and lemon jam, tinned fruit and tomatoes, and condensed milk. Bony found several cartridge-cases fitting Dash's Savage, and two fitting Dot's Winchester, besides a few fitting a twelve-bore gun.

There were many things in that camp-site to indicate the tastes and characters of its one-time occupants, and Bony examined it with care. Of tracks there were none other than those of innumerable rabbits. The ashes on the fireplace spoke of a tenancy lasting several weeks. There was nothing peculiar about it. The wind had levelled the ash-heap and partly covered it with sand, and it was entirely on impulse, born of memory that a fireplace is a gold-miner's favourite cache, that Bony began to excavate a hole in the centre of where the fire had been habitually built.

The mixture of ash and sand was loose and fine. Bony worked with his hands, and he had scooped out a hole two feet deep when he felt the touch of metal. A little further trouble, and there lay exposed a neatly made box fashioned from a four-gallon petrol-tin.

Slowly he lifted it up. The lid was fastened down by a wire catch, and with his lips compressed into a straight line he opened the box. Within was a parcel wrapped in black waterproof cloth, used at one time for protecting fracteur from damp. With firm unhurried fingers he undid this parcel, and suddenly smiled gently when he saw many neat packets of one-pound treasury notes.

There were twenty-three of these packets. He counted the notes in one of them. There were fifty. The total was eleven hundred and thirty pounds; and as though to prove that the money had belonged to Marks there was a bank draft for two hundred pounds made out in favour of Thomas Marks, and payable at Perth, Western Australia.

For this "find" the cupidity of Dot was responsible, so Bony believed. His was a nature that could not bear to see good money destroyed. He knew it was good money, since the notes were untraceable. He knew that he could spend them any time he chose. Why had he not already done so? Was it natural cunning or natural covetousness, or just plain fear? Or was it because his partner was the dominant figure, and they waited for an agreed period of time to expire before they divided and left Windee?

Bony had made an important step forward. He had obtained evidence—of a sort. It was not conclusive evidence that Marks was murdered, for the partners might have *found* the box and contents, and it could be suggested that Marks had cast it from him whilst he aimlessly searched for a path leading to a human habitation and life.

He thought for a while, and then, suddenly smiling, wrapped up the notes again in the cloth and set the parcel aside. The tin box he securely fastened and replaced at the bottom of the hole. Lastly he filled in the hole and smoothed the surface carefully, leaving no trace of the spot having been disturbed.

Taking up the parcel of treasury notes, he looked over the campsite before walking back to the junction of the roads, where he took off the sheepskin sandals and found a fresh hiding-place for them in a hollow tree. The result of his afternoon's work was highly gratifying to him, for, although it was not conclusive, it was a further proof that Time was on his side.

When he entered his bunk-room, shared with Jack Withers, the cross-eyed man put down a novel he was reading, and, with one eye looking out through the open door and the other fixed at a point several feet above Bony's head, he drawled: "Ole Noonee bin along looking for you. 'Pears quite upset like. Says Moongalliti et summat wot made 'im feel like throwing a seven. Wants you to go along and look 'im over."

"Ah, perhaps someone has been pointing the bone at him," Bony surmised with a smile.

"'Taint likely, unless it's the ole bloke wot's just arrived."

"An old man? Stranger?"

"Yaas. Embly says 'is name is Illawalli."

"Indeed!" Bony's surprise was hidden by blandness. "Have you seen him?"

"Yus—and smelled 'im. 'E's about a 'undred and fifty years old, and as 'igh as any black wot 'as offended me nose. Must be old Moongalliti's great-great-grandfather, come to life from Noah's Ark."

Chapter Twenty-four

Secrets of Ind

AFTER DINNER that evening Bony wandered down the creek to the blacks' camp, which he found partially deserted, many of the tribe having gone hunting. Several gins vanished inside their rude humpies (huts) at sight of him, and one of them was Runta, apparently fearful that Bony might be suffering from his "sometime now" malady. Gunda, however, came to meet him, and her not bad-looking face betokened curiosity.

"Well, Gunda, ole Moongalliti bad, eh?" Bony said.

"Him plurry crook," was Gunda's emphatic answer.

"What's the matter with him?"

"Him all bad here," Gunda explained, pressing her hands to that part of her body below her waist; then added naively: "But bimeby him all right. Blackfeller come long way. Ole feller Illawalli, him make Moongalliti good soon."

"Ah, take me to Moongalliti, Gunda."

The chief was lying on some old chaff-bags spread out beneath a box-tree; he was groaning deeply and writhing in quite an alarming fashion. Noonee, the mother of Ludbi, was seated at his feet, her body rocking from side to side, and from her lips proceeding long, high-pitched, doleful wails. At Moongalliti's head was seated a tall, marvellously emaciated patriarch with snow-white hair and a white beard fully a yard long. This person was dressed in new cheap shop-made clothes, which Bony instantly guessed had been provided by the police before he was forwarded on his long journey south. Seeing Bony approach, Illawalli jumped to his feet with astonishing agility and ran to Bony with a joyful yell. His trouser-encased long legs, the light brown jacket, and the pink kerchief about his neck reminded Bony of the time, long gone, when he and several other boys had dressed an emu in an old suit of clothes and let it go.

"Bony! Bony, my son and my father!" Illawalli shouted, and reaching out his skinny arms he clasped the half-caste in an affectionate hug. The warmth of his greeting recompensed the detective for the odour—not of sanctity—the old man emitted, and behind his keen black eyes he saw a hint of amusement which flashed now and then, as though some stupendous joke rivalled the affection. And while Illawalli hugged he said softly:

"Ah, Bony, you want me, eh? You sent police, eh? You 'member ole Illawalli tell you him son and his father. I come! I come on the horse that goes on wheels and I rode on the emu that flies."

"Were you not afraid, Illawalli?"

"Ya-as. Then I not 'member it. Oh, Bony, I laff and I laff, 'way up there. I look and see clouds from top."

"Well, well! You're a lucky man. Now let us see what's wrong with Moongalliti."

"Him all right. I gibbit him blackfeller's dope make 'im crook; then I gibbit 'im whitefeller's dope make 'im well. Me great man Nor' Queensland; now me fine feller Noo South Wales."

"Why did you do that?" Bony asked curiously.

"Well, you see, like this. Moongalliti not like poor ole Illawalli. Him think I'se be chief here. So I put stomach debil in 'im tucker; then 'e sing out loud and I fix 'im up. Him all right bimeby."

Now with gentle firmness Bony put his friend from him, and together they went to the recumbent Moongalliti, who had ceased his groaning and was regarding them with unfeigned interest. Bony seated himself beside him and, taking up one thin wrist, felt the pulse. It was almost normal.

"Bad! Me bin plurry bad," said the patient shakily.

"You been eating too much," Bony told him sternly.

"Naw."

"Yes, you have. You eat nothing till to-morrow, or you get bad again. You nearly die." The old gin began to wail louder than ever. "Illawalli, him fine doctor. He make you well. Good feller, Illawalli."

"My plurry oath," agreed Moongalliti, sitting up. Then with startling suddenness he yelled to the gin: "You'm shut up! Wa' for you make that row?"

Almost as old as Moongalliti, the woman's fat and ugly face brightened at the now normal tone of her husband. Her black eyes glistened, and about her mouth dawned a tender smile that fascinated Bony's attention. Moongalliti also saw her expression of tender affection for him; but he was a man, and men must not be weak with women. There was a heavy waddy within his reach, and Bony caught his arm just in time to prevent its being hurled at the wife. Hastily she arose and fled.

"Do you feel stomach-debil now?" Bony inquired seriously.

"Naw. He bin almost dead."

"Just so. Almost dead, but he may come to life again," the half-caste warned the chief. "You go slow now. Don't you get up. Illawalli and I go hunting for tree-leaf which will kill your debil for ever. Now, hear! Don't get up!"

"Orl right, Bony," Moongalliti promised, memory of the recent pains still vivid. Then he clasped Bony's hand in his saying: "You good feller, Bony. You good feller, Illawalli."

Illawalli grunted. He and Bony got to their feet and strolled off down the creek whilst the box-tree leaves glittered as flakes of gold in the setting sun. They had walked nearly half a mile, and, arriving at the ironstone hillock crowned by the ancient and mysterious pavement of rock squares, they seated themselves at its base and made preparations to smoke. All round them rabbits fed on fallen leaves and scratched small holes in search of grass-roots, and from out its hole crawled a gigantic monarch goanna, six feet in length, moving slowly with deceptive sluggishness.

In the vernacular Bony related to his companion the mystery of Marks's disappearance, described the blackfellow's sign, and told what he had learned from Runta.

"Ole Moongalliti, him cunning feller," Bony went on. "Ludbi, his son, told him he saw a car come through the bush with this whitefeller, Marks, fighting with another whitefeller. I believe Ludbi told Moongalliti who killed Marks and how, and Moongalliti threatens the pointing-bone to any one of his tribe who says a word about it."

"What-it whitefeller gotta do blackfeller?" the ancient asked, intelligently placing his finger on the crux of the affair.

"That's what I can't understand," Bony admitted. "Me good friends with Moongalliti." He whispered three words, and Illawalli's eyes gleamed with aroused interest. "No good to me he tell me on sign of the moon. Then I can no tell no one. He not see sign on your back same as me. You read his spirit-mind, Illawalli, and what you read you tell-it me, eh?"

For a little while the old man made no reply. His seamed face was as that of some ugly heathen god, but, whereas the god expresses evil, there was in the face of Illawalli a look of placid benevolence. "Me grow old," he said at last. "P'r'aps me can't look into Moongalliti's spirit. You one plurry fool, Bony. 'Member me wanted teach you how to look in men's spirits ? Mine father learned me, an' my father's father learned 'im, an' 'is father learned my father's father. From the land of Ind, before the waters rose an' made this land roun' as is the sun, came the secrets my father learned me. No son have I to pass on the power. You are my son and my father, Bony, and you will have none of it."

The half-caste sighed. Illawalli's hypnotic power was stupendous. Twice had Bony experienced it, and gladly would he have become possessed of the power had there been any other than the precise condition accompanying the offer. In his profession the secrets of the art, handed down through countless generations to Illawalli, would have been of inestimable value; but the condition on which the old man insisted in return for the knowledge was that Bony should forsake the white man's civilization and become chief of Illawalli's tribe when the latter died. And that was a condition Bony felt he could never accept. It would mean surrendering all the interests in life which the white man's education had given.

"It cannot be, Illawalli," he said a little sadly. "Yet do as I ask. for I have had you carried on the emu's back that you might do it."

"Have no fear, Bony. As the missionary at Burke turns the leaves of his book and reads the signs therein, so will I read the pictures in the mind of Moongalliti. Say, now, am I getting old?"

Bony was idly watching the goanna waddling over the ground, its gait belying its tremendous speed when hard pressed by a dog. Idly, his mind occupied by the possibilities of Illawalli's power, could he but possess it without the damning condition, he watched it make a small circle, then stand still for a second before raising itself on stiffened legs and swelling out its neck to an alarming thickness.

A rabbit drew near and crouched down facing the goanna. Another joined it, also crouching and looking into the bright eyes of the reptile. Then at short intervals other rabbits came and gazed at the goanna till presently there was a complete ring about it. Rabbits were scurrying towards the reptile, and after a little while a second ring was formed outside the first. When that was completed a third ring was formed, and yet a fourth, a fifth, sixth, and seventh. Seven rings of grey fur, and in the centre the motionless, evil-looking, gigantic lizard.

Seven perfect circles, one within the other! Bony watched, and saw possibly a thousand rabbits move as one, so that they sat up on their hind legs. As one, that host of rabbits bowed in deep obeisance to the monarch seven times. At this point remembrance came to Bony and he laughed. He realized that Illawalli was hypnotizing him. Yet knowing it, quite aware that what he saw did not really exist, nevertheless he continued to see it as plainly as though it did exist. In spite of what he knew, he plainly witnessed the rabbits disperse as they had formed the circles, and when the last had gone he watched the swelling of the reptile's neck subside, saw the long grey-green body sink nearer to the ground, then proceed on its way.

"You are yet strong in spirit," he said, chuckling.

"You say to yourself that ole Illawalli is a great man," the ancient countered.

"I did," Bony admitted. "There is nothing hidden from you, O reader of men's minds! Come, let us go back, and you read me the mind of Moongalliti."

They arose and walked to the camp in the quiet stillness of the new-born night. Arrived at the camp, they found that the hunters had all returned and were eating in the light of several large communal fires. When they joined Moongalliti, Illawalli handed to him a few berries from a box-tree, after he had made many mystic signs over them. And Moongalliti took them and chewed, and because he was given faith he was cured.

The three sat alone and maintained a long silence. About them the tribe ate or wrangled or conversed with much laughter. The wrangling was only sporadic, the laughter continuous. Children chattered and shrieked, dogs yelped and growled over titbits tossed to them, and the scene was lit by the glowing fires that tipped the tree-leaves with scarlet and put out the stars above.

Bony broke the silence that had settled about him and his two companions. He said to Illawalli:

"You 'member Arney? He killed a blackfeller near Camooweal little time ago. Black trackers caught him on the Diamantina, and when a white policeman was taking him back to Camooweal in a motor-car he escaped."

"Ah!" Illawalli sighed non-committally, for he had never heard of Arney.

"Yes. On the way Arney attacked the policeman who was driving the car, nearly killed him, and escaped. They haven't caught him yet."

"Ah!" Illawalli said for the second time, but there was something very significant in the sound of this second "Ah". Bony felt satisfied. He knew then that the fictitious story regarding Arney and the policeman fighting in the motor-car had brought to the surface of Moongalliti's mind the story told by Ludbi. And, having set memory going as a wound-up clock, Bony fell into silence again. Moongalliti did not speak; he was making a cigarette, and whilst he made the cigarette Illawalli was reading his thoughts as one reads the printed page. A minute elapsed. Then Illawalli sighed as though he awoke from a long sleep. His forehead was damp with perspiration, and he rubbed his hands as though they were cold. When he looked at Bony, the half-caste saw in his parchment-like face the faint light of triumph.

Chapter Twenty-five

The Strange Lady

THE FOLLOWING DAY Illawalli disappeared as mysteriously as he had arrived. His visit to Windee had been arranged with creditable expedition and privacy by Sergeant Morris, so that none ever knew that the old man had been police-conducted. Illawalli returned to his tribe by slower but none the less interesting methods of locomotion, and the excursion proved to be the crowning experience of his life.

The day after Illawalli departed. Bony learned that one of the station trucks was leaving for Mount Lion to bring back a load of rations. Instead, therefore, of walking in company with Jack Withers to the site of the new stockyards he and the cross-eyed man were building, he sought and found Jeff Stanton in the station office.

"Morning, Jeff!" he drawled pleasantly. "I hear Ron is going into Mount Lion this morning, and as I want some clothes, will you allow me to go with him?"

Stanton relit his half-consumed cigarette before replying: "I've got no objection, Bony. You're on contract work, and time is your own. But I'm paying Jack Withers wages. Can he get along by himself?"

"Most easily. He knows exactly what to do."

"All right. But don't forget to come back."

Bony smiled at the significance in the other's voice.

"I will return in order," he said. "But I had better take ten pounds. Father Ryan is sure to tax me. Besides, I run no account at the stores."

"Ten pounds, Mister Roberts," Stanton snapped, and, while the cheque was being written, he said to Bony: "You come from Queensland, don't you?"

"I was born and educated there."

"Then what possessed you to come to New South Wales?"

"Change of scene chiefly." And then, as though to qualify this statement, he lied blandly: "Also to get a holiday away from my wife."

"Humph!"

Roberts placed the cheque-book before him, and Jeff Stanton signed the form filled in for ten pounds. When taking the cheque Bony sensed that his employer was not satisfied with his explanation; a faint glint of suspicion remained behind the grey eyes fiercely regarding him beneath the white pent eyebrows.

Whilst walking from the office to the waiting truck loaded high with kangaroo skins, the property of Dot and Dash, he wondered how Jeff Stanton had become suspicious of him. That it was merely suspicion, and not fear, Bony was satisfied. But what it was, or what had occurred to start the suspicion, as well as to cause the change in Marion Stanton's attitude towards him, the detective was unable to understand. Unless it were that Stanton and his daughter were fully cognizant of the details of Marks's disappearance.

Ron, the fresh-faced Englishman, climbed behind the truck steering-wheel on seeing the half-caste hurrying towards him. He was a stalwart youth, not much over twenty, and represented the cream of the British immigrants, those who penetrate to the heart of Australia in preference to slaving for a "cocky" (small farmer) for next to nothing or wandering about a city in a ridiculous quest for non-existent work.

"Old man a bit off-colour this morning?" he asked, as though fully convinced of it, himself.

"Not more so than usual," replied the smiling Bony.

"He's a card all right, but I'm sure there is not a better man to work for in this country or in England. Pays me four pounds a week and keep to drive this truck, when other squatters only pay two-fourteen-eight, arbitration wages. What I can't understand is that, although he pays big wages, he has become a millionaire. It is not as if he has only just started to pay big so's to get rid of some of his cash. Jack Withers says he has always paid more than anyone else, even when he was battling on his first selection."

"It is not a difficult problem," Bony said reflectively. "There is no waste, nor is there any deterioration going on through neglect of plant. As for the wages aspect of the affair, I remember a parable in your Bible, which once I read from cover to cover, which illustrates a fundamental truth. I refer to the saying—the precise words escape me—that bread thrown on the waters will return greatly increased. Only a very few big employers have realized that, and they must smile inwardly in these days when the universal cry is, 'Wages must come down', whereas the universal cry should be, 'Waste and inefficiency must cease.'"

"You're right there," Ron assented. "There's old Jones on the other side of Mount Lion. He's got to pay the Arbitration Court wages to white men, so he employs nigs at less than a pound a week, and he sees to it that they spend their pound a week on tobacco and clothes which he sells them. Well, you know what nigs are. They're good workers when worked alone, but no good when worked in a mob. Old Jones employs a mob. They were supposed to look after his stock, and they became too tired to overlook a bunch of expensive rams and show them their way to water, so that the rams hung in a corner of a paddock and perished. Sixty-seven of 'em, and they each cost eight pounds."

"'A fool and his money ...'" quoted Bony.

"True enough. But there's a deuce of a lot of fools in this unsettled world. By crumbs! Remind me to call on Mrs Swale for a parcel for Miss Marion."

About half-past ten they reached Mount Lion, where Ron pulled up outside the police-station to obtain from Sergeant Morris the necessary permit to dispatch, per storekeeper's truck, the kangaroo skins. Bony stayed on the truck seat whilst the Englishman was within the sergeant's tiny office, and through its window he could hear Morris's barked questions as though Ron and Dot and Dash were habitual criminals. Carrying the permit, the truck-driver emerged with a slightly flushed face, and when he joined Bony it was to say, a little resentfully:

"Poor down-trodden England can rightfully boast of the civility of its police, at least."

"Never mind," murmured Bony indulgently. "You can always counter incivility with politeness."

"Well, I've got to see Hugo about the back loading, but we'll have a drink first."

Within the hotel they discovered Mr Bumpus entertaining a lady over a glass of beer, and at their entry host and guest straightened up and abruptly stopped what obviously was a most confidential conversation. The Englishman called for the drinks, and while Bumpus served them Bony examined the lady cautiously through a mirror behind her.

She was of medium height and dressed fashionably but loudly. Her face was rouged and painted in no niggardly manner, her hair was yellowish golden, and from even a short distance her age appeared to be about twenty-five. Bony's penetrating observation, however, stripped her of the appearance of youth created by peroxide and rouge, and he saw in the mirror a forceful woman nearer sixty than fifty years of age, a woman of vitality and not without character of a kind.

Having served them, Bumpus sidled along the bar to his previous position opposite her, and without the slightest self-consciousness she produced a florin and requested that his and her glasses be refilled. It was so odd for a woman to drink openly in a public bar that Bony found Ron winking at him; but then the oddity was lessened by the fact that Mr Bumpus's hotel was situated in Mount Lion, and not in the thriving city or town. They were on the verge of leaving, when the woman ceased her low-spoken conversation with the publican and approached Ron. Bony she ignored.

"They tell me you're driving for Mr Jeff Stanton," she said. "I want to see him. Will you give me a lift to Windee?"

"Yes—why not?"

"When are you starting back?"

"After lunch."

"All right, I'll be ready. Here, mister, fill 'em up."

So Mr Bumpus refilled the glasses, and Ron and Bony gravely wished that the lady might continue to enjoy good health. Politely the Englishman offered to "shout" in turn, but the woman declined, saying:

"I travelled all yesterday from Broken Hill. Reckon I'm tired, and I'll have a lay down before lunch. See you boys after. So long!"

Smiling at each in turn, she swept from the bar with a swish of knee-high skirts, her figure helping to support the lie regarding her age. On her exit, Bumpus winked significantly and Bony smiled with obvious mirth. Said the publican:

"Queer party! Got hopeless last night on whisky, and all the morning drinking beer. Stands it better than I could."

"What's she here for?" Ron inquired.

"Dunno. Wants to pay a visit to Jeff Stanton. Bit of a hard doer. P'rhaps she wants a job cooking or house-maiding."

"Ah well! We'll take her out. I must go and hunt up Hugo. See you later, Bony."

Whilst the half-caste followed Ron outside the hotel, he paused on the sidewalk to roll a cigarette and to scheme to interview Sergeant Morris without being observed. The street was deserted when the Englishman entered Hugo's weatherboard store, and silent, too, until the cockatoo in its cage hung from the store veranda roof observed with its usual distinctness: "How dry we are!"

It was then that Bony, looking up, saw Father Ryan coming out through the whitewashed wicket-gate in front of the sergeant's house. The little man obviously had cut short his studies on seeing Bony through his window, for he was dressed in tussore silk of a bright yellow colour and wore a very much used Panama hat. There was geniality and purpose in his gait when crossing the road.

"Good day, Bony!" he greeted, with his wonderfully sunny smile.

"Good morning, your reverence!" Bony replied, with a slight bow. "Being such a warm day, would you care for some refreshment?"

"I honestly believe I am entitled to refreshment this hot morning, but I rather fear meeting a somewhat extraordinary lady who arrived here last evening."

"The track is clear. She has retired to her room," laughed the half-caste.

"Then I no longer fear"—and, taking Bony by the arm, the little priest drew him through that door which led to Mr Bumpus's private room. When the publican followed them in, Bony looked interrogatively at Father Ryan.

"A glass of wine, Mr Bumpus," he said, his eyes twinkling.

"Bottled beer," stated Bony.

Mr Bumpus withdrew.

"What is your opinion of the visiting lady?" questioned Bony softly. Father Ryan's eyes clouded.

"My opinion is hardly formed," he said. "Obviously she drinks to excess, and yet there is something very straightforward in her manner as well as her speech. I approached her to solicit a subscription for my benevolent fund, but before I could speak she said to Bumpus: 'A drink! A drink for the Church! A double whisky!' I was obliged to drink at least half the spirit, for which I do not care; and during the rest of the half-hour I was with her I couldn't get a word in edgeways."

Mr Bumpus came in with the drinks on a tray. After he had offered the wine to Father Ryan and taken his drink off the tray, Bony placed thereon the cheque for ten pounds and asked Mr Bumpus to change it.

"I suppose Mount Lion does not see many strangers?" was Bony's next question.

"Well, no, excepting the mail-car passengers, and invariably they stay only one night. Really, I think the last visitor we had was a fellow named Marks, the man who got lost in the bush and presumably perished. A very sad and a quite mysterious affair."

Mr Bumpus came back with Bony's change, which he counted out on the table in notes and silver. Bony was about to pick it up, when Father Ryan cut in:

"It might be as well to subscribe ten shillings to my benevolent fund," he said jovially. "You will find it a sort of insurance against indisposition."

Bony chuckled, and offered a pound note, saying:

"I was fully expecting it to be more."

"You have yet to prove yourself. I may have to raise the premium, but I sincerely hope not. Come! If you will accompany me to my rooms, I will write you a receipt; also I have a volume by Nietzsche in which he says a lot about human progress being an illusion, and that mankind advances and retreats alternately in historical cycles. This, I think, from something you said on the tin-kettling night, is something like your belief. I am much afraid you are a Pagan."

"Perhaps. Anyway, I believe with some of the Greeks that every event in the past will be repeated in the future," Bony rejoined gravely. "I am forced to that belief by Nature, since cycles of life are so pronounced among animals. And man, after all, is but an animal."

"You are wrong," the little priest said stoutly. "So was Machiavelli when he said that, as human passions are always the same, so their effects must be always the same. You must read Bernard Bosanquet and ponder on what he has to say about idealism."

Reaching the wicket-gate, Father Ryan, talking volubly, was leading Bony to the side-door of the house when Sergeant Morris called loudly for the half-caste to go to his office. The priest's hand fell on Bony's forearm, his appealing eyes looked up into the dark face, and he said softly: "Come and see me when the sergeant's business is over. I want to talk to you, for I realize you are a man of intelligence. It is many years now since I talked with an intelligent man."

"I shall be delighted," Bony assented. "But I shall bring my friends, Marcus Aurelius and Virgil, with me."

Chapter Twenty-six

"A Little Experiment"

"I HAVE some official letters for you," stated Sergeant Morris in his crisp manner when greetings had been exchanged and Bony was seated. "How did your experiment with Illawalli turn out?"

"Not quite up to expectations, my dear Sergeant. He told me all that Moongalliti knew, but that was not quite all I wanted to know."

"What did it come to?"

"I will tell you when I find out the little he, Moongalliti, doesn't know. With your permission, I will just scan these letters."

The half-caste proceeded to read his mail. The first communication was from the Research Department, Police Headquarters, Sydney, relating to a boot-sprig. The second was far more lengthy and dealt with Marks's early history and that of a certain Mrs Thomas. Mrs Thomas's history was obtained chiefly from official records. The third letter was from Colonel Spender demanding to know when Bony anticipated returning to his duties in Queensland, as the murder at Longreach was baffling everybody. The fourth letter was from his wife, and this he decided to read later. The fifth letter related to a small silver disk, and the writer was Sir Alfred Worthington, a very famous Australian.

From his letters Bony's eyes rose slowly to the impatient face of Sergeant Morris. Bony's eyes were veiled to hide the triumph in their blue depths, and from the sergeant they wandered to a police trooper engaged on clerical work at another table, and from him came finally to rest on two emu eggs set up on the mantelpiece as ornaments.

"I want an urgent telegram dispatched," he said at last. The sergeant reached for pencil and telegram forms. Dictated the half-caste: *To Inspector Sutley, Criminal Investigation Branch, Sydney. Wire personal particulars Mrs Thomas—mail photo if possible.—B.*

The message was given to the trooper, who was ordered to dispatch it at once. On his leaving, Bony picked up from the mantelpiece the two emu eggs, and, examining them, saw that they had at each end a small hole through which the contents formerly had been blown.

"Can you lay your hands on a .44 Winchester or Remington rifle and a .22 Savage rifle?" he asked softly.

"Yes. The trooper has a Savage, and I can borrow the Winchester. Why?"

"It is necessary to carry out a little experiment. Can one in your back garden be observed by any of the neighbours?"

"I don't think so. But what's the scheme?"

"Go and borrow that Winchester. If you see the trooper, tell him to bring away his Savage. We might want two cartridges for each rifle."

Sergeant Morris rose obediently, even though he saw the incongruity of a uniformed police-sergeant obeying an aboriginal half-caste. When he was gone, Bony searched the officer's desk till he found a half-sheet of postage stamps, from which he detached a strip of the gummed border. Tearing off two rough squares, he stuck them over a hole in each of the eggs, and over the paper he melted ordinary sealing-wax.

Returning with the borrowed rifle, Sergeant Morris found Bony lounging down in his chair, the back of his head supported by clasped hands, a cigarette between his lips.

"The trooper has gone to his lodgings for his Savage rifle," he told Bony, who thereupon rose and picked up the large, blue-green eggs.

"These will more easily be filled with water if they are submerged in a basin. Perhaps Mrs Morris will oblige?"

"You're darned mysterious, Bony. What is the idea?" demanded the sergeant, with prominent determined jaw and glinting grey eyes.

"Patience, friend, patience; and perhaps, in a few days, I will describe the perfect murder. However, I do not promise. Let us fill these eggs with water."

Together they made their way to the kitchen, where Mrs Morris was discovered making pastry. A dish was procured and filled with water from a rain-tank, and after a little trouble the eggs were filled to Bony's satisfaction. Back in the office once more, Bony sealed the remaining openings in the shells as he had done the others, and by that time the trooper appeared carrying a well-kept .22 Savage rifle. He and his superior followed Bony carrying the eggs into the neat garden at the rear of the premises. There Bony selected an earth border surrounding a tiny grass lawn that was the pride of the sergeant's lady. Making sure that beyond the fence there was nothing but open common, he then formed two golfing tees and on them set the eggs firmly up on end.

"Which of you is the better rifle shot?" he asked his perplexed audience. "Rowland is," Morris admitted promptly.

"Very well. Now, Mr Rowland, I want you to lie down about twenty feet from these eggs. I want you to fire a bullet from the Winchester exactly through the middle of one of the eggs, and a bullet from the Savage exactly through the middle of the other. Take your time and don't miss, for probably we could not find another emu eggshell in Mount Lion."

The trooper loaded the Winchester and took up the specified position. When the rifle cracked the egg very slowly fell from its supporting tee, and Bony, picking it up, said: "See, the bullet has passed through the egg, making a very neat round hole through each side. With my penknife I will mark it with a 'W'. Now the other, Mr Rowland."

The action of the bullet from the Savage rifle was markedly dissimilar, as was the report of the exploding cartridge. The egg collapsed at the moment its water content was whisked away in spray. But one small piece of shell remained, the rest having been dispersed in a thousand fragments. On that one piece of shell Bony scratched the letter "S".

"Thank you!" he said. "The experiment was entirely successful. Let us return to the office."

Again seated in his chair, with Sergeant Morris in position at the farther side of the paper-littered desk, Bony fell to making his eternal cigarette with the long thin fingers bequeathed him by his mother. With his head bent to the task he nevertheless now and then looked up at the stern military face of the police sergeant, a ghost of a smile playing about his mobile lips.

"Once, I think, I told you that murder generally is a very sordid affair, yet to a man of my intelligence a crime very easily finalized," he drawled softly. "The number of men—and doctors are included among them—men of mental ability who have tried and dismally failed to destroy the bodies of their victims, is remarkable. Perhaps the difficulties that confront a murderer desirous of utterly destroying the body of his victim should make law-abiding normal people very thankful. Equally thankful, too, the police who investigate crimes of this kind."

"I should say so," Sergeant Morris interjected sharply.

Bony waved his hand airily. "The chief and overwhelming evidence against a murderer is the victim's body, or part of it. A body, or identifiable parts of a body, being found, convicts ninety-nine murderers in every hundred. The odd one escapes justice not through his own cleverness, nor by good luck, but because the investigating officer is a fool."

The sergeant frowned. Bony continued blandly: "In British law a charge of murder made when no body or part of a body is found is almost unknown. There is one case recorded, and one only. A woman named Perry and her two sons were hanged for the murder of a farm bailiff without the production of a body by the prosecution. It may be surmised, therefore, that when, a few years later, the supposed murdered bailiff turned up alive, he caused no little surprise. This case may be the cause of the judicatory authorities being very particular about making a human body the basis of a murder trial.

"In any case, if a killer can manage to destroy without trace the body of his victim, his chance of escaping due punishment for the crime is excellent. You remember that I told you I knew six wholly different and effectual methods of destroying utterly a human body with agencies and implements obtainable by anyone. Windee has revealed to me a seventh.

"I know now how the murder was committed and the body destroyed. I know that there were two, possibly three, men implicated in it. I know the name of one man, and may be excused for guessing the name of the second. The third man I do not yet know. To complete my case I want this third man's name and also the motive.

"You may say that to establish a motive for murder is the most important part of a prosecution. I agree. In this case, however, it has been necessary first to establish the fact of murder, because the body of Marks, or any recognizable part of it, does not now exist. The discovery of the motive will indicate the third man, whom as yet I cannot name."

"Who are the other two?" Morris demanded.

Bony's smile contained a hint of scornful remonstrance.

"I believe," he said slowly, in a manner which implied that he believed nothing of the sort, "I believe that all great detectives in fiction, Mr Sherlock Holmes. and Dr Thorndyke among them, never divulged their progress in a case until it was finished, so far as they were concerned."

"But, damn it, we are not book detectives!"

"Your objection is perfectly legitimate, my dear Morris. On the other hand, although I am not a book detective, neither am I an ordinary policeman in plain clothes, despite my official rank and connections. I am a man who has never yet failed to finalize a ease allotted to me. Why? The answer is simple. I have from the beginning refused to be bound by red tape. I have never cared a tinker's curse for chief commissioners, advancement in the service, instant dismissal from it, or any other of the many things that govern a policeman's career." Bony rose to his feet. "Nothing influences me in my profession but the elucidation of some mystery, which often is extremely simple. Permit me to leave you now. I have an appointment with Father Ryan. I am taking with me Marcus Aurelius and Virgil."

"Who the devil are they?" exploded Sergeant Morris.

"They are, I think, strangers in Mount Lion," replied Bony, walking out.

Chapter Twenty-seven

"A Bloomin' Corker"

BONY PASSED an hour with Father Ryan, and the little priest, although he failed to convert the half-caste from Paganism, revelled in the luxury of a mental bath. The light and airy room which his host used as his study, the shelves of books on theology, history, biography, and philosophy, as well as the great table used for writing, delighted Bony, and made him feel a rare regret that he had not given his life to the practice of the arts instead of the detection of crime. When at last he rose to leave, Father Ryan waddled round the table and clasped in his the two hands of his visitor, exclaiming:

"My son, you leave me with memories of a delightful conversation, and a little touched with sorrow that the Church failed to call you as a young man. What a missionary you would have made! What convincing arguments you would have put forward, and with what eloquence! Almost you have convinced me that the Greek philosophers were right and Christ wrong. You have touched my mind, but you have not weakened my faith. The reason why your philosophers are wrong, the reason why man ever marches forward and upward, is because of the faith which is within him in an ideal, which is God. Au revoir, and my heartfelt gratitude!"

"Your reverence is kind—and a most worthy antagonist," Bony replied, smiling down into the round chubby face. "I will call on you again before I leave the district, which I regret I shall have to do soon. I, too, say 'au revoir'!"

At the gate the trooper joined him, asking him to return to the office, because Sergeant Morris wished some further talk with him. With a hint of amusement in his blue eyes, Bony entered the office, and with assumed resignation slipped into the vacant chair and at once proceeded to make a cigarette.

"There are one or two points in this Marks case which I would like you to explain more fully," the sergeant said persuasively.

"Well, go ahead."

"You say that you know how Marks's body was destroyed. Am I to understand that it was destroyed utterly?"

"That is the fact I endeavoured to explain."

"It is going to be very difficult, then, to satisfy a judge and jury that Marks is dead." For a moment Sergeant Morris paused. "Have you hope of bringing forward other evidence to prove it, or in an effort to prove it?"

"Decidedly. I possess proof that Marks is dead, even though we cannot produce the body," Bony said with a trace of triumph in his voice. "Even though we cannot produce the body, I can prove how he died."

"How can you prove that?"

"By a little silver disk which might have come from the back of a wristlet watch, but did not."

"Explain, man! Damn it, explain!"

"Not now, Morris. I am not quite ready. What is the visiting lady's name?"

"Thomas—Mrs Rose Thomas. Interested in her?"

"Not personally," answered the half-caste, faintly smiling. "She has business with Jeff Stanton. Ron is taking her to Windee this afternoon. By the way, if the reply from Headquarters does not arrive whilst I am in town, I want you to get it to me as soon as possible." Bony rose to go, and added: "Never hurry in detecting crime. So many people scoff at coincidences, and yet coincidences are the toys of Father Time, and Father Time is pre-eminent as a crime investigator."

When Bony walked to the door of the office Sergeant Morris bit a fingernail. Of all the strange men he had come across during his long official career this half-caste surely was the strangest. His methods were unique, his philosophy of crime detection most original, yet for all that Morris felt utterly sure that Bony would be completely successful. There was the inevitability of fate in the man's make-up.

"Oh, by the way," the half-caste drawled, returning to the desk, "you might put this stuff in your safe for security."

The sergeant, with widened eyelids, saw on the desk before him wad after wad of treasury notes which appeared with baffling quickness from various portions of Bony's dress. "What the deuce ...!" he began.

"That is the money which Marks had with him at the time of his death," interrupted Bony in the quietest of tones.

"The devil!"

"No. Marks, not the devil." And before the astonished policeman could exclaim further Bony had vanished, and was heard swinging back the wicket-gate.

It was then a little after noon, and the two stores were closed during the lunch hour. Knowing that a further twenty minutes was at his disposal, Bony sauntered to the hotel, and, seating himself in the shade of one of the flanking pepper-trees, he produced the letter with the Queensland postmark, opened it, and proceeded to read.

Dearest Bony,

Your letter written November 25th reached me this morning, and I am so glad to know that you are all right. All day I have been laughing at your description of Runta and the way you frightened her off marrying you. You be careful now, or I shall be losing you yet. I will send on the dress for her. A figured print one-piece garment in an out-size should suit her, and I do trust it will repair her broken heart.

Remember, though, that if you don't come home soon your Marie will be suffering a broken heart, a broken heart which will take all your attention and all your affection to mend. ...

Come home, Bony dear! We all want you; and write soon to

Marie.

Smiling gently, the detective re-read the letter, and pictured in his mind the tall, robust figure, almost regal in its grace, and the dark brown face with its clear-cut features and wide-spaced fearless grey eyes. Every time he saw his wife, every time he thought of her, he experienced a sense of prideful satisfaction that she was his mate—she was so worthy to be the wife of Detective-Inspector Napoleon Bonaparte.

He was still thinking of her and his family when the lunch-gong sounded from the hotel, and, seeing Ron coming from the direction of the store, he rose to meet him. They decided to have a drink before lunch.

Within, they found Mr Bumpus in his shirt-sleeves drying glasses. With deep and intense boredom depicted on his round, red face, he served them with tantalizing slowness.

"I'll come along and give you a hand with the loading after lunch, if you like," Bony volunteered to Ron.

"The job's done," was the triumphant reply. "All I've got to do now is to do the errand for Miss Marion, collect the mail, have one more drink, and rope in our fair passenger. Then ..."

With the utmost caution Mr Bumpus leaned over the bar till his face was between their empty glasses and about on a level with them.

"She's a corker!" he whispered. "Gonner stay at Windee at least one night, and got the lubrication 'arf hour ago. Two bottles uv whisky and one uv gin. Strike me pink! Fancy being married to 'er!"

"Must have more money than I've got," Ron commented.

Mr Bumpus refilled their glasses. "She's a bloomin' corker—a bloomin' corker," he whispered again. "If she wus my wife, I'd—I'd ..."

"What?" inquired the delighted Bony.

Mr Bumpus once more wormed himself across the bar. His face had become purple with honest indignation. He spoke with conviction: "I'd cut her ruddy throat!"

He did not share their low laughter when they left the bar and walked along to the dining-room. Here, with all the windows open and the blinds three parts drawn, the air was a little cooler. There were three tables, and at one of these sat the lady who called herself Mrs Rose Thomas. On seeing them she smiled and invited them to sit with her. An anaemic young lady waited on them.

In the darkened room Mrs Thomas did indeed appear youthful. She was gay, possibly a little too gay. Her small, very modern hat was pulled well down over her head, but beneath it was to be seen the highly peroxided hair. On her fingers there flashed several rings, whilst resting on her breast was an enormous diamond pendant which, if genuine, must have been worth considerably more than a hundred guineas. Throughout the meal she addressed herself entirely to the Englishman, without studiously avoiding Bony, and for this the detective was thankful, for it enabled him to observe her carefully and to listen.

She appeared avid for information about the Stantons and about Windee. Regarding Jeff Stanton, she asked of Ron several questions at intervals. How old was he? What was he like in appearance? How long had he occupied Windee? Bony came to wonder what was her actual reason for visiting the squatter. Her hunger for information appeared excessive in a woman supposedly seeking employment as cook or maid, and when the time came for them to leave the table Bony had become deeply interested in her. Ron promised to be ready to leave at precisely two o'clock.

It wanted but twenty minutes to the time of departure when a boy gave Bony a telegram. It was addressed to Sergeant Morris, and read: *Age fifty-eight—height five-seven—peroxide hair—brown eyes—flashily dressed—wears much jewellery—speaks rapidly, shrilly—maiden name Green.*

No indication was given of the sender. It had been sent from Sydney. Bony's blue eyes became almost invisible between the narrowed eyelids. Why was Marks's sister visiting Windee?

Chapter Twenty-eight

A Squatter at Home

JEFF STANTON was working at his own particular table in the Windee office on the morning Bony paid his visit to Mount Lion. Spread before him was a large-scale map of Windee Station, with every paddock named thereon, every well and dam and natural water-hole. The map was affixed to a drawing-board, and in it were stuck two-colour pins and miniature white flags bearing black numbers. From data supplied him every evening by his overseer at Nullawil and his lonely boundary-riders, he could tell at a glance the condition of the natural feed in a paddock, the supply of water, and the number and classification of the sheep within its five-wire fences. The map served the squatter as other maps serve a military commander.

A sheep-run of over a million and a quarter acres is not exactly a farm, and the well-being of seventy thousand sheep calls for constant attention and thorough experience, for, whilst a man can go bankrupt in a year or two through bad farming, it is possible for a squatter to fail in one month when drought is beginning to grip the country and the water supplies are failing. Allow sheep to remain—say three thousand—in a paddock when a hot sun has sucked up what has been considered a week's supply of water in a dam, and, because those sheep have become used to a drink every day, they will all have perished within a week. And wow! there goes four thousand pounds.

Now and then Jeff Stanton scribbled a note on a sheet of foolscap. A flock of four thousand sheep in such or such a paddock will have to be yarded—two thousand drafted off and put into another paddock where the water supply is greater. From yet another paddock the sheep will have to be removed to an empty paddock, and these for three days shepherded near the well till they have learned to find their way to the water without being driven.

Such decisions were taken at these times only at the last minute that permitted a margin of safety, for, so soon as the sheep were concentrated into a comparatively small number of paddocks having abundance of water, the increased number would the more quickly eat down the available feed, which would not be replenished until the rain came. If as much thought were given, when transferring the unemployed of Great Britain to the Dominions, as a successful squatter is obliged to give to his flocks, the British Empire would be far more prosperous than it is.

Here and there over Jeff Stanton's map were placed tiny red flags. There were five of these flags, and they indicated the dams and wells at which the rabbits were watering in force. Observations have shown that forty rabbits will drink one gallon of water when there is no green feed for them to subsist on. It will be understood, therefore, that when two thousand rabbits pay a nightly visit to an open dam, or water-trough supplied by a well, the water supply for the sheep will be affected. Whilst such a drain on a well that is fed by an underground stream is a matter for consideration, such a drain on a surface dam with its limited bulk is of vital consequence, for the nightly presence of a vast number of drinking rabbits means that the water of the dam will become far more quickly exhausted than if it were taken by sheep only.

Stanton picked up the telephone on his desk and gave two long rings—for Nullawil, since there were half a dozen boundary-riders' huts connected by the same line. Then: "Good day, Mrs Foster! Put me through, please, to Carr's Tank. Very warm this morning."

"It is, Mr Stanton," came the feminine voice of the bride, oblivious of Stanton's objection to "mistering". "Our thermometer is up to ninety-eight already."

"You're lucky. Ours registers just a hundred. ... Yes, all right!"

Another wait followed while Jeff restudied his map. Then came the pleasant drawl of Hugh Trench.

"Good day, Dash! How's things out there?" inquired the squatter.

"We have almost finished for the time being," came the reply.

"Good! How many have you got?"

"Not quite seven thousand. We have cleaned up all the 'roos."

"Humph! Well, look here, Dash. I'm told the rabbits are watering in millions at the Frenchman. Will you go along there as soon as you can, say to-morrow?"

Dash demurred. "Can't very well. You see, we have three wool-packs ready for dispatching, and it won't do the skins any good to keep them. They will lose weight."

"I'll send a truck out this afternoon," Stanton countered. "You could load it up this evening, and the driver could come back to-morrow and take 'em into Broken Hill. I've got to send a truck to the Hill for iron. How will that do?"

"That will suit us. There is no netting at the Frenchman, is there?"

Stanton pondered. "No," he said.

"Well, what about sending out about four hundred yards? The driver could drop it when he reaches the branch track to the Frenchman, and it would save us the time rolling up the netting in use here. Besides, in a month's time there will be a fresh mob of rabbits drinking here, and we can come back."

"Good-oh! I'll do that," Jeff agreed. "And you'll go to the Frenchman to-morrow?"

"Yes. It's keeping dry, isn't it?"

"It is, but we are not feeling the pinch yet. Ned tells me that the feed your way is knee-high and dry as tinder. It'll be a good year for a fire. Dry thunder-storms now will be a worry."

"We may be lucky," Dash pointed out. For four seconds he was silent, then: "I shall be in at the homestead on Christmas Day. You will remember that this Christmas marks the end of the probation period."

"Does it?" asked Stanton slowly.

"You know it does. I've kept my word made to you nearly two years ago. You cannot say I haven't proved myself. Jacob didn't do more in his seven years than I've done in my two."

"I'm not arguing the point!" the old man suddenly roared, causing Mr Roberts to mar his ledger with a blot of ink. "My word's my bond. I said you could speak again in two years' time, if you were of the same mind, and proved yourself a man by roughing it during that time as I had to rough it when I was your age. Damn it, I'm not growling! Come in on Christmas Eve, and do your damnedest first thing Christmas morning."

"All right!" Dash cut in, happy laughter in his voice. "I think you and I will get on all right."

"Get on all right?" Stanton snorted. "Don't I get on with anyone all right? Why, I haven't sacked a man these last twelve years. But don't you be too cocksure. It takes two to start a lifelong argument, remember."

"It does. But—but—it will be damned hard if I come a cropper."

"Well, well!" Stanton said more gently. He waited, but evidently Dash had broken the connection, for he did not speak again. For a long while the squatter sat and smoked, and looked vacantly down on the map. He did not see Mr Roberts close his ledger, go over to the typewriter-table and begin to type letters, nor did he hear the clacking of the machine until half an hour later, when, the book-keeper having finished, the silence brought him out of his reverie. Then he looked at the clock hanging on the wall. It was a quarter to twelve.

"Put me through to Bumpus," he requested abruptly.

Three minutes later he heard the publican's voice.

"Has Ron reached town yet?" Jeff asked.

"He came in an hour and a half ago."

"Is he leaning up against your bar?"

"No, he's up at Hugo's."

"Is Bony drunk yet?"

"Not him. He went over to the Padre's quarters some time ago, but the sergeant called him into his office."

"Oh, what's he done?"

"Nothink that I knows of."

"Been there long?"

"He ain't left yet, to my knowledge, which ain't saying he ain't left."

"Well, well, it's none of our business, Bumpus. Don't you let either of 'em get drunk. I want 'em back here to-day. Send out a dozen of port, will you?"

"Good-oh, Jeff!"

Once more the old man fell into a reverie. He wondered. He had wondered a lot about Bony ever since Dash had mentioned casually over the telephone that Ned remembered Bony as being a successful police-tracker. Why was Bony in New South Wales? A half-caste so seldom leaves his native State, and rarely the district where he was born. Bony's long interview with Sergeant Morris seemed significant.

He was still thinking of Bony when the station lunch-gong sounded, and on Mr Roberts saying something about the heat it took a mental effort to banish Bony and make a suitable reply.

Together the two men walked to the bath-room, the young man erect and soldierly in movement, the squatter lithe yet strangely sluggish, as though he felt momentarily the onset of old age. In the dining-room they found Marion, cool and lovely, awaiting them. Mrs Poulton was pouring out tea at a separate table, and when she had set the cups before them she, too, became seated.

"I shall be glad when Christmas is over," she exclaimed, fanning herself with a handkerchief. "I always think it is so much hotter before Christmas than after."

"It is hotter after Christmas, but by January our blood has thinned and we feel the heat less."

"I suppose you are right, Jeff," she said in her cheerful way. "We should be thankful to be living in a large cool house instead of one of those dog-kennels you call boundary-riders' huts."

"It is surprising what you can get used to," he said grimly. "In my youth I lived in an affair which was no better than a black-fellow's humpy. Anyway, my lads are better housed than the majority." With that Jeff relapsed into silence. An unaccountable foreboding was pressing on his mind, but he put the feeling down to a touch of liver. Mr Roberts and Marion started to talk books, a subject that served throughout the meal.

Afterwards Stanton passed out through the wide-open french windows to the cool, blind-shaded veranda, where he sank into a wickedly luxurious lounge-chair and proceeded to roll a cigarette. He was not thinking of Bony now, but of his daughter. He was still thinking of her when she came and sat on the arm of his chair, saying:

"Will Jeff be here to-day, Dad?"

"No. He has to move sheep out of Whittocks into Deep Bend. By the way, I am sending a truck to Broken Hill to-morrow. If there is anything special you want for Christmas, send in your order."

"Very well, Dad," she said, smiling softly. "Christmas is a long time coming. I think I will buy you a cigarette-making machine. That one you are now smoking looks like a camel in a fit."

Stanton laughed ruefully. "Perhaps you will be so kind as to make me a handsomer one," he said. "Christmas is not so far away, and afterwards you may not have the time to make me cigarettes."

"Why not?" Deft fingers were busy at cigarette-making.

"Because Dash will be here on Christmas Day."

For quite a little time Marion gazed searchingly at her father. "You think he has not forgotten or changed his mind?"

"I know that he has not forgotten and that he has not changed his mind. Have you?"

Marion's dark eyes closed for a second. When they opened they were like stars.

"How could I forget when I have been counting the days?" A blush dyed her cheeks. Slipping off the chair-arm she stood looking into his grim, life-scarred face, and added: "You are a hard man in some ways, Dad, but you're a wise man. I've come to see that." Then she fled.

Jeff Stanton sat on the veranda until Ron with his passengers arrived. He watched the truck pull up before the house-gate, and when he saw a lady descend he leaned forward in his chair and stared. And in the flight of a few seconds Jeff's face was drained of its colour, and his eyes became glassy with fear.

Chapter Twenty-nine

The Stolen Bride

THE DAYS that followed Bony's visit to Mount Lion provided much food for thought. The first stage of the case was almost complete, but not quite.

Proof that Marks was dead constituted the first stage. The nature of the silver plate was vouched for by Sir Alfred Worthington, but as evidence of Marks's death it was not absolutely conclusive. Assuming that further evidence was obtained which would emphatically establish that Marks was dead, the finger of fate steadily pointed to Dot and Dash as the murderers, for not only was Marks's money discovered buried in the fireplace of the partners' camp, but also the kangaroos shot by Dot had been burned where had been discovered a boot-sprig, suggesting that a human body had been disposed of by burning as well as those of the kangaroos.

As the case now stood Bony was just short of sufficient evidence to prove that Marks was dead. Nor did he think he was justified in arresting the partners on suspicion of murder, although they could be arrested for having concealed Marks's money. On that ground he would have ordered their arrest had it not been for the fact that the man seen by Ludbi fighting Marks and revealed through Moongalliti by Illawalli was *neither Dash nor Dot*.

The coming of Mrs Thomas had disarranged the threads the half-caste was disentangling so laboriously. Certain facts regarding her supplied by Headquarters indicated that Marks was not killed for his money. Now had arisen a suspicion that the motive of the crime was far deeper than the lust for material gain—if Jeffrey Stanton had been christened Joseph and his father's surname was North.

In her youth Mrs Thomas had figured in a romance that had gained for her much newspaper publicity, as well as the deep interest of the police. This romance had occurred forty years before. Mrs Thomas's maiden name was Green, and she was the daughter of a small selector who lived a few miles out of Louth, on the River Darling. At the age of eighteen Rose Green was a very pretty girl, and, as was natural, was much sought after by the young men of the district. Her favours apparently were bestowed about equally on Joseph North, a young but prosperous boss-drover, and Thomas Thomas, who owned a neighbouring selection. Of these two young men the girl's parents preferred the latter.

The parental preference may have decided Rose Green eventually to give her hand to Joseph North, for she was a wilful girl, and in the opinion of that time considered bold. She promised to marry North when he returned from a droving trip that was expected to last seven weeks, and before he left he bought a plot of land in Louth and made arrangements with a Wilcannia builder to erect a wooden house.

North having gone off on his trip with six thousand sheep, the Greens brought pressure to bear on the daughter in favour of Thomas Thomas. Rose Green at last surrendered, and the arrangements for the wedding were hastened to ensure that when North returned it would be too late for the girl to change her mind again. It was too late, even though North arrived back a week earlier than was expected.

It appears that he knew nothing of his sweetheart's altered programme until he entered the hotel at Louth to pay off his men and groom himself before rushing to his adored one. On that same day Rose Green was married to Thomas Thomas. North entered Louth precisely one hour after the bridal-party left the township for the wedding-breakfast at the bride's former home.

Besides the bride and groom there were seated at that breakfast no fewer than fourteen people. It was the last day of June, and, the weather being cold, the feast was eaten in the main room of the house. The room was crowded. The chatter of the guests was enlivened by a thirty-six-gallon cask of beer set on a stand in a corner. It was a day of days. Everyone was exhilarated, especially the men. And then in upon them walked Joseph North holding in each hand a nickel-plated man-size revolver.

In appearance North was the superior of the bridegroom. He wore a navy-blue serge suit of the then fashionable cut. On his feet were tan shoes, and on his head a black bowler hat. In the lapel of his coat was a single white rose. Apparently he would have appeared thus had he actually led Rose Green to the altar.

Filling in the blanks, Bony easily visualized the scene that followed. The half-caste's sympathies were entirely with Joseph North, then and throughout. North threatened to shoot any person there who attempted to rise from his or her seat. Doubtless the young man's facial expression was extremely earnest, for not one disobeyed him, not even Thomas Thomas himself when he was minutely instructed in the task of binding his guests to their chairs with lengths of rope, undoubtedly brought there by the jilted North. Afterwards he had the unique experience of being himself bound to a chair by his bride of an hour.

"I think you will be fairly secure for some time," North told them in general. To the girl's mother he said: "You tricked me, didn't you? You knew that I was making a home for Rose, yet you bullied her into marrying Thomas. Had Rose been given a fair chance to decide between me and Thomas, and she had chosen Thomas, I'd have said nothing. But no, not only did you bully her into marrying Thomas, but you stopped word reaching me, and it was only because I got through my contract a week ahead that I got back to Louth to-day.

"It was lucky for me that I did get back, for now Rose is as much mine as ever she was. A few words spoken by a parson don't amount to much. I'm wearing my bridegroom's clothes, and I'm going to be Rose's bridegroom. She is going away with me as my bride. Rosie, get your hat and put on a pair of riding-boots."

"I won't! You must think I'm mad," objected the bride.

"All right, come as you are, then!"

Amid a babel of lurid language from the men and shrill invective from the women, Rose Green began to cry. Yet the hubbub and the tears had no effect on Joseph North. He took the girl by the arm and led her out of the house dressed in her wedding finery and without hat or coat. Afterwards the listening guests heard the thudding of horses' hoofs growing fainter and fainter, and when the first of them freed himself and hastily freed the others, they rushed out to see no sign of North or the bride.

The police were informed. Search-parties were organized. Every station homestead in the State was frantically telephoned for news. All Australia was thrilled and delighted by the story, which was headlined "The Stolen Bride".

Yet neither the bride nor her abductor was traced. The great heart of Australia had swallowed them utterly. Weeks became months, and months became a year. It was three o'clock in the morning of the first of July in the following year that the licensee of the hotel at Louth heard horses' hoofs outside his bedroom window. A minute later his front door was thumped by a human fist. Partially dressed, he took a hurricane-lamp and went to open the door. On unbolting, he heard again the sound of horses' hoofs passing along the road. Mystified, he opened his door and, holding aloft his lamp, saw a figure crouched on the low veranda without. The figure was bowed, and from it came sobs. And when he lowered the lamp and gently raised the bowed head, he looked into the face of Mrs Thomas, nee Green.

"Return of the Stolen Bride" was the star attraction of the papers for weeks. Yet beyond the headings there was but little news, for Mrs Thomas resolutely declined to say one word of what had befallen her during the twelve months. It was she who insisted that the warrant for the arrest of North should be withdrawn. It was she who told a sergeant of police to stop worrying her with fool questions and to mind his own blank business. It was she who went to Thomas Thomas and informed him that since he was her husband it was his duty to support her.

Apparently Thomas accepted the responsibility, for the "Stolen Bride" lived with him until his death, fifteen years later. He left her some four thousand pounds, and nine thousand in trust for their son, aged twelve years. The seasons being good, the selection was sold for a further two thousand five hundred, and Mrs Thomas then migrated to Sydney, where she went into the hotel business. She had prospered, and at the time of her coming to Windee was the licensee of a popular sportsmen's hotel in George Street.

A remarkable woman, Bony considered her. A strong woman, for never a word had escaped her regarding that year's sojourn with North in Central Australia.

At that time North would be about twenty-three years old. He was an active man, a good horseman, abstemious in his habits, and careful of his money. He was of medium height, with grey eyes and black hair. Stanton was of medium height, and his eyes were grey. Marion Stanton's hair was black.

Was Stanton Joseph North? If so, had the business that had brought Green, alias Marks, to Windee something to do with the abduction of the bride forty years before? It seemed feasible that the brother had come to Windee to execute some scheme, and, since he had failed and disappeared, the sister had come to make inquiries. The future appeared pregnant with drama. The tangled skein was even more hopelessly entangled by Fate.

Bony waited expectantly for something to happen. In Time's cupboard lay a skeleton than only Time would bring to light. Bony went on working at his sheep-yards, assisted by the cheerful Jack Withers. Yet nothing happened. Mrs Thomas apparently settled herself for a prolonged stay, yet, when Bony was beginning to think that she had become a fixture at Windee, she suddenly departed, being driven into Mount Lion in Mr Bumpus's car, which she had bespoken by telephone.

The perplexed Bony still waited patiently.

Chapter Thirty

Reconciliation

IT SO HAPPENED on the day after the departure of Mrs Thomas that Jack Withers, feeling unwell, did not accompany the half-caste to their daily work. On most days the two men rode to and from their work, but the day Bony worked alone he walked and carried his noonday lunch with him.

Throughout the day his mind was continuously revolving the visit made by Mrs Thomas and the mystery that lay behind her departure in a hired car. It wanted but two days to Christmas, and it was peculiar, if Mrs Thomas was a welcome guest, that she should not have stayed over the holidays.

At half-past four, when he ceased his labours, after rolling a cigarette he picked up his billy-can and lunch-bag and started his mile-long walk to the homestead. It had been a windless day, and hot. Widely separated, deep thunderclouds lay almost motionless in the sky like aerial icebergs. Birds were stirring from their daylong drowse, and a party of crows settled about the place where Bony had eaten his lunch.

Pensively smoking, he walked along a bank of the dry creek, welcoming the shade cast by the box-trees and trying to decide whether he would wait longer for Time to aid him or whether he would act without Time's aid. His investigations had reached a point where they might be materially forwarded if he stirred up the human factor by ordering the arrest of Dot and Dash, or even by ordering the detention of Mrs Thomas. Something, certainly, should follow either step.

He walked with his head bent, his eyes noting sub-consciously the tracks of animals and insects which he crossed. He failed to see Marion Stanton riding Grey Cloud, and, because her mind was occupied with Mrs Thomas, she failed to notice him until they were so close that, when recognition was mutual, Bony swept off his hat and she reined in her magnificent steed. It was a meeting for which Bony had long hoped, and he said gravely:

"Good afternoon, Miss Stanton."

Instead of replying, Marion regarded him steadily for several moments. In her eyes Bony saw the temptation to ride away without uttering a word, and he recognized that here was the opportunity to discover the reason of her displeasure.

"I fear that in some way I have offended you," he told her un-smilingly. "If I have done so it has been done unwittingly, I earnestly assure you. Perhaps I could explain."

"I am not sure that I would be interested in an explanation," came the coolly spoken reply. He was struck by the immobility of her face, the different shade of beauty her displeasure created. The eyebrows now were straight and the eyes shone with the ice-cold gleam of—sapphires. She saw how easily he stood, with deference but without servility. She saw, too, a very faint hint of amusement in his dark eyes which aroused at once her antagonism. Seated still on the immovable grey gelding, she said sharply:

"You remember, do you not, that once you told me of your wife and your boys in Queensland?"

Bony nodded.

"You described to me what a wonderful woman is your wife, and how proud you both are of your sons. You interested me in them, and also you interested me in yourself and in your philosophy. You led me to think that you possessed the instincts as well as the education of a gentleman. Explain, therefore, why you made love to a gin named Runta!"

The surprise of the accusation figuratively stunned Bony. Having made up his mind that her coldness was the effect of suspicion that he was connected in some way with the police, the real cause was so unexpected that he wanted badly to sigh with relief. Nevertheless, he could not render the true explanation. Without the slightest hesitation he invented an explanation which possessed, at least, the saving grace of a grain of truth.

"Possibly my making love to Runta is inexcusable, Miss Stanton. Yet I remember that even worse sins have been committed by scientists in search of truth. Before the blacks returned from their walkabout, I discovered one evening a low hill of ironstone near the creek below the homestead. The top of the hillock is flat, and I saw that it had been used for centuries by the blacks in connection with some mystic ritual.

"I have always been interested in the aboriginals, their folklore, ceremonials, and ways of life, and intend to write a book when I have sufficient data. As you know, I am a stranger to the blacks here. Being a half-caste, I am looked down on by the blacks, just just as a half-caste is looked down on by white people. Moongalliti and the members of his tribe at first regarded me with suspicion, and, in order to gain their confidence, I made harmless love to Runta, knowing that she was not matrimonially attached at the time."

"Even so, I can see no excuse for such conduct. What is worse, Bony, is the manner in which you drove her away."

Now Bony did sigh audibly. He tried hard not to smile, and she saw it.

"Unfortunately Runta became very serious," he said. "I am inclined to think that equally with me she loved my peach pies and toffee."

"What would your wife say if she knew—knew of your scientific zeal?" Marion asked less coldly.

"No man is a hero in shining armour to his wife. My wife knows her husband very thoroughly. In her last letter to me she said so. At my request she sent me a very resplendent dress for Runta."

"You told her?"

"Believing that Runta is entitled to compensation, I asked Marie to send me a present for her. It arrived two days ago. I took a peep at it. The background is Chinese yellow and there are large purple spots all over it. I am assured that it is an extra out-size, so it should …"

He broke off to listen to the most delicious laughter he had ever heard. The girl's head was thrown back and her eyes became half closed. Bony's face became lit, too, with the ecstasy her beauty created in him, and she saw it and felt glad because of it, and slipped from her horse to stand in front of him.

"Bony, you're the most extraordinary man I have ever met!" she said, laughter still in her voice. "The two gins helping Mrs Poulton told her about your love affair, and I thought it was one of the common sordid cases. I was disappointed in you, and now I am glad it was so harmless after all. I am glad for another reason. I have been wanting to ask your advice. Would you give it?"

"To do so would make me a very proud man."

"Then let us walk on home."

Together they turned towards Windee, she with the horse's reins slipped over her arm, he carrying the blackened billy-can, the horse following softly. For nearly a minute Marion did not speak. Then:

"You were on the truck when Ron brought Mrs Thomas to Windee, weren't you?"

"Yes. I first saw her in Mr Bumpus's bar."

"What did you think of her?"

"I considered that she was a remarkable character."

"She drinks—horribly."

"So I observed, and so I was emphatically informed by Mr Bumpus."

"Did she say why she was coming to Windee?"

"No, but I understood she was seeking employment."

"It was not that at all," the girl said sadly. "I wish it had been. I wish I knew. To me she is an utter stranger, yet she knew Father years ago, and taunted him in a veiled sort of way about something which had occurred. She frightened Father. She's made him positively ill.

And the other night when she was drunk—drunk, mind you—she accused father of murdering that man Marks who got lost in the bush four months ago."

"Mrs Thomas's departure must be a relief to you," Bony said softly and reflectively.

"In a way, yes; but Father is still suffering from her beastly accusations and the secret of the past which has so suddenly been flung in his face. I don't know what to do. I don't know how I can help him. Would it be wise to urge him to share that secret with me?"

"Most certainly it would," assented Bony. "If it were but a youthful folly, the sharing will lighten the load. Do you know why Mrs Thomas left so hurriedly?"

"No, Bony, I do not. She and Father had a terrible row the other night. They were in the dining-room with the door shut. Mrs Poulton and I were on the veranda. We could hear the squeak of her voice and then Father's roar when he shouted, 'I won't!' many times. But—but, Bony, there was despair in his voice."

"As though, in spite of what he said, he knew he would have to give in to her wishes or demands?"

"Yes—like that."

For a little while they walked in silence, a silence broken by the girl, who exclaimed: "And I was looking forward to such a happy Christmas. The Fosters are coming, and Father Ryan. Dot and Dash are coming in, and Father is giving all the men a Christmas Dinner."

The next day was Christmas Eve, and the fact that Dot and Dash were coming into Windee occupied Bony's mind equally with the fact that Mrs Thomas was making demands on Jeff Stanton. It was almost proof that Jeff Stanton was Joseph North. Was she blackmailing? Did she know something about Marks's death? It appeared so. Or was the urgency of the demands based on the case of the "Stolen Bride"?

Bony came to believe that the best way to help the girl who had given him her friendship was to force on this Marks case, and the best way to do that was to order the arrest of Dot and Dash. He would settle with Mrs Thomas. Mount Lion was a police-controlled town, Sergeant Morris could order her to move on.

To Marion Bony said in his gentle way: "That cloud up there is black underneath, yet its middle and top are snow-white. In the morning there probably will be no clouds in the sky. Induce your father to confide in you by all means. A shared load is a lightened load."

And when Marion gazed into Bony's smiling face she came to believe it.

Chapter Thirty-one

Joseph North

IMMEDIATELY after his dinner Bony wrote a letter to Sergeant Morris in which he ordered the arrest of Dot and Dash on the charge of having murdered Luke Green, alias Marks. Also he gave precise instructions that the arrest was to be made without divulging his connection with it, and that the partners were expected at Windee on the following day, an opportune time and place. This letter he sent per one Warn, a blackfellow who owned a horse as well as a silent tongue.

It was the custom of Jeffrey Stanton to sit on the main veranda of Windee every evening after he had spoken per telephone to his overseer at Nullawil and his riders east of the range. Invariably his chair was placed in one position, which was midway between the drawing-room door and the fine-mesh-wire-screened front of the veranda. There he smoked his eternal cigarette and glanced through the *Wool Growers' Gazette,* or leaned back with closed eyes and a strangely softened face whilst Marion played the piano in the room behind him.

It was the only spell of relaxation he permitted himself. Seated alone on the veranda, listening to the piano, the old squatter was an entirely different being from the one who faced the world in his image during the day. Possibly none other than Marion knew of this unsuspected softening, unless it was Bony, who often, when the night was dark, stole through the wicket-gate and drew close to the outside of the wire screen, able to see within, but himself invisible.

At other times he had come to hear Marion play, and share with the Boss of Windee the witchery of her music. The evening he dispatched the order for the arrest of Dot and Dash he entered through the wicket-gate with his usual noiselessness, and with a further object than that of hearing good music.

After his conversation that afternoon with Marion, Bony considered it likely that she would act on his advice and seek the old man's confidence that evening, selecting the psychological moment after she had been playing for some time.

When he arrived and sat himself down against the edge of the veranda the girl was playing something from *Lohengrin*. In his then position Bony's head was above the level of the veranda floor, and he knew from experience of previous visits that no word spoken behind him would be unheard. Now and then he turned and looked in at the squatter revealed in his easy-chair in the subdued light of the scarlet-shaded standard lamp beside him. Beyond, the room where Marion played was more brilliantly lighted. He could see neither her nor the piano, but he knew that presently she would cease playing, come out and pass along the veranda, to return in a few minutes with a small tray containing cups of coffee. And then, whilst she and her father drank from the cups, they would talk of the affairs of the day in rare companionship.

It is to Bony's credit that previously he never had stayed to eavesdrop on them. Unscrupulous though he was sometimes, ordinary spying was a thing he abhorred, but this night he considered the act excusable if thereby he might learn what lay behind Mrs Thomas's threats, which so gravely upset Jeff Stanton, and in hardly less measure the woman who had always been kind to him. Once in possession of the facts lying behind the woman's visit, he deemed it possible to render her in some way innocuous.

Sitting there in the darkness, listening to the piano, and idly watching the soft flicker of lightning in a cloud low on the horizon, he wondered what would follow the execution of his order to Sergeant Morris. When under arrest, would Dot and Dash confess to the acts he believed them to have committed and implicate the murderer of Marks? Or would they remain grimly silent, admitting only that one of them had found Marks's money and hidden it, on the principle that finding justifies keeping?

These two men were eminently sane. Bony judged that beneath Dash's grandiloquence and Dot's peculiar humour there were tremendous still depths. He rather admired them for it, but he never lost sight of the fact that he was there to bring the murderer of Marks to justice, and the accomplices, before or after the fact, as well.

Of all this was Bony thinking when Marion rose from the piano and came out to the veranda. Jeff Stanton had been leaning back in his chair, his head resting on his clasped hands, his eyes closed. His expression that evening was one of weariness, and for the first time Bony thought he looked much older than his actual age.

"Tired, Dad?" the girl asked gently.

"A little. I've had a worrying day," he replied with a strained smile, adding, as though to emphasize that the cause of the worry was not Mrs Thomas: "Young Jeff is having trouble with a mob of wethers beyond Range Hut. He doesn't expect to be able to get in for Christmas."

"Oh, that's too bad, Father. Couldn't he be relieved?"

"Yes, he could be, but he was sent out to do the job, and he knows he's expected to do it. I have been beginning to suspect lately that he is acquiring a liking for booze, and that is why I am giving him plenty to do at a fair distance from temptation. In any case, I think he would be ruffled if he was relieved when his mind was on his job."

"You are right about that, Dad. It would annoy him. But I know nothing about the booze, and can't believe it of him. He is not the type."

Marion left then to bring the coffee, and Bony, with a twinge of conscience, squirmed in his comfortable seat and longed for a cigarette. The ensuing five minutes passed slowly, and he wondered if Warn had by then delivered his letter at the police-station, and whether Sergeant Morris had fallen out of his chair with astonishment. Then Marion returned and, giving the squatter a cup, sat beside him on the arm of his chair and at once opened the battle.

"It's not only Jeff who is worrying you, Father," she said softly. "It is that terrible woman who has upset the serenity of our lives. You're nearly worried to death about her. Tell me—tell me all, and let me help."

"Your knowing things wouldn't help me," he said gruffly, but, reaching out, took in his hands one of hers.

For a little while neither spoke. Then: "A thousand soldiers are better able to defend a fort than five hundred, Father. I know already just a little. I couldn't help hearing the other evening you tell her repeatedly that you wouldn't do something she wanted you to do. And you spoke so desperately."

Jeff Stanton sat and silently stared straight at that part of the veranda netting beyond which sat Bony. His white brows almost met in a continuous line of shaggy hair. Yet his usually firm mouth drooped as though with senility. The girl slipped her coffee-cup on the table and covered his imprisoning hands with her free one.

"Father!" she said.

Stanton continued to stare with unseeing eyes.

"Dad!" she insisted.

Suddenly he raised his face and looked into her starry eyes, and, seeing the despair in his, she suddenly released her hands and, throwing her arms about his neck, pleaded:

"Let me share the trouble, dear. What *does* she want? What does she demand of *us*?"

And then from his lips came the words, low but distinct: "She—wants—me—to—marry—her!"

"To marry her? You? To marry *her*?"

Stanton nodded. "I was to have married her years and years ago," he said. And Bony knew that sitting there was Joseph North, hero of the affair of the "Stolen Bride". The old man sighed, for indeed he looked old and frail sitting there in the pink light. "I'll tell you, Marion," he said slowly, "but when I've finished remember—don't forget to remember—that I am your father."

Jeff Stanton prefaced his story with a short account of his life and circumstances in his early twenties. Then he went on to describe his courtship and his cruel jilting, and how he dressed with care and went out to the hotel horse-yards, where he saddled three of his horses, two with riding-saddles, one with a pack-saddle. He told how he led them to the store, and how he floored one man who asked him where he thought he was going in his best clothes.

With his pack-bags full and two old suits of dungarees rolled within four blankets, he described his thoughts whilst riding to his lost sweetheart's home, and precisely what happened when he got there.

"She wouldn't change her things, so I dragged her out of the house in her wedding rig," he said slowly. "She wouldn't mount the spare horse, and I told her that if she didn't obey orders I wouldn't waste a bullet on her, but I'd cut her throat. I would have done, too. I was mad, absolutely mad. I hated her, and yet I loved her. She was very pretty in her white dress, and her hair shone like gold beneath a gauzy kind of veil.

"She began to cry, but she must have seen her danger in my eyes, because she mounted the horse and we rode like lightning till it grew dark and we reached an empty hut and a well. The first thing I did after hobbling out the horses was to make her discard her wedding finery and put on one of the suits of dungarees. I burned the dress and her shoes as well, and gave her a pair of riding boots. She screamed and fought like a wild cat when I cut her hair short with a killing-knife. More than once I was tempted to slash her throat.

"I bent her to my will that night, and thrashed her in the morning because she refused to cook the breakfast whilst I was away bringing in the horses. She made no attempt to escape me, knowing I'd track her down. And after that she was more reasonable.

"For three days we rode westward, keeping well wide of station homesteads. The fourth day we rode north, and at noon reached a selector's house occupied by an old school-pal of mine. He knew about the hold-up—a police party had ridden by the day before. I asked him to let me and my bride stay there in hiding, and he agreed. It was Fred who drove my three horses fifty miles towards home, where he left them to wander back by themselves. Dressed as she was, no one would think Rosie was a woman, for I had run the clippers over her head to make the haircut a bit more professional. She kept house and did the cooking, and was obedient, and I came to ask myself if she really hated me or loved me. She was a mystery altogether.

"One day, Fred and I came home from mustering sheep and found five horses tethered outside the garden gate. As we rode up a policeman came out, and I knew I was done. But, instead of arresting me, he greeted us affably, and said he hoped my pal wouldn't mind him and his mates having a snack, because the lad had been insistent. In the kitchen we found Rosie feeding four more troopers. She had on her old felt hat, and there were smears of soot all down one side of her face. The girl had deliberately done what she could to further her disguise. She was a peculiar girl.

"After that she seemed to hate me less and love me more. You see, she always had loved me, but she was influenced against her will by her people into marrying Thomas. Still, for all that, I no longer loved her. I smarted too much beneath the lash of ridicule, and my stupid pride was seared and burned.

"A baby was born, and I was doctor and nurse, because I was afraid to send her to Wilcannia. The baby only lived a week, and that I believe brought about the climax. Had the child lived, I would have stuck to Rosie through thick and thin. It affected her in that she suddenly took to complaining about everything and everlastingly nagging. One can stand most things, bar a nagging woman. Fred got tired of it. Short of gagging her there was no stopping her. She sort of let herself go, only half-dressed, and some days wouldn't even wash her hands. The baby dying must have done it. She swore I killed it. In the end I decided I had had enough. I thanked Fred for what he had done for me, and I had paid him by working for him almost twelve months for nothing. I took Rosie back to Louth, timing to get there about midnight, and outside the hotel I left her, having first knocked up the licensee.

"I never saw her again until the other day. The man Marks was her brother. She found out about me years ago, seeing my photo in an illustrated paper. The brother was something of a blackguard even to his mother, and during a weak or drunken moment Rose Thomas told him of her abduction and all about me.

"Strangely enough, she had no desire to force herself upon me or seek revenge. She prospered in Sydney, but the brother saw a way to blackmail me, and he did so for nine years. When he last left Sydney he intended to clear out of the country, and called on me to make a final and big demand for money. ... Not hearing from him, his sister thought he had left Australia, and did not know until just recently that his assumed name was Marks.

"Now she is accusing me of having killed him. She said that for having killed him—of which, of course, she has no proof—she intends to force me to marry her and to disown you and your brother. If I refuse and have made no definite arrangements for the marriage by New Year's Day, she intends to expose me as the abductor of the 'Stolen Bride'."

The even voice suddenly ceased. Marion continued to sit very still. When she spoke only her lips moved.

"Let her expose you, Dad, but marry her you shan't!"

"I shall have to," Stanton said wearily. "You see, before he died, my old friend, Fred, left a document, signed and witnessed, in which he describes helping me bury a dead baby. He did so apparently under duress himself, fearing exposure of his part. The woman's brother told me that he had this paper. He showed me a copy of it, and it formed the basis of his power. Now Rose says that the copy was all he did have. She still has in her possession the original. If I don't marry Rose Thomas I shall be cast down into the dust."

Chapter Thirty-two

Spring-Cleaning

NEARLY EIGHT HUNDRED rabbit-skins, each stretched over a U-shaped length of stiff fencing wire with the two points thrust into the loose sandy ground, represented the last catch at White Well secured by Dot and Dash.

The partners, having breakfasted late, since that morning there was no skinning to be done, proceeded to pack this last catch in the wool-bale that finally would contain three thousand skins. The four corners of the open bale were secured to stout posts five feet high, and into the bale, already three parts full of skins, climbed Dash, being a heavier man than his partner. Dot now deftly gathered up a dozen skins on the wire bows, with one movement pulled away the wires, and with another handed to Dash the stiff, board-hard pelts. Dash then proceeded to build up a corner within the wool-bale, and to stand on the skins in that corner whilst he built up another. Thus with this human press the bale, when at last it was sewn up, presented a solid mass weighing nearly two and a half hundredweight.

Four other full bales lay near the truck, and, since the price of skins that summer was good, Dot and Dash expected to clear a hundred and fifty pounds on their last consignment for the year.

It wanted an hour to noon when the partners sat down to a pint of tea and cigarettes, having completed the fifth bale and having loaded the five bales on the truck.

"I guess I ain't looking forward with eagerness to shaving," the little man observed ruefully, pushing his fingers through a flaming beard. "Ole Samson musta felt the heat some afore that tart shaved 'is 'air and 'is whiskers. Me, I'm fearful of catching a chill. Couldn't we—wot about leaving 'em on?"

Dash frowned with mocking gravity. "When in Rome we must ape the Romans. Out here in our 'vast open spaces', surrounded by our inspiring 'natural resources', we may please ourselves whether we cut our hair or not. At Windee we find ourselves among civilized human beings, who do not grow red-hot whiskers. In about ten minutes you may have the pleasure of cutting my hair very carefully, and my beard closely and without care."

"Wot about me?"

"I will render you a like service. It will be the last time we shall so serve each other."

"Wa'-do'-mean?"

"Precisely what I say. I do not anticipate that ever again I shall grow such whiskers as I now sport."

"Are you gonna hire a vally?" gasped Dot, looking extremely hot, although he had discarded his undervest, the upper part of his powerful body being naked.

"Not in the immediate future. I am, however, earnestly hoping to get married."

"Married!"

"Is the idea so preposterous?"

"Married!" Dot's voice was a harsh screech. His expression was a combination of anguish and horror. "You ain't serious, pardner?" he implored, almost in a whisper.

"Yes, Dot, I am." The assumed grandiloquent manner fell from the Englishman. It was as though he discarded mask and cloak, and stood revealed in his true personality. Dot received yet a second shock. Dash went on. "In the old days a fellow by the name of Jacob worked for fourteen years for a girl named Rachel. The work he did during that time was identical with the work he had done all his life. Before I became your partner I was and lived as an English gentleman, an allowance made me by my father enabling me to live without having to work.

"Five years ago there came over my house a financial cloud, and in order that my father and my dear mother might continue to live in reasonable comfort, I surrendered to them four-fifths of my allowance, threw up my commission in the finest regiment on earth, and came to Windee as a jackeroo, as you know.

"At Windee I fell in love with a lady with whom you are acquainted. In spite of my poverty, I dared to tell her I loved her. Dot—she accepted me. My next step as a man of honour was to ask Old Jeff for his sanction. What do you think Old Jeff said?"

"Get to hell outer here!" Dot replied promptly.

"He was a little more ambiguous than that, but his meaning was the same," Dash went on unsmilingly. "In his usual blunt fashion he told me he thought I was hunting his girl's dollars. Since he was an old man I couldn't hit him, and, besides, he was Marion's father. I did tell him, though, that I was prepared for him to test me, and without hesitation he set the test."

"Wot was it?" Dot asked with interest.

"That I would work with you for two full years."

"Humph!" The little man lit a cigarette and smoked pensively. Whilst inhaling and exhaling the tobacco-smoke he regarded his partner as though he had met him for the first time, and during that regard it dawned on him that Jeff Stanton's test was unduly severe. He knew how Dash hated the killing and skinning of kangaroos and the skinning of rabbits but nevertheless never shirked his share of the work. At that moment Dot realised what his own mode of living must have meant to one with his partner's upbringing. Two years is quite long enough for a man to gain an intimate knowledge of another man's habits, mental outlook, and ideals. Yet now was the first time it was borne in on him that Dash must have suffered mental degradation every time he handled carcasses, every time he ate and drank from tinware, every day he had to deny himself a bath, and all the time he had to associate with such as he.

"I ain't surprised at your acceptin' the test," he told Dash, "but I am kinda surprised that you've won out. I'm mighty glad you've won out, anyway. You an' me have got on well. No arguments, nothing. I'll feel kinda at a loose end when I'm on me own. You see, a man sort of gets used to a bloke."

"I know, Dot, how it is," Dash said earnestly. "Our partnership has been successful, and it has smoothed away the rough edges of a rough life."

"When's the two years up?"

"To-night at midnight," Dash replied. "Old Jeff knows that, and knows, too, that we are going to Windee to-day, and that to-morrow I shall, with his sanction, ask Marion to marry me."

"Wot are you gonna do then?"

"I don't know, really. I thought of buying a small place in the hills out of Adelaide, a fruit-farm probably. I have enough money for that."

"Well, if your bank runs dry, don't forget I am your milking-cow. I got a lot o' money wot you're welcome to. I got more'n you think."

"Then you must possess a great deal," Dash said, getting up with a smile, to add with sudden earnestness: "Nevertheless, old man, although we dissolve partnership, we do not and never will dissolve friendship. Where are the scissors, do you know?"

They spoke but little whilst each worked on the other. Dot evidently was somewhat depressed, for he shaved without his usual humorous complaints. The metamorphosis that was accomplished within half an hour was not a little surprising. From wild-looking bushrangers Dash became a well-groomed Army officer, and Dot's round shining face bespoke a priest in disguise.

The coming severance with his partner weighed heavily on him, for he esteemed Dash, and held him in great affection. Nevertheless, there was something else which weighed on his mind, and after a while Dash became conscious of it. He said quietly:

"What has gone wrong, Dot?"

"Well, seeing as 'ow we're going to bust up, I'd like to sort of confess me sins," came the somewhat surprising answer. "We shall have to wind up the business part of it properly, and give each other a receipted bill. It seems kinda right that we should part, too, with receipted minds, if you get me. Do you?"

"Well, not quite."

"I shall have to touch on a matter which we have made taboo," Dot said in a strained voice.

"Oh!" The other's voice was suddenly metallic.

"Yes. It's gotta be done. I guess I was a fool, a poor avaricious boob. You'll sort of jump on me when I tells you, and I'm thinking I'll deserve it. You remember the money wot I was supposed to have burnt?"

"Yes. What of it?"

"Well, I didn't burn it, that's all."

Dash, who was lacing up his expensive shoes, with great deliberateness rose to his feet and stood looking down at Dot with amazement, chagrin, and alarm all expressed in his clean-cut face.

"What did you do?" he inquired calmly.

"I hid it. I put the notes in a kerosene-tin box and buried 'em in the fire ashes at our camp." The little man's blue eyes winked with the force of his self-condemnation. "Gawd! I just couldn't burn good money. I just couldn't destroy orl them thousands of dollars——" He broke off suddenly, to continue looking at Dash with appealing eyes. Then: "Wot er we gonna do, bo?"

"We are going to sneak along to that camp to-night, and I am going to watch you burn those notes one by one," Dash said slowly.

"Orl right! I reckon I ain't got no kick coming if you orders me to eat 'em."

Chapter Thirty-three

Bony Lights a Fuse

CHRISTMAS EVE was a day of intense heat, the oppressive heat presaging an electrical disturbance. Until eleven o'clock the sky was clear of clouds. Then, in the manner peculiar to Central Australia, they began to appear. When Bony, working with Withers at the new sheep-yards, first saw the first cloud, it was less than the size of a man's hand. Nature, the Great Enchantress, made and fashioned it from nothing: in the beginning a wisp of white smoke that grew and grew into an enormous white-capped solid-looking mass. Other clouds were born and magically expanded, and for quite a long while hung motionless in their distinct, solitary grandeur.

The workers watched them during work, wishing earnestly that one would move across the sun and shield them from its scorching rays. At times it looked as if their wish would be granted, when a cloud was seen moving towards the sun with stately slowness, but always to move round and past it. Not until four o'clock did the many clouds begin to find mutual attraction and drift into huge blue-black masses, within which the shimmer of lightning flickered and thunder rumbled.

When Bony and his companion returned to the homestead it was to see the arrival of Sergeant Morris and his trooper, both mounted on magnificent police horses. Their advent set up speculative comment among the hands who were preparing themselves for dinner, and the number of the men at Windee that evening was far in excess of that at any other time of the year.

The two policemen were met by Marion Stanton, astride Grey Cloud. They saluted her and spoke with her, the three horses bunched. Then Marion rode away up along the creek, seizing the opportunity thus early—since later she would have to welcome her guests—to take her daily ride. From the door of his bunk-room Bony smiled, and watched the uniformed men ride to the stockyards, where they left their horses, thence to walk with military stiffness to the station office.

Having set the match to the gunpowder train, he prepared himself to enjoy the spectacle of the explosion.

For nearly twenty minutes the office door remained closed. Then emerged Mr Roberts, hatless and carrying a notebook. He moved in his usual deliberate fashion round the house towards his room. For two seconds the angle of the walls concealed him, and when he reappeared Bony saw him pass out of the side wicket-gate, glance back once, and hurry away up the creek.

A few minutes after that the sergeant and the trooper came out. With significant purposefulness they crossed to the men's quarters and asked for Bates, the custodian of the Windee plant, and of him required a half or three-quarter inch wire rope. Neither so much as glanced at the amused Bony.

He watched them accompany Bates to one of the store-huts, and saw the three of them come forth carrying a long length of wire rope, which they took down the curving road leading out over the plain and to Nullawil.

"Surely they ain't going to hang Bates," Withers suggested.

"Naw, they're going to put up a swing for the Christmas party," Ron announced, making motions with a toothbrush.

"I'll go along and see what is doing," Bony said loudly, and proceeded to follow the police party by slipping from tree to tree. He found them stretching the rope across the track, securing it to a tree-trunk on each side so that a car-driver coming to the homestead would see it just before he would be obliged to decelerate in order to get over a fifty-foot stretch of loose sand.

Facing along the outward track from the rope through the western fringe of creek trees, the vast expanse of plain appeared as though it were a grey patchwork carpet. Vast irregular areas were darkened by the cloud shadows, and between the areas the low salt-bush gleamed and shivered in the mirages. At a great distance, probably ten miles, a slowly mounting cloud of dust appeared stationary. It was, in fact, caused by a rapidly moving automobile.

"They are coming now," announced the trooper.

Morris grunted, and satisfied himself that the blocking rope was securely fixed before he, too, gazed out over the plain. To Bony these preparations for the arrest of Dot and Dash seemed almost absurdly excessive, yet he also foresaw the difficulties that the partners in their truck could raise against mounted men. They had but to see them to drive at and past them and escape. Morris, seeing the danger of frustration or resistance, had cleverly selected a place where the driver of the truck would be obliged to stop, and that place being sandy would prove exceedingly awkward for a man to turn a truck, for, once out of the formed wheel-tracks, it would bog, and before he could reverse out on the hard ground the policeman would be able to board him.

For no definite reason Bony remained carefully concealed, now a mere onlooker, amused and entranced, his mind busy with speculation as to the various possibilities of his coming arrest.

The gong for the men's dinner was struck by Alf the Nark, yet Bony felt it impossible to leave his chosen post of vantage. Bates moved away at its call, but Sergeant Morris halted him, saying that he might need his assistance, and in any case did not wish a crowd to collect there, as assuredly would be the case if it became known what was pending.

The approaching dust-cloud became appreciably nearer, and it was some five miles away when the waiting men saw a second dust-cloud far beyond it. Separated by four miles, two motors were speeding to Windee, but whether the first was the partners' truck or the overseer's car was not known, since the stock-riders at Range Hut were then at the homestead and there was no one at the house in the hills to answer the telephone.

Now, had not the small pinion-wheel in the differential of the car first seen shed its cog-teeth, subsequent happenings on Windee might have been quite different. The breakdown occurred about one mile from the homestead, and it was signalled to the watchers near the wire rope by the nearer dust-cloud, which suddenly dwindled and vanished. The second machine came on steadily, and with obvious impatience Sergeant Morris rolled a cigarette blindly, his attention fixed on the plain. At that distance it was impossible to tell whether it was the car or the truck which had broken down, but it mattered little, since the passengers by the first would assuredly be brought on by the driver of the second.

Twenty minutes elapsed. By that time the second machine was quite near the stationary first. Bony then saw that the attention of the sergeant and his trooper was taken by something north of them, and on the edge of the plain. Bates's round face was alive with interest. Two minutes passed slowly before Bony's curiosity was allayed.

Across the plain, from a point above the homestead, there sped a grey horse and a white-dressed rider. The flying hooves sent up a long trail of greyish dust. The animal's head was low: its rider sat a little crouched forward, a rose-pink veil floating out horizontally behind her head. Riding Grey Cloud, Marion Stanton was rushing towards the disabled car.

With no uneasiness but a thrill of admiration, Morris watched the beautiful action of the horse and the easy seat of his rider. It was natural to surmise that Marion Stanton, having observed the breakdown, should determine to ride and learn the fault. The significance of Mr Roberts leaving the office before the policemen and hurrying up the creek when Marion Stanton had already ridden that way was not realised till later.

They saw her reach the stationary machine at the same instant as the second drew up. The two machines, now that the dust-cloud had left them, looked like a pair of black ants, about which tiny objects moved no larger than pinheads. With his keen vision Bony distinguished two people about Grey Cloud. No effort was made to examine the faulty machine, which indicated that the fault was serious and not to be repaired in a hurry.

Precisely what was going on out there the watchers were unable to decide. Nothing happened for several minutes. Then Grey Cloud moved a little apart. There arose a faint haze of dust. Through the still air Bony's ears just caught the hum of an engine. One of the machines was moving. A cloud of dust arose and hid it. The dust-cloud became elongated, lengthened as though a destroyer was creating a smoke-screen. And the machine that raised the dust was going away from Windee, was racing back to the hills towards Nullawil.

The grey horse came slowly towards the watchers. Time seemed to drag. Eventually they could see that Grey Cloud carried two riders. Two men moved about the broken-down car. The other car was speeding westward. Bony was delighted. Marion Stanton had warned Dot and Dash of their impending arrest, having been informed of it by Mr Roberts.

Chapter Thirty-four

The Strike

VERY SOON it was evident to the waiting men that the riders of Grey Cloud were women, obviously Marion Stanton and Mrs Foster. Beyond them several figures moved about the broken-down car, and later it was learned that these were Harry Foster and the two stockmen, merely waiting for a station truck to arrive and tow them to the homestead. Why the fur-getters had gone back was a mystery that only the women could solve.

When a quarter of a mile from the waiting policemen, Grey Cloud was turned off the track on a more direct line to the big house, and Bates was then asked to remove the obstructive wire rope while the sergeant and his trooper went to intercept the riders between the creek and the stockyards. Outside the homestead they met Marion and her companion, who dismounted.

"How do you do, Sergeant Morris?" Mrs Foster said gaily, with the faintest trace of mockery in her tone.

"Very well, Mrs Foster. What has happened?" Morris's voice was sharp. He was visibly annoyed. The flush on Marion's face, her obvious excitement, aroused his suspicions. Mrs Foster, standing before him and looking up at him, smiled with her mouth but revealed in her eyes a flash of malice.

"Something went wrong with the differential," she explained, when Marion had led her horse away. "Naturally we counted on coming along on Dot and Dash's truck; but when Dot and Dash learned that you were after them they turned tail and fled. Oh, what have they done, Mr Morris?"

"From whom did they learn we were to arrest them?" the sergeant barked.

"Why, Marion"—the hard eyes resting for a moment on the white-clad figure near the yards. "You see, Marion rode out to find what was wrong, and happened to mention to Mr Dash that you were here."

"Oh she just told them that we were here?"

"Yes, that's all."

"But a moment ago you said they learned from Miss Marion that we were here to arrest them."

"Did I? Well, really, perhaps I should not have said that. I must have imagined it. Do you—what are you arresting them for?"

"There seems to be a mystery here," Morris growled. "I cannot understand how Miss Marion came to learn that we wished to arrest Dot and Dash. Rowland, ask Miss Stanton to join us."

Across the open space in which they stood a voice roared out for "Mister Roberts", and, turning his head, Morris saw Jeff Stanton standing on the veranda outside the office door. Waiting for Marion, Morris impatiently looked in the direction of the men's quarters, to see the bookkeeper hurriedly leave and walk swiftly towards his employer. When Marion came back, he said in his bluff manner:

"Who told you, Miss Stanton, that we are here to arrest Dot and Dash?"

Peculiarly defiant, she answered: "Does it matter?"

"Not much, probably. It matters more that apparently you conveyed a warning to Dot and Dash. Why did you do that?"

"Really, I hardly know," Marion told him easily, but with an expression much like that on her father's face in his grimmer moments. "I rode over to find out what was wrong with the car, and mentioned conversationally that you and Mr Rowland were here. I trust they have done nothing serious."

"This is beside the point, Miss Stanton," Morris objected stiffly. "Doubtless you mentioned the fact without thought that by so doing you were interfering with the course of my duty. Excuse me, I must speak with your father."

The two men walked to the office. Little Mrs Foster, slipping an arm through one of Marion's, told her softly:

"I am afraid, dear, that I have put my foot in it this time. It was I who told the sergeant you told Dot and Dash about him waiting for them. I am so sorry, but I am so eaten up with curiosity to know what they have done. It was so silly."

"Never mind. Sergeant Morris will forgive me some day, I know."

They walked over to the main door of the house. Outside the office Sergeant Morris was saying to Jeff Stanton:

"Your daughter inadvertently warned Dot and Dash that they were wanted, and they have cleared off back. I want to use your telephone to warn all homesteads and neighbouring townships not to supply them with petrol. Have you any idea how much they would have with them?"

"No idea whatever," was the gruff answer. "However, not more than a case of eight gallons and what was in their tank. Perhaps Foster could give you a closer estimate."

"We must ask him. Whilst I am telephoning, will you loan us a truck and three or four cases of petrol? A driver, too, as neither Rowland nor I can drive, as you know."

"You can take my car if you like," agreed Stanton, unable to offer less.

"Good. It is far faster than Dash's truck. The chase will last until their petrol gives out, when probably they will abandon their truck and go on foot. As it is likely that we shall want a tracker, go along, Rowland, and get old Moongalliti."

Jeff Stanton and the trooper moved away together when Sergeant Morris entered the office, a general prepared evidently to check every move of the enemy. There was no doubt in his mind that Stanton's outside estimate of the partners' petrol supply was fairly accurate. In such case, at the farthest, they would have to replenish within the distance of two hundred miles. His duty was to warn the towns of Wilcannia, Tibooburra, Milparinka, and eight station homesteads that lay within the radius of two hundred miles.

Eventually Dot and Dash would be forced to abandon their truck, take to horses if they could procure them, to foot if not. He recognized the importance of overtaking them before they left the truck, or as quickly afterwards as possible. Should the thundery conditions culminate in rain, their tracks might well be washed out, and, being experienced bushmen, their complete getaway probably would follow. The telephone engaged him for half an hour and when he had shut off all probable petrol supplies he left the office without a word to Mr Roberts.

It wanted about an hour to sunset. A mass of blue-black cloud emitted lightning and thunder far to the north, whilst another threatening mass was coming up from the western horizon. Anxiously scanning the sky, Sergeant Morris walked rapidly to the men's quarters, where he saw Jeff Stanton talking angrily with his men, or rather with Jack Withers, who stood a little in front of them. Stanton's eyes, when he turned them on Morris, were ablaze.

"A strike! By Moses, they've gone on strike!" he roared, adding, as though it were impossible to believe: "*My* men have gone on strike, *my* men, mark you!"

"What are they striking for?" Morris demanded, not yet realizing how this strike would affect them.

Stanton threw up his arms in a gesture of helplessness. He was a man incapable of appreciating the causes in face of the devastating effect. He knew full well that incompetent parsimonious Australian employers were always dealing with strikes, but always had he regarded those employers with supreme contempt. He thoroughly believed that strikes were most easily avoidable by treating employees in a fair, straightforward manner, and by paying good wages to good men. Yet here were his men striking when always he had treated them straightforwardly and generously. How his rivals who had hated his methods would have the laugh of him now! The fact of the strike wiped from his mind the reason for Sergeant Morris's visit.

"I told my men they could come in for Christmas," he roared. "Most of 'em are here. I'm providing 'em a flash dinner to-morrow; and now I come along and ask five of 'em in turn to drive my car for you. Ask 'em—ask 'em yourself why they won't."

Jack Withers lounged before the sergeant and the squatter. His poor eyes were almost at right angles, but his mouth revealed the iron will that the eyes tried to conceal.

"We reckon," he drawled, "that, seeing as 'ow to-morrow is Christmas Day, the boss oughter recognize that we poor slaves 'as 'elped to make 'is millions, and that extra to the Christmas dinner 'e should make us a momentary [monetary] present, or bonus. We 'ave decided not to do no more work till 'e does."

"What utter rot!" Morris barked. "In any case, Jeff is loaning me his car, and *I* am asking for a driver. I'll pay the union rates of pay, whatever it is, for overtime and double time. Now, Ron, get out the car, quick."

The Englishman shuffled on his feet. "Nothing doing!" he stated emphatically. "I'm no blackleg."

"Well, I want one of you to drive," the now exasperated policeman snorted. "I'm not concerned with your strike against Jeff Stanton. Any one of you who drives me can't scab on his mates. Come now!"

"There ain't nothing doing," Withers rejoined slowly. "We ain't gonna do no more work till we gits that bonus."

"Well, damme, what are you aiming I should give you?" roared the old man, thinking far more of the way the affair would smirch his reputation than of obliging Sergeant Morris.

"Oh!" Withers indolently exclaimed. "Now we're talking, Jeff. What do you say to five hundred pounds per man?"

"What!"

Jeff Stanton's mouth opened and shut several times. With stunned blankness he looked around him, sub-consciously noting Bony standing apart and looking highly amused, seeing Roberts walking from the office towards them, and the gathering black clouds low in the western sky. Five hundred pounds per man bonus! It was ridiculous. They must all have gone mad, or perhaps it was he who had suddenly lost his wits.

Then Roberts was close to him saying something about fire and telephones. What was it? Lightning had caused fire in one of the north-west paddocks. Ned Swallow had reported it. Six thousand sheep prisoners in the paddocks. Just telephoned. And then Ron and Evans started racing towards the motor-shed. Two men were running towards the store with Roberts. And Jack Withers was thumping him on the back and yelling:

"The strike's off, Jeff. We gotta smother that yer fire in quick order, or we'll miss our Christmas dinner. And we shan't be able to spare anyone to drive the sergeant orl over the scenery neither."

Then Jeff Stanton came to life.

Chapter Thirty-five

"Great Doings!"

THE EFFECT of Bony's explosion, deliberately brought about, proved most satisfying to the half-caste detective. From the moment Dot and Dash's truck turned and rushed across the plain towards the range, Bony lived from second to second. He began to watch, second by second, the actions of certain people governed by the peculiar circumstances he himself had created.

It presently became evident that when Sergeant Morris and Trooper Rowland first entered the station homestead they found there Jeff Stanton and Mr Roberts. To the old man Sergeant Morris had explained his mission. The bookkeeper, unavoidably overhearing him, had slipped out of the office at the first opportunity, and, knowing that Marion had ridden up along the creek, had gone to meet her on her way home, in order to acquaint her with the imminent arrest of the partners.

Marion had urged Grey Cloud over the plain at the precise moment that the Fosters' car had broken down. The breakdown had been a fortunate coincidence. To a certain extent it masked her intention of carrying a warning to the wanted men.

On his return to the men's quarters Bony found Mr Roberts telling them that the police were waiting to arrest Dot and Dash, and saying suggestively that he supposed no one wanted the honour of driving any car or truck Sergeant Morris might commandeer with which to pursue them. It occurred to Bony then that this was a plan formulated between Marion and Roberts, with a secondary plan behind it to deal with the situation had it been the partners' truck and not the Fosters' car which had come to grief.

The resultant discussion among the men had given Bony vast amusement. One of them, who could drive, objected to flatly refusing Sergeant Morris on account of the intimidation he would receive from the police when next he visited Mount Lion. The objection applied to the other men also; but the balking of Sergeant Morris still seemed a very attractive idea, if it could be accomplished safely. To Jack Withers had come the brain-wave of a general strike, and very quickly it was agreed to strike for a bonus of five hundred pounds—an amount that certainly would not be granted, and at the same time would not be so fantastic as to allow Morris to guess that the strike was really aimed against him.

And, again, the battle of words between Jeff Stanton and Jack Withers gave much joy to the half-caste. Here was being enacted a play of mingled comedy and drama simply because he had willed it; but it was a play that when once started passed out of his control, placing him in the position of a mere spectator in the stalls. So far its results were highly gratifying. If a mystery could be invested with personality, this one had been discovered in a lethargic state that apparently became dormant. Bony's order to arrest Dot and Dash had quickened it into a living thing, had given it a fresh lease of life that might well strip it of its enfolding draperies and obliterate it for ever.

Certainly his orders to Sergeant Morris had been followed by several surprises. Bony had counted on this when he sent his instructions to the sergeant. The greatest surprise to him was afforded by the action of Marion in warning the partners. How could it possibly concern her what happened to either or both? Less surprising was the action of Roberts in rushing to tell her of the partners' impending arrest. Whilst the bookkeeper's name was still down on Bony's list of fish, it was so merely because it had not been proved not to be the sting-ray. Now it appeared that Mr Roberts was greatly concerned, and had most astutely schemed that Sergeant Morris should be cheated.

To Bony the incident of the fire was inopportune and most annoying, since it was likely to check the actions of the performers, halting the drama in the middle of the second act. It was obvious that immediately Jeff Stanton recovered from the surprise, first of the strike and secondly of the news of fire which had so abruptly terminated it, he would put into action plans laid long before to cope with the fire demon should it rear its head. It also was obvious that the strike was farcical, for no sooner had the book-keeper announced the outbreak than the strike was swept off the board in proof of the strikers' genuine loyalty to their employer.

Lightning had fired the knee-high grass near the north-west boundary in one of the paddocks ridden by Ned Swallow, who had elected to remain at his job. From the hut where Dot and Dash had camped when they shot the kangaroos he saw a thin spiral of smoke rising skyward at a distance of several miles. He waited, watching it, to make sure it was not a chance blackfellow's signal, and saw the spiral become a column, and the column rapidly become a whirling black mass.

Immediately he was convinced that it was a bush fire he had telephoned the fact to the homestead. He stood by the telephone until Mr Roberts had called Jeff Stanton, watching the smoke become a high menacing cloud in the northern sky through a wide space between the wall-sheets of the hut.

Whilst Stanton was hurrying to his office two men ran to the motor-shed, thence to bring out the powerful motor-cycles and charge them with petrol in view of expected orders. The remaining men hurried after the squatter and collected outside the office, ready and willing to be rushed to the fire zone to put out the conflagration before it reached uncontrollable dimensions. As for Sergeant Morris and his trooper, they were ignored for the time being, and Bony, who stood on the outskirts of the little knot of men, saw with twinkling eyes the furious anger in the sergeant's face.

Presently Stanton emerged from the office, calm, cool, and resolute, a born leader, far-sighted, radiating confidence. Standing on the veranda, thereby seeing over the heads of the men, he said in his gruff, barking voice:

"The lightning has started a fire at the back of Black Horse Paddock. As you know, all that country is ripe for a fire. It'll take a lot of putting out, and I'm glad to see that you are justifying my faith in you, and that your damned strike was a sort of Christmas joke. Every day that we are engaged in putting out this fire your wages will be the usual pound a day.

"Most of the sheep in Black Horse Paddock are now coming in to water, and Ned Swallow will hold 'em near the tank. Jim and you, Tom, go out on the bikes and give Ned a hand. There are several spare hacks out there. Roll your swags and leave 'em here before you go. Ron, fill up with petrol and take three cases of extra petrol on the Chev. All you men roll your swags and leave 'em here. All of you will go with Ron. Ed, see to the Reo—take plenty of spare petrol. Jack and Bony will give you a hand to put aboard one of those four-hundred-gallon tanks. That done, pull up here and pick up the swags and the tucker Mr Roberts will set out. Get busy!"

Men rushed to their quarters, and, hastily rolling their blankets, raced with them back to the office veranda. First one and then the other motor-cycle engine roared and sputtered. The cloud-hidden sun was just setting when the first red-painted machine skidded off in a cloud of dust, followed in three minutes by the other—machines ridden by expert but fearless, dare-devil riders. The policemen, ignored and wrathfully helpless, saw the first of the trucks, loaded with men, move off into the dust raised by the second motor-cycle, and with perplexed annoyance Morris saw Bony helping to lift a huge square iron water-tank on the powerful Reo truck, as though he were just an excited, loyal station-hand, and not a detective-inspector of the Queensland Police.

The situation was one wholly governed by time. Every second added bulk and strength to the devouring fire-devil. Every second added to the danger menacing the flocks of sheep imprisoned by the far-flung wire fences.

"Sorry, Morris, but we can do nothing to help you now," Stanton said gruffly. "The fool strike snookered you, or you would have been away in the car before we received news of the fire. Now we need every machine that will go."

"It seems a mess-up from the start, Jeff. First your daughter warns Dot and Dash after being told it was Dot and Dash we were after. Then the men pretend to go on strike, for it certainly looks like a put-up stunt. Things will have to be sorted out later. I'm going back to Mount Lion to dispatch telegrams and to get a car of some sort. Rowland will ride after their truck, for it is quite on the cards that they will abandon it. They will know full well that they'll be safer on foot. You might lend old Moongalliti a horse so that he can go with him."

Jeff nodded. "The groom is out after the horses right now. He'll fix Moongalliti. I am sending half a dozen nigs out to the danger zone on horseback at once."

Half a minute later a mob of some thirty saddle-horses was brought to the yards by the groom, quite invisible on his stock horse in the dust they raised. The policemen were walking to the yards for their horses, and, passing Bony, were halted by him, since just then there was no one to see them.

"Great doings!" he said, with flashing blue eyes.

"Too right! But we'll get 'em in the end. I'm——"

Sergeant Morris stopped speaking. An expression of dawning surprise spread over his brick-red face. Then: "By the way—you told me you could drive a car, didn't you?"

"Yes, I think I remember having done so. Why?"

"Then why in thunder didn't you offer to drive when none of the men would do so?" demanded Morris.

Bony laughed softly.

"Because it is not so very important that Dot and Dash should be arrested to-day, or even to-morrow."

"But you ordered their arrest!" gasped the astonished policeman.

"I know I did, Morris. But, after all, their arrest was not so important as what would happen when it was known they were to be arrested, or were arrested. However, it will be as well to gather them in. Charge them with murder, although I am almost sure neither committed the murder. This mystery is going well. The murderer of Marks has but to make one slip."

"You are a most unorthodox detective."

"Everyone says that," Bony murmured. "I am, however, the greatest detective in Australia."

Chapter Thirty-six

Father Ryan Acts

FATHER RYAN had eaten his dinner at the policeman's table as usual, and was seated at his desk gazing over it and beyond the open window towards the hotel with meditative eyes. The sun was on the verge of setting, and but two sounds drifted in upon him from the silenced world—the voices of several children at play in the street, and the occasional reiterated phrase, "How dry we are!" screamed by the cockatoo in his cage on the store veranda.

But of these sounds Father Ryan was unconscious. He was thinking of the only guest staying at the hotel, and wondering what on earth kept her in Mount Lion. He was a little afraid of Mrs Thomas, but felt no dislike for her. She shocked him, certainly. Her outspokenness had at times really pained him. On the other hand, save for her indulgence in liquor, her behaviour was above reproach. Had Mrs Thomas been a man, her drinking would have aroused no comment, though her generosity in "shouting" would have done. Her ability to consume liquor was a never-failing marvel to Mr Bumpus, who was even more afraid of her than was Father Ryan. In fact, she was the topic of conversation among the whole population of Mount Lion. She was at once the giver and the withholder; she gave her money in "shouts", and she withheld at all times any information about herself.

Father Ryan, however, knew a little more about her than did the other inhabitants of the bush town. To him had Mrs Thomas come asking questions, many questions, questions that sought to find out if within recent time anyone had risen to affluence even for a short period. In his capacity as a Roman Catholic priest she had confided that she was the sister of the missing man, Marks. That was about all she did confide. Father Ryan knew nothing about the case of the Stolen Bride, and was but told the relationship between her and Marks to secure his sympathy and aid in her search for the truth. For the official statement concerning the disappearance of Marks she did not believe, knowing that her brother was a bush-man born and bred.

The grounds of her belief in foul play had been communicated to him with a downright clarity that had brought Father Ryan to believe, with her, that Marks had not died simply from exposure. It was the apparent fact that in his district there was a man who had killed and robbed which so disturbed the little priest. He had been so sure he knew the hearts and minds of all the people who were his friends that he was like the husband who was told that his wife was unfaithful.

Into the calm water of his life, so seldom disturbed by human passion, had dropped a stone that had agitated it for some considerable time. That evening the agitation was subsiding, for Father Ryan was making himself believe that Mrs Thomas was suffering from hallucinations; and, just when he was congratulating himself on having arrived at this decision, another and heavier stone was dropped by Mrs Morris, who came bursting into his study.

"There's been trouble out at Windee, yer reverence," she exclaimed, dropping him an habitual curtsy. "Oh, such trouble! Morris has been out to arrest Dot and Dash, and they've escaped, and the place is on fire, and it's Christmas Day to-morrow and——"

A large blue neckerchief smothered her wheezy voice whilst being used to wipe the perspiration from her broad face. Her body, almost as big in width as in length, appeared to sway on the small feet.

"One item at a time, Mrs Morris!"

The priest's deep and musical voice seemed to reach her as a cooling wind. She felt his hand on her forearm, felt herself urged backward and into a wide-armed chair.

"Now, then. Tell me your news—slowly—and in sequence," he said gently. "From the beginning, please."

"Morris has just rung me up," gasped the woman, still all of a flutter. "He and Mr Rowland left for Windee this afternoon, but he never told me what job he was on, which isn't like him. He says they are after Dot and Dash, and when I ast him what for, he said: 'N—i—x!' You know what he is when he says: 'N—i—x!' don't you, Father? It ain't no use arguing. Says Dot and Dash was warned he wanted them and they escaped. Then at the same time old Jeff gets word that all the back of Windee is afire, and about thirty thousand sheep in danger of being burnt up. He's coming home, is Morris to get Slater's car, and chase Dot and Dash. Oh, what could they have done? That snip of a Dot! No one can help liking him. An' poor Mr Dash! A proper gentleman in every way——"

Father Ryan let her run on. No longer was he following her. His mind was flashing back and forth between Dot and Dash and Mrs Thomas. Mrs Morris continued to drone on, but upon the tablets of the priest's mind had at last become written in letters of flame: "Dot and Dash? Dot *or* Dash?"

Was it one of these two, or was it together that they were responsible for the disappearance of Marks? Was Mrs Thomas's seemingly unfounded suspicion really substantial? Dash—Hugh Trench—Marion

Stanton. Marion—Marion, who had waited two years! Marion, whom he had regarded with such sincere affection ever since she was little!

Mrs Morris was still voicing complaint and speculation when the fact of the fire wriggled into the ambit of his mind. The back of Windee alight—thirty thousand sheep in danger—all hands rushed to the scene—thirty thousand sheep—thirty thousand! Old Jeff gone out there too. Even Roberts would go. Marion and Mrs Poulton, likely enough, left behind. And Marion—Marion thinking of Dash, wondering, wondering, wondering! Alone and wondering. And Dash fleeing with Dot—the law on their heels. The law—and Marion!

Out of the mental welter stood the name Marion—the little girl whom he loved, and who loved and confided in him; the woman he loved, and who still confided to him all her secrets, little and big. She would be wanting him at that moment. He must go, at once.

Without speaking, he snatched up a light coat, but failed to remember choosing a hat, and left the now breathless Mrs Morris to follow him to the gate, there to stand and watch him cross the road to the hotel. She saw him make straight to the public bar door and disappear within.

Mr Bumpus's main bar was a spacious room, which was not too large in the far-gone prosperous days, but now always seemed uncomfortably big. Within, Father Ryan found four men playing two-up—everyone knew the police were not in town—and Mrs Thomas seated on a barrel at the farther end of the bar drinking from a glass mug reputed to hold an imperial pint. Mr Bumpus was drawing drinks for the two-up players, and the entrance of the little priest made him pause in the act of pumping beer, and the gamblers freeze into statues of almost ludicrous guilt.

On the round, cherubic face of the priest was no evidence of the perturbation of his mind. Having caught the men red-handed, he seized the slight additional power the situation afforded him. Softly he said:

"Ah! Two-up! An illegal game. Played on public premises, too. Your premises, Bumpus! Very serious. Bumpus, call your wife!"

"Tell her she's wanted by the Church," put in Mrs Thomas.

"Wot d'you want her for?"

"Call your wife, Bumpus!"

"The Church demands your wife, Bumpus. Render unto me beer and plenty of it, and unto the Church your wife," Mrs Thomas said very loudly, but distinctly.

One of the gamblers, raw-boned, unshaved, one who appeared in visage and dress as if he had stepped off the deck of a pirate ship in the "Jolly Roger" days, sauntered along to the woman, whom he addressed in a slow, drawling voice and regarded with a facial expression so truly terrific that even Mrs Thomas was awed.

"Yous ain't meanin' no offence to Father Ryan, are yous, mum?"

Mrs Thomas, fortunately, held her peace.

"I'm kinder glad uv that," proclaimed the man, known to every policeman in West New South Wales as "Stormbird". The fingers of one huge sun-blackened hand fondled his throat significantly, and dimly Mrs Thomas realized that chivalrous regard for her sex was a weakness unknown to Stormbird. Before Father Ryan could intervene, Mrs Bumpus entered the bar.

"Good evening, everybody!" she exclaimed with a giggle. "Hallo, Father Ryan; good evening!"

"Good evening!" replied the little priest, smiling broadly. "I asked for you because I want you to take charge of the bar while Bumpus drives these four boys and me out to Windee in his car. See that you have enough petrol, Bumpus, before we start."

"Wot's the stunt, Pardray?" demanded Bumpus.

"Just a little commission for you, Bumpus. Hurry up! Now, you boys, one drink apiece before we start. There is work and plenty of it waiting us at Windee."

"Tell us the idee, Father," the Stormbird pleaded, obviously careful of his speech.

Father Ryan paid Mrs Bumpus and lighted a cigar of the kind which her husband always boasted was the best Havana procurable.

"I understand the back of Windee is afire. I'm after thinking every man of us will be needed. I intend going along to do what I can, and I know quite well that you all would consider yourselves insulted if I went without you when men are wanted."

"My ...! Yes, Pardray, uv course," drawled the Stormbird. "Uv course!"

"Naterally," interjected a second man.

"Don't you men be such fools as to go away from here this time of night! Have a drink on me!" shrilled Mrs Thomas, slipping off her barrel and coming towards the group via the bar counter, needed as a stay. She brought up against the Stormbird, who, stooping, leered down on her.

"Yous ain't meanin' no offence, are yous?" he asked softly.

Mrs Thomas sat on the floor and began to weep.

From out of the evening twilight beyond the door Mr Bumpus's motor-hooter told them he was waiting.

Chapter Thirty-seven

Man and Dog

PICTURE A CIRCLE one mile in diameter, as dry as the Sahara, as bare of bush and tree as that great region, and the loose ankle-deep dust covering it finer than any on the Sahara, almost as fine as flour. In the centre of the circle a great earth tank, windmill, and watering troughs, and near it a ramshackle structure by courtesy called a hut. Across the circular desert a fence cutting it exactly in halves. On one side of the fence a slow-moving, milling mass of sheep from which the red dust floats upward in a long slant to the south, with a horseman on the outer edge of the mass moving slowly in a larger arc, to and fro, keeping the mass in one place hard against the fence. On the other side of the fence a similar mass of sheep, moving, ever moving, as a dull white circular disk, and—on that side farthest from the fence, and therefore farthest from the horseman—a single slow-trotting dog.

In this manner Ned Swallow and his Kelpie bitch held some six thousand sheep until help should arrive.

Beyond the hut, towards the hills, four saddle-hacks raced about the fenced horse-paddock measuring precisely one square mile in area. It was noted by the solitary man that horses always galloped so when rain was approaching, but when the sun went down this evening their liveliness was not caused by the approach of rain, but by the huge menacing cloud rising from earth to sky-vault in the north. Even the horse ridden by Ned Swallow telegraphed nervousness to his rider.

In the north-east sky hung a great mass of clouds, blue-black underneath, its west and southern edges wonderfully deep and brilliantly lit in tones ranging from white, through gold, to purple by the sun already sunk before the mulga-line horizon. The mass was passing slowly eastward. From it lightning flickered and thunder grumbled, and here and there from its black base hung diaphanous veils of falling spray, hanging but a short distance from the main cloud body, as though the spray was turned into gas or steam when it met the heated air nearer the earth. From this cloud, forty minutes before, had fallen the demon, fire.

Here and there over the remainder of the sky space sailed the iceberg clouds as seen earlier in the day by Bony, so mighty in aspect that it seemed wonderful they did not crash on the world from their very weight.

The galahs were retreating from Carr's Tank to their roosting-places among the eastern hills. The last battalion left in the magic light that in a few minutes would be gone. Above, so high that the sunlight still held it, flew a giant eagle, no larger, as seen from the ground, than a gnat. From all sides the kangaroos came hopping in to drink, unhurried, as yet unfearful of the smoke-cloud to the north. And from the north the wind blew gently, very softly, but steadily.

Now the light on the plain died down. The edge of the scrub appeared to rush away from the man and vanish in the gathering darkness. Up from the now invisible plain eastward rose the range of hills, to remain visible for yet a little longer—hills that seemed to rest on a carpet of dark grey velvet. Constantly Swallow's eyes searched the hills generally, and one thrusting spur in particular, for round the spur lay the track from Windee. At the last second, just before the shadows of the plain swept upward to envelop the hills, the watching man saw a rapidly lengthening ribbon of dust rise from the top to half-way down the spur, and then, cut out, become lost in the rushing shadows. Relief was coming.

The task set Ned Swallow and his dog by the Fire Demon was not a light one. One flock of sheep he could have managed to work into the mile-square horse-paddock with the help of his dog. But his dog was urgently required to keep in one place the second flock of sheep in the other paddock. To have attempted to box the two flocks, to have endeavoured to put the dog's flock through the gate beside the dam to mix with the one he held, meant that they would lose either one or the other. One of the flocks, knowing of the attempt to hold them, would have broken away for the scrub and the miles of grass which lay in the present path of the fire. And, once there, the fire would sweep on them, chase them to the south boundary fence of the paddock, and there devour them at its will.

Swallow's chief anxiety was the rapidly falling darkness. His dog, he knew, would not fail. It would shepherd the great flock it was sent to shepherd all night long, and not one animal would break. He, a mere man, would be less efficient than the dog. His limited eyesight would be a handicap that all his knowledge of sheep and all his bushcraft could not overcome. He would be unable to see a sheep break away, and unable, therefore, to block it and turn it back.

Along half the section of the northern horizon flickered a ruddy glow, dark red for long periods and here and there suddenly brightening into vivid scarlet, silhouetting the tops of the outstanding trees. A beam of light, brilliant and yellow, moved up and down as a searchlight on a warship, and told the anxious guardian that the car was crossing the many water-gutters that cut the track at the foot of the hills.

Presently the beam grew steady, became pointed at him as a single star of hope, a star that magically grew in size and brightness to first-magnitude dimensions, and told Swallow that the car was at last on the open plain and would reach him in a few minutes.

The plaintive baaing from the tens of hundreds of sheep drowned the roar of the racing engine, but by the continuous sound Swallow knew he still had his flock in hand.

Then he saw a star of the fifteenth magnitude burst into sight just below the edge of the blackest shadow that denoted the hills. It winked, disappeared, shone, disappeared, shone, and faded time after time, but always sinking lower to the plain. A second star of the fifteenth magnitude flashed into being, to pass through the same evolutions as the first; and Swallow wanted to shout, would have shouted, had he dared risk stampeding the sheep, for he rightly guessed that these two far-away stars were the head-lights of motor-cycles.

The lights of the car began to fall on the milling sheep, swing away, return, ever more distinctly revealing them and the dust column rising above them. Alertly Swallow watched and slowly trotted to and fro in the arc that hemmed in the flock to the fence. He saw the car pull up beside the hut. He heard then, above the chorus of complaining sheep, the low hum of the engine, and knew when the engine had been shut off to permit the occupants to listen.

Of all the men whom Swallow thought might reach him first, the very last to be thought of, if at all, were Dot and Dash. Yet it was they who reached Carr's Tank first. Their hurried plan to escape the law had been formulated before the sun had set, and before they had reached the eastern slopes of the hills. Arrived at the summit of the hill road when dusk was deepening, Dash almost wrecked the truck against a giant boulder when he saw to the north the great whirling cloud of black smoke set on a crimson base.

"It kinda looks as if we're in fer a rough passage," Dot gave out as his opinion.

"If we can get to Quaker's Swamp before the fire sweeps south and blocks us, it will certainly block for a while the police and their trackers, Dot."

"I guess you is right, old son," Dot agreed. "Still, we gotta keep going like greased lightning if we want to keep ahead of them trackers. Me, I'm not afraid of the bulls, nor was I ever feared of Sheriff Dawlish back in ole Arizonee, but I kinda shiver at these yere Australian black trackers. Blood'ounds ain't in it. Injuns are blind men compared with 'em."

"Still, with two good horses, which I am sure Ned will not see us take, we've a good chance," countered Dash cheerfully. "Besides, you've been right up into the Northern Territory this way twice before, and know the location of the water-holes."

"You're right there, ole feller. Still, I maintain that if we 'ad gone on to Windee and said 'ow-de-do to Sergeant Morris, 'e could have done little but bark if we kept our mugs shut. Providin', that is, 'e wants us to tell 'im if we seen Marks that day."

"My dear Dot," Dash said, returning to his grandiloquent mode of speech, "I am not in the slightest degree perturbed as to that affair. We finalized it—as one would say in the quartermaster's office—most satisfactorily. The only fly in our ointment is the Third Person. As I pointed out to you before, our bolting as we do lays the scent, no matter how faint, to us and away from him. Believe me, our actions have been dictated by pure altruism, and no man has made a greater sacrifice than I."

"'Xactly!" Dot said with sudden warmth. "You make me feel as I did when the lady missionary came to our city at home and held revival meetings which Four-Eyed Brady bet me ten dollars I wouldn't sit out. Hm! Don't see no light in Ned's comfortable Main Street residence— four bed, two recep., kitchen and bath h. and c., thirty-two dollars per month. Must be out."

"May be after the sheep."

"Some job if he is."

Pulling up beside the unlighted hut, both men got out, whereupon Dot shouted for Ned Swallow. Just then Dash thought he heard the voice of many sheep and shut off the engine to hear the better. In the sudden following silence the sound of the two great flocks reached them as a great wave. For half a minute both men listened. The direction of the sound did not vary.

"He's caught the sheep when they came in to water, and evidently is holding them till help arrives," pronounced Dash with conviction.

"Sure thing, by the sound of it. Looks as if help or the bulls is gonna arrive quick."

In the reflected glow of the headlights Dash saw his partner gazing back towards the hills, and, looking back too, saw the wide-spaced glowing stars of the two motor-cycle headlamps. As Dot had said, it meant either the police or help for Ned Swallow—Ned Swallow alone out there in the dark, working to hold six thousand sheep.

"What's what?" demanded Dot succinctly.

For a moment of two Dash was silent. Then:

"The odds are against the police," he drawled coolly. "As we cannot muster Ned's loose horses without his hack, which he is sure to be riding, we had better join him, lend a hand with the sheep, and get a horse apiece when they are mustered."

"But if it is the police?" objected Dot.

"Well, there will be only two of them, and we are, I fondly hope, two grown men."

"I should say! Come on! Ned must kinda be getting weary. Bet yew a level dollar 't ain't the police?"

"No takers, Dot. You're on almost a dead certainty."

Chapter Thirty-eight

"The Place Fer Us"

NED SWALLOW'S SURPRISE was complete when out of the darkness two figures emerged, one of which hailed cheerfully:

"How are you enjoying yer holiday, Ned?"

"Nicely, thank you," Swallow replied with studied politeness. "Was thinking of you drinking pints in Mount Lion. What about running your truck out hereabouts and throwing your lights on this ruddy mob? Afraid they'll break in the darkness. Anyways, what blows you out here?"

"Explain, Dot, while I go for the truck," requested Dash.

Whereupon the little American told Swallow that the police wanted them, but what the hell for they weren't wise, and didn't much care. They planned to get away up into the Northern Territory, if only for the sake of annoying Sergeant Morris. It might be he wanted them because they had failed to return Income Tax statements. As though he, of all men, would pay money to the Government so that politicians could go a-gallivantin' around the world.

"Hear, hear!" Ned agreed heartily. "What kin I do?"

"You can lend us a 'orse each, Ned."

"You can take yer pick."

"We knew that, which was why we headed this way," Dot said emphatically. "We can't go on for ever on the truck, 'cos we can't make gas outer mulga scrub. And ole Jeff, 'e'll get our returns for the last load of kangaroo skins, which'll pay 'im for the 'orses."

At a strategic point Dash stopped the truck. The whole flock was clearly outlined in the beam of the lamps. It revealed the rising dust created by the hoofs of the flock guarded by the dog beyond the fence. It cowed, too, the more restless sheep, quietened the vast mass, and turned all heads in its direction. Even the bleating subsided a little, and they were permitted to hear the roaring exhausts of the motor-cycles when they reached the hut. Passing it, the riders came out and straddled their machines close to the three men. Cheerful greetings were exchanged, and Dot and Dash informed of the strike and its results.

Dot chuckled. One lamp's rays fell on him, and they could see how his button of a nose wrinkled when his face widened in a gurgling laugh. Dash did not even smile. He was thinking and trying to guess exactly how much Marion Stanton knew.

"What's your next move?" inquired one of the cyclists.

"We——You had better not know, pardner. The less you know the better for your health," the little man said, still chuckling.

"An' the better for your 'ealth the sooner you clear out," was Swallow's advice. "Run in them 'orses, Jim." Then, to Dot and Dash: "Give us a hand to get these woollies into the 'orse-paddock, an' I'll fix you up with saddles. I'll have to loan you my own, so take care of it."

The motor-cyclists skidded away to the horse-paddock gate, which they closed behind them. Those with the sheep heard them yell with youthful excitement whilst they tore away through the paddock, in and out of low scrub, curving round scattered boulders, their headlights sweeping in wide arcs, their exhausts roaring. It was the modern way of mustering horses, and far more sporting than doing the job with a hack.

With yells and honking claxons they discovered the four horses at the farther side, and because these animals had become used to being driven into the horse-yards in a corner nearest the hut, they raced for those yards with the yelling fiends behind them.

By that time the partners and Swallow had got the latter's flock past the windmill and dam, and jammed against the horse-paddock fence. In spite of the darkness and the dust, there was no confusion, each man knowing precisely what to do and where to be in position to edge forward the rapidly milling mob. Thirty minutes after the arrival of Dot and Dash the two flocks were safely within the small horse-paddock, there so easily to be brought out again on the plain if the fire threatened. Six thousand out of thirty thousand sheep were safe.

"Ain't nothink we kin do till old Jeff gets out here," Swallow announced whilst the five men drank scalding hot tea outside the ramshackle hut.

"Anyways, whatever we do won't suit, and, as I heard Bony say the other day, 'When in doubt do nothing'," Jim said slowly, a young man hardly twenty. "Clever bloke, Bony! Cleverest half-nig I ever knoo."

"M'yes," Swallow agreed. There ensued a silence lasting a full minute, during which all faces were kept eastward, and all eyes were centred on that spot in the hills where first would become visible the lights of the trucks and the car. Swallow spoke again deliberately. "I was forgettin' Bony," he said. "Yes, I was forgettin' Bony." Turning to Dash, he added: "Some'ows I don't like your chances of gettin' clear."

"Why?" Dash asked imperturbably.

"'Cos wot I recolleck of Bony makes the betting heavily in his favour. When I was in Queensland he was just King Tracker."

"If he's put on our trail we'll give him a good draw," promised Dot cheerfully.

"Orl right," Swallow said resignedly. Then, with surging hope in his voice: "I'll lay you even money he gits you."

"Right! How much?"

"Ten quid"—eagerly.

"Make 'er twenty-five. A level hundred dollars."

"You're on. She stands at twenty-five quid."

"Look! You'll win if he's on the first truck. Here it comes," the second rider announced.

"It may be the car," Swallow lit his cigarette with care. Then, jumping to his feet: "I'll take two to one against old Jeff's car."

"A quid!" jumped Jim, grinning.

"An' he'll have the bulls with him for shore," Dot said decidedly.

"Course! You blokes git! Come on, give us a hand to saddle the 'orses. Get 'em away quick, or I'll have it again me conschuss when I take Dot's cash."

And ten minutes later, when the lights of three motors were leaving the foothills of the range:

"Well, so long, Dash! So long, Dot! Keep agoin' and keep straight for Darwin," Swallow advised hurriedly.

"So long, everyone!" Dot drawled.

"We'll tell 'em you headed due west. You ain't goin' west, are you?"

"We are!" Dash confided. "Yes, we are going west. Tell them, if you *can* tell a lie, that we have gone south."

"You run a danger of the fire pinching you," the second and more silent cyclist told them.

"We'll chance that. Well, good-bye, fellows! Thanks for your help."

"That's orl right, Dash. Hooroo!"

"Hooroo!"

To the little knot of men standing outside the hut the partners immediately vanished in the darkness. As Dash said they would, they rode due west with the fire now so near that they could see its flickering tongues a bare two miles away on their right flank. To both men came the same thought. If they could clear the path of the fire without turning south to escape it, it would sweep down from the north and for a little while balk pursuit. The fire also would obliterate their horses' tracks to a very great extent.

"You are now the commander of this party, Dot," remarked Dash, after they had ridden for half an hour in silence. "What are we going to do?"

"Go back, face the bulls, and tell 'em to be damned," was Dot's instant reply.

"Do not let us become wearied by fruitless argument, my dear man. Let it be final that there is to be no going back."

"Well, there is no reason why you can't go back."

"Please, Dot, no further discussion on that topic. We go together. Where do we go?"

"You're the most obstinate cuss wot ever drank beer. Howsomever, west o' here is Freeman's Run. Windee's west boundary is marked by the border fence. There or in South Australia we'll strike the track from Freeman's homestead to Nullawil. It's a hundred to one ole man Freeman 'as bin told of the fire and will be sending orl 'is 'ands to join up with the Windee push to smother it. We'll ride that track till we hear 'em acomin'. We'll then leave it and head north-west. They will ride over our tracks so that even Bony won't foller 'em, champeen tracker an' orl.

"On the north-west boundary of Freeman's Run there's a ole friend of mine cooking for two boundary-riders. 'E won't go to no fire, 'cos 'e's nigh seventy years of age and rheumaticky. From 'ere to 'im is about forty-seven miles. We'll 'it 'im to-morrow at noon. We'll rest up till nightfall, and then head into the Never-Never. Understan', when we leave my pal we git off the station country on to the open country, and when once there we got to chance the water-'oles."

"Do you mean that we shall have passed beyond the edge of the settled, fenced country?" asked Dash.

'Jest so. Up away beyond the stations is that scattered that it's possible ter get to Darwin without passin' through a gate or climb a fence."

"But surely we have not to make for Darwin?"

"No. We'll hole up on the shores of Lake Eyre."

"What sort of a place is that?"

"Hain't you never 'eard about the shores of Lake Eyre?"

"No."

"Well, jest you imagine what this yer world will be like millions o' years ahead, when the earth 'as kinda run down and there ain't no sea-tides and no people, no nothink but insects and sand and mud and withered things wot look like trees; a place where the souls of orl the bad blokes and blokesses hover about awaiting 'ell—and then you'll git Lake Eyre. It's a place wot must make even Satan feel the draught up and down 'is back. Just the sort of place fer us, ole pard!"

Chapter Thirty-nine

Bony's Dilemma

DETECTIVE-INSPECTOR Napoleon Bonaparte was helping to load rations from the store on the second truck when he saw Marion Stanton standing nearby watching the operation. With Bony was the driver and a second man. Mr Roberts remained within the store. It was whilst the driver was busily engaged in arranging and stacking the load and the second man was inside that Marion gave Bony a note, before walking away. Not until the loading was finished did Bony get a moment of time to read the message unobserved.

"I want to see you before you go. Come to the north end of the house."

The opportunity to slip away presented itself immediately afterwards, and he found the girl waiting for him in the doorway giving entry to the north veranda. Without speaking, she beckoned him to follow, and led him into the house and to a room that in furnishing was between a drawing-room and a study. It was her own sitting-room, which no one ever entered excepting when invited. She herself closed the door.

"Sit down, Bony. I want to talk to you," she said.

Bony sat down. He saw that the girl's face was very pale, and there was emphatic evidence that she had been crying. Her voice was tremulous, and because he saw that she was hurt the half-caste detective's sympathy at once went out to her. Patiently he waited for her to speak again, his face revealing the sympathy he felt. Then:

"Someone told me—I forget if it was you or my father—that you are an expert tracker. Are you really?"

Wondering, Bony acknowledged it. "In Queensland I have shown aptitude in that direction," he murmured.

For what seemed to him a long time she gazed at him with disconcerting steadiness. It was a silence which he broke.

"If you want me to do any tracking for you, Miss Stanton," he said quietly, "I shall be very happy indeed to serve you."

"Why?"

"Why?" For a moment Bony was nonplussed. Then with complete frankness he answered: "Because you, who are the daughter of a millionaire, a white woman and lovely, have been kind, not condescendingly kind, but with the kindness of an equal, to me, a—a—a nigger. Because you are the one white woman who has been kind to me that way there is nothing I would not do to show my great appreciation of it."

For a further many seconds she regarded him in silence. Bony again wondered, but veiled from his eyes the alertness of his mind to meet a second shock. It did not come—yet.

"Remembering the incidents of this afternoon, you know how the trooper set off on horseback with Moongalliti and Warn to arrest Dot and Dash," she said slowly and utterly without passion. "Have you any idea what kind of trackers those two are?"

Bony began to wonder what lay behind this fresh turn. Without hesitation, however, he replied:

"I have only the faintest idea, based on the fact that these two men were present at the search for the missing man Marks, and that it appeared then that their tracking ability was poor. But, they having gone after Dot and Dash, what are they to do with—us?"

To this counter-question Marion made no immediate answer. Watching her intently, Bony saw that she was making up her mind to say that for which she had brought him there, and thinking carefully the words she would use. Before him he saw a very resolute woman—saw, too, how like she was to old Jeff Stanton when he stood outside his office and addressed the whilom strikers.

"Supposing Moongalliti and Warn failed to find and keep on the tracks of Dot and Dash, they might ask you to do the tracking; in which, of course, you would succeed?"

"I should be astounded were I to fail," he said, a victim to his vanity. It brought to her face a ghost of a smile, and seeing it he added: "Both Moongalliti and Warn are full-blooded aboriginals, Miss Stanton. It is well to remember that, and also to remember that I am a half-caste. The aboriginals are clever trackers. Individual feats of tracking by them are amazing. Nevertheless, the aboriginal's intelligence is not very high, and in him imagination is almost non-existent. He will follow what his eyes reveal to him. From my mother I have inherited the black man's vision and the black man's passion for the chase, as well as his bushcraft. From my father, however, I have inherited imagination and reasoning power. When there is nothing which a black man's eyes can see he comes to a halt. I go on, because I reason this and imagine that, and presently come again on the tracks which were lost. I have followed tracks three months old."

"Then, were you asked to find Dot and Dash, you would find them?" was her question, spoken with a shade of anxiety.

"I have no doubt about that," he said simply, and this time there was no hint of vanity in his voice. He spoke as he would if stating his belief that the sun would rise on the morrow. He added that which brought a flash of fear into her eyes. "Do you wish me to track Dot and Dash?"

"Bony——" He saw her bite her nether lip. His question had brought her to the point which had been responsible for this conversation. "Bony—oh, Bony!—can I trust you? Can I?"

For a moment he failed to respond. The appeal in her face made his pulses jump into a racing throb. It occurred to him that he had never seen her look so lovely, and the vision wiped from his mind memory of what and who he was. He forgot entirely that he was a half-caste, that his skin was ruddy black, and that he was also a detective-inspector of the Queensland Police. His own voice sounded strange in his ears. It seemed as though another man was speaking. The voice held a tone of hauteur.

"I might remind you that just now I said there is nothing I would not do for you. Now permit me to repeat the word 'nothing' with emphasis."

"Thank you, Bony; you make my task easier."

"Forget that it is a task, Miss Stanton, and command," urged this extraordinary man grandly. He saw her smile, and thrilled to the loveliness of her. Her words came in a rush.

"I want you to volunteer to track Dot and Dash, or in some way to prevent Moongalliti and Warn from getting them."

"That will be easy. I shall not fail to bring them in."

"But I don't want them brought in. I want them to get away, and I want you to volunteer to track them, so that you can make it possible for them to get clear, even if you have to mislead the police."

It was then that Bony stared at her, subconsciously noting how her lips remained partly separated, as though she was frightened by the words she had uttered. He remembered then who he was, and what he was. He remembered that he it was who had ordered the apprehension of these men. For seconds he was mentally stunned by her appeal. And then his old command of himself returned. Into his mind came flooding back all the alertness and all the cunning which so largely made up this man Bony.

"Why do you wish this?" he asked coolly.

She sensed the change in him, but, seeing she had gone too far to withdraw, proceeded to fight on as her sire would have done.

"That is a question I would rather not answer," she told him. He felt the stiffening in her attitude. "You said you would do anything for me. Do this without questioning. Please, Bony!"

"The circumstances are unique, Miss Stanton. Knowing your position in life, and knowing, too, that of Dot and Dash, you must excuse my feeling some surprise. Wait, please! In Queensland I have by no means a poor reputation at tracking—a reputation of which I may be excused for feeling proud, as I have never yet failed in tracking-work set me to do. You decline to give me a reason for asking me to do what would destroy my reputation, what would cause the finger of scorn to be pointed at me. I feel sure when you understand how much you want of me that you will give me the reason why you wish it."

Whilst he was speaking he saw the blood mount slowly to her cheeks and brow. He saw her hands clasp tightly and the fingers work in and out among the others. Genuinely astonished by her request, he failed to divine the motive that prompted it. The motive might be one of many things. Was it fear that prompted this request? Did she fear something consequent on the arrest of these two trappers? If so, then he had let her out of his net too soon. If so, then he had failed dreadfully on one point. He had failed in his reading of her character. And failure in anything stung him always, lashed his self-esteem, struck at his vanity, tended to make mock of "the greatest detective in Australia".

"You will not do this which I ask unless I explain why I ask it?"

He nodded. "You ask a great deal, Miss Stanton. Give a little. The more powerful the reason of your request, the more enthusiastic will I be to accord it."

"You will promise never to repeat a word?"

Again he nodded. Beyond the house he heard Jeff Stanton roaring his name. Then he heard that which brought him to his feet, spoken with bowed head, softly:

"It is because I—I love Hugh Trench."

He stood as a man of stone. Even his eyelids remained seemingly fixed whilst he stared down at her bowed head.

"You love—Dash?"

He saw her head sink a little farther in acquiescence.

Old Jeff Stanton continued to roar out his name, but Bony hardly heard. He could hear hardly anything but Marion Stanton's slow sobbing, and think of nothing but the fact that this woman, to whom he owed so much, loved the man he was hounding down.

Chapter Forty

The Necessity for a Wedding Present

PRESENTLY OLD JEFF ceased to cry Bony's name and the man himself heard the sound of a motor-engine roar for a short space, slow down when the driver changed gears, speed up again, slow once more, again speed up and its sound grow faint. The truck had gone without him.

Still he did not speak, nor did Marion raise her head. He heard footsteps coming along the corridor without, listened with strained intentness to their passing beyond the door, and to the gentle tapping that followed. To them came Mrs Poulton's voice.

"Marion!"

Bony began to think the girl would never speak. Then quickly she stood up and, whilst looking at him, said:

"Yes, Mrs Poulton. What is it?"

"The master is just leaving for the fire. He would like to say good-bye."

"Tell him I will come at once."

They heard Mrs Poulton departing, and, when her steps sounded no more, Marion gazed steadily into Bony's blue eyes, saying:

"Well, will you do what I ask?"

Bony's face was drawn. Had he been white, his complexion would have been whiter than usual. Then:

"You present me with a mental battle," he said slowly. "Leave me here while you farewell old Jeff. You must give me time—indeed you must. You ask of me a hard thing, a far harder thing than you can guess."

And so that she should not see the pain in his eyes he turned away from her, and was but dimly conscious of hearing the door open and close behind her. His feet almost faltering, he reached a chair placed beside a writing-table, and, sinking into it, covered his face with his hands, his head falling forward, his elbows resting on his knees.

If ever a man was impaled on the horns of a dilemma, Bony then was that man. The tip of one horn represented pride; the tip of the other, a fierce admiration for the pure and the beautiful.

Pride! Yes, pride in achievement. He had been born with the white man's blood in him and, as is sometimes the case, a skin as white as his father's. From an early age he had felt his superiority over the other little boys at the mission station, most of whom were black, or of that dark putty colour there is no mistaking. At eighteen years of age he had fallen in love with a girl at the high school both attended. Life and the passion of life were opening to him as a flower-bud will open, and he revelled in his power to make the girl love him.

With the inevitability of fate his long-dead black mother claimed him from the grave, claimed him and held him. He was bathing with several companions one afternoon, and one of them remarked how peculiar it was that his legs were darker in colour than the upper part of his body. The horror, the agony, which succeeded that afternoon! The realization, the knowledge that, after all, when he had been so certain that the black strain in him would never show, it was at last asserting itself!

His soul in torment, he told the girl of his mixed ancestry. At first she would not believe it. To her honour, however, she clung to him for a year; but at last, when the colour mark had crept up his body and reached his face, she had to believe. Even so she would have married Bony, had he permitted it.

But Bony put her from him. The act cut out of his life temporarily all the joys of youth save one, and that one the joy of knowledge. Yet always was he acutely aware of his inferiority to the full-blooded white man. He strove and excelled the white man in one thing: knowledge; he equalled the white man in one other thing: personal honour.

The hereditary influences that had battled for him ever since his early manhood wearied him at times to the point of exhaustion. He seemed never to escape them, never to be free from them. He had so wanted to become a great scholar, had so dreamed of becoming a famous Australian; and, when the call of his mother, and through her the call of the vast bushlands, clashed within his soul, he knew his ambitions to be but dreams, and his dreams the epic of absurdity.

His mental gifts and natural faculties, plus fortuitous circumstances, led him into police circles. The life of a detective, especially one specializing in bush crimes, suited his complex racial make-up, and to this calling he had given his talents gladly, and lived for it and of it. The white man's ambition denied him, the black man's life repugnant to his finer instincts, there was but one thing left. Pride of achievement, pride of success, the joys of mental victories. His tremendous vanity was bred from his absolute immunity from failure. Never had he failed at a case entrusted to him, and in consequence he sat in the seats of the supermen.

And now this! For the first time since he had renounced the love of his youthful sweetheart he had met a white woman who never had looked down on him from a higher plane, who aroused in him the ecstasy of the worshipper of beauty, who had made him forget his inferior birth and status, and who recognized unreservedly his spiritual superiority. Knowing not who he was, she had besought him to fail in a case, had urged a service that would mean but one thing. And that thing was that his chiefs would know he was as other men, as other men who sometimes failed.

There was the torturing point of these two horns drawn together into one. This case of the missing Marks was all but complete. It was the deepest mystery he had ever had to unravel. It revealed almost the perfect crime. He was morally certain that he would complete this case as he had completed all others. Yet, knowing that, and because of Marion Stanton, was he to go back to Headquarters in Sydney and admit failure, and then on to Colonel Spender, in Brisbane, and admit to him as well that he had failed? Easily could be visualize the Chief Commissioner's expression of astonishment, of disbelief, and finally the look of disillusionment deep in the fierce grey-blue eyes.

Failure! What a word to include in his vocabulary!

If he allowed Dash to escape, it meant that Dot also would escape. Should he drop the case against Dash, it meant he would have to drop the case against his partner and that third man whom Ludbi had seen fighting with Marks in the runaway car. There was no way of saving only Dash. There was no way out for him, Bony. There was no loophole of escape for him from his plighted word that he would do anything for the white goddess to whom his spirit went out in worship.

When his hands fell from his face and he held up his head to gaze vacantly on the littered writing-table, beads of perspiration gathered on his fine forehead. His shoulders drooped as though the load he bore was beyond human strength to carry. And, whilst sitting thus, his eyes rested on a sheaf of letters filed on a long, straight wire with a wooden base.

In spite of his mental preoccupation he could not but be interested by the fact that this table belonged to a woman so methodical that her business letters were kept for possible reference. There must have been fully thirty of these letters bunched on that wire file, and almost at the bottom the edge of one stood out a little from those above, and there was revealed to him in block letters the name of an Adelaide firm of jewellers.

For some while he stared at it uncomprehendingly, and then words formed at the back, as it were, of the thoughts filling his mind, words that became joined as the links of a chain. Almost without conscious volition he reached forward, pulled the file towards him, slipped up the covering mass of letters and read the letter from the jewellers. Then was the cup of his anguish filled to the brim, for there beneath his eyes was the proof that was the corner-stone of the structure he had raised from the past with fine red sand.

If only he had known the direction of his drift! If only he had known, he could have steeled himself against the dark-haired, wonderful white woman with the magnetic personality. If—if he had but known at the very beginning the riddle of Dash leaving his position as jackeroo to become a trapper, at which he now shrewdly guessed! If he could have known this and have had reasonable ground to suspect what the jewellers' letter contained, he could have thrown up the case much earlier and retired with honour.

But there were those letters to Sydney asking for vital information; there was the sending there of the small silver disk; there was lastly and not least his orders that Illawalli be brought down from the far north of Queensland. How now to explain all that without admitting failure? How at this stage could he countermand the order to Sergeant Morris regarding the arrest of Dot and Dash?

The other point of view he did not then remember. It was not till later that he thought of his duty to the service to which he belonged, his duty to the majesty of justice. For, after all, the man Marks had been murdered, and his murderer still lived. To lay down his cards, to put before his superiors the complete chain of proofs—wanting but the body of Marks—would mean striking down the woman he had come to revere, to whom he had given his word that for her he would do anything.

So preoccupied was his mind that he was utterly unconscious of removing from the file the jewellers' letter, as he was unconscious of hearing Jeff Stanton's great car go purring off into the night. So preoccupied was he that he did not hear the door of the room open and close, and did not see Marion Stanton until she stood directly before him.

"Bony—why are you so troubled over the little thing I have asked of you?" she said with a frown.

He stood up and gazed deeply into her eyes, so deeply that she became uneasy, not with fear of him, but because she saw that in his face which reminded her of pictures of St Joan of Arc tied to a stake, and of King Charles standing beside the headsman's block. It was a look that indicated renunciation, or sacrifice.

"I am no longer troubled," he told her with a smile she saw was forced. "I promised to do anything for you, and you have asked me to do that something. I will do it. But how I wish I had known you loved this man Dash!"

"Why—why?" Once more he saw the blood dye her cheeks and, guessing rightly what was in her mind, hastened to correct her.

"To me, Miss Stanton, you have been most kind," he said, and would have taken her hands had not she drawn back. "You have been kind in a way which no white woman has been before. To use a well-worn phrase, yet one very apt, you have stooped to conquer. From an Olympian height you have bent down to one in the mire, and my feeling for you has more of spirituality in it than of earth. I rejoice that you love this man, who is so well known and respected as Dash, the partner of Dot; and not only will I see that he does not fall into the hands of the police, but I will also guarantee to restore him to you."

"You will? Oh, Bony, tell me, tell me how?"

"That is a question which one day he himself will be able to answer. Then you will understand how it is that now I am unable to explain. I am reminded of a task I must perform at once. Immediately afterwards I will go after him and bring him back."

"You will, Bony—true?"

"As sure as that I shall be lectured by your father for missing the truck," he said, with his old smile back once more. "There is, however, a little matter I would like you to explain, if you would be so generous."

"What is that?"

"Tell me how it was Dash became a trapper."

And without hesitation she explained the one battle she had lost to old Jeff: how, in spite of the harshness of his decision, she had seen its justice and its far-sightedness.

"The probationary period is over to-day, Bony," she said softly, "and instead of welcoming him here, I had to warn him about Sergeant Morris. Oh, what could he have done, Bony? Nothing, nothing dishonourable, I am sure."

"I, too, have grounds for assurance that it was nothing dis-honourable," he cried, with a smile of dawning comprehension, as one who sees a light after a long period of darkness. "Ah, all is clear now. I see—I see!"

"See! What do you see?"

But she saw the growing light of triumph fade from his blue eyes, saw it replaced by an expression of hopelessness, and then again by his old gaiety. It was all so swift that she failed then to analyse these expressions, and said again swiftly:

"What is it you see?"

For the second time he made to take her hands, and this time she permitted him to succeed. In the dim light cast by the shaded lamp she saw his face as it was ever to remain in her mind. His teeth flashed in a laugh, gentle and cultured.

"I see," he said, quite slowly, "I see that I shall have to get you a wedding present. I will get it to-night."

And, before she could say a further word, he had bowed with old-world grace and left her—left her wondering wherever he had learned to bow like that.

Chapter Forty-one

Young Men and Young Ladies

IF MRS THOMAS's outstanding vice was a susceptibility to alcohol, doubtless acquired in the course of "working up" hotel business, she had never permitted it to loosen her tongue regarding matters of business concern. It was a mental make-up of which she was proud. Her body was so inured to the stimulant that it required a very great deal of it in a short space of time to reduce her to the condition vulgarly known as being drunk. She was drunk the night Father Ryan called for volunteers to go with him to Windee, which is to say that she reached the stage when to weep was far easier than to laugh. This being the first time she had reached this stage during her sojourn at Mr Bumpus's hotel, it fell to Mrs Bumpus to decline to serve her with more, and at first persuade, then command, the guest to go to bed.

Mrs Bumpus, however, was not a woman who could command with assurance of being obeyed. Had she continued her persuasion she might have won the unequal battle, for it was humanly possible to persuade Mrs Thomas, but humanly impossible to exact obedience, especially when she had arrived at the weeping stage, which occurs about midway between sobriety and utter stupor.

Mrs Thomas wept loudly and without ceasing, and told Mrs Bumpus that she would continue to weep even more loudly if she, Mrs Bumpus, refused further to serve her with a drop, just a little drop, of brandy. However, on the point of brandy Mrs Bumpus was firm, and her guest was forced to swallow small glasses of bottled beer, with long intervals between glasses. Mrs Thomas was seated on the barrel at the farther end of the bar-counter, crying softly now, and Mrs Bumpus was glaring at the clock on the wall every half-minute and making up her mind, ever more firmly, to give Bumpus the very devil for leaving her there with that terrible woman.

The two ladies had the bar to themselves for over an hour, a seemingly endless hour for Mrs Bumpus. At half-past eight Sergeant Morris came in to inquire if Fred Slater was about, and, since Mrs Thomas said never a word whilst he was present, he did not interfere with her enjoyment, but left in search of the desired Slater and his car. Half an hour after that, when Mrs Bumpus was preparing to shut the door, eject Mrs Thomas with the help of the yardman if necessary, and close the bar, she heard her husband's car coming bumping along the miniature hills and valleys forming the main thoroughfare of the town. She knew it was his car because of the metallic screech made by a loosened mudguard.

The car stopped before the front entrance for precisely two seconds, and then was driven round into the shed in the yard behind the building. After a further thirty seconds her husband appeared behind the counter.

"Back at last!" he said, cheerfully snatching up a glass and swooping down on the bag-covered bottles of beer.

"'Bout time, too! I'm sick of this, Bumpus," snapped his lady. "It's gone time and the sergeant's in town, so close up and let's get to bed while there's a chance of a night's rest."

"You can go on, Ethel," Bumpus said after he had drunk and sighed with ineffable satisfaction. "That half-caste fellow Bony came in with me from Windee. Says he's got a cheque and is goin' ter spend it."

"Give me a drink, Bumpus," demanded Mrs Thomas, fumbling with her handbag.

Surveying her, Bumpus was on the verge of refusing, but just before then he had been examining the contents of the till. It had been a poor evening financially. And Mrs Thomas threw down before him a florin.

"What'll you 'ave, Mrs Thomas?" he asked familiarly.

"Brandy and soda, quick! I been drinking coloured water. Your missus got no idea of running a pub, 'deed she hasn't. Have one yourself."

Mrs Bumpus vanished, leaving with her husband an impression that she would deal out the beans later, probably when he was comfortably tired and was about to fall asleep. He and his guest were toasting each other for the second time, when Bony entered the bar and, after one swift glance round, smiled broadly, glanced at the clock, and closed and bolted the public entrance. Then:

"Good evening, Mrs Thomas! I thought you were spending Christmas at Windee."

Mrs Thomas sat up more regally on her barrel, regarded Bony with slightly bemused eyes, and, without pause between words, said in welcome:

"Good—evening—Mister—couldn't—stick—Windee—girl—stuck-up—ole—man—always—grumbling—no—comfort—come—here—for—merry—Christmas—have—a—drink—with—me."

"With pleasure," accepted Bony, walking to that end of the bar which appeared to have become Mrs Thomas's favourite corner. "A glass of beer, please."

"Brandy 'n' soda—haveoneyourself."

With laughing good humour Bony drank, and ordered the glasses to be re-filled. He laughed gaily at and with the suddenly rejuvenated Mrs Thomas, and noted with satisfaction that the task he had set himself would not be nearly so difficult as he had expected. For be it noted that he had come to Mount Lion with the intention of getting Mrs Thomas very drunk.

He now beheld Mrs Thomas already very drunk. He observed, too, with interest, that Mrs Thomas, although very drunk, could speak distinctly and knew what she was about when producing money from her handbag. Without her hat, with the marks of tears running vertically down her powdered and rouged cheeks, swaying slightly on her barrel, the woman presented a striking contrast to her appearance on the first occasion he had beheld her. A drunken man is a disgusting sight; a drunken woman is a tragic one.

Still, Bony had his plans. He drank beer and Mrs Thomas drank brandy but whereas Mrs Thomas drank to the last drop, Bony drained most of his into the long trough of sawdust at the foot of the counter. And whilst he drank and slyly wasted his liquor, and "shouted" and watched Mrs Thomas drink, he marvelled at the command she retained of her speech, even as he marvelled to see by perceptible degrees her eyelids become heavier. It was to him a fresh manifestation of the effects of alcohol on the human brain—a subject that interested him both scientifically and professionally.

Finally the point was reached when no longer could Mrs Thomas keep open her eyes, although her mind was still active and her speech clear and sensible.

"Well, what about bed?" inquired Mr Bumpus yawning.

"The word has a good sound," Bony agreed. "What's my room?"

"Number four."

"Good! Now, Mrs Thomas, permit me to escort you to yours," Bony murmured gallantly.

"All right! Give us a Doch and Doris, Bumpus, and a half-bottle for the morning," and Mrs Thomas fumbled blindly in her bag and produced a pound note. She held out her right hand gropingly, and Bony placed the full glass within the clutching fingers. She drank with her eyes shut.

"That will do me," Bony said colloquially. "My arm, Mrs Thomas. What number is your room?"

"Seven, Mister Bony. Seven it is. Where's me reviver?"

"I have it here safe."

"Righto! Good night, Bumpus! You're all right, but missus, missus no business woman. Yes, I mind the step. Got me reviver? Yes? Blessed dark—can't see a dratted thing!"

Raising the flap in the counter-top, Mr Bumpus winked at Bony in a manner supposed to be devilish significant; and Bony, pretending to be slightly muddled, winked back quite in the generally approved manner.

Although she stated that the world was drattedly dark, Mrs Thomas came to be aware of the darkness of the passage leading to the bedrooms. In a tone of voice startlingly like that of a girl of seventeen, she giggled, and Mrs Bumpus, lying awake in her bed, heard her say:

"Only to my door, Mister Bony. Young men only escort young ladies to their doors. Ah, naughty young man! Well, if you must, just one!" And, to Bony's horror, she made a loud sound with her mouth indicative of kissing.

Too busy in the bar counting the day's takings, Mr Bumpus failed to light his guests to their rooms, so that with his free hand Bony was obliged to strike a match to find room No. 7. Fortunately they stood outside it at that moment.

"Bed! Lead me to it, Mister Bony," commanded the astonishing woman. "You brought my reviver? Good! Set it on the table with a glass so that I'll find it in the morning." Bony had got her to the bed. She felt for it with her hands and rolled forward on it. "Good night, dear friend!" she cried. "Well, if you must, just one," and again she made that most suggestive sound.

Bony fled, feeling hot all about his ears, but he withdrew and pocketed the key before he closed the door loudly. And a second or so later his own door closed as loudly.

He gave the inmates of the hotel two hours to fall asleep, and at the end of the third hour he had discovered the confession of one Fred Sims relative to a dead baby being buried by Joseph North.

At seven in the morning he was interviewing Sergeant Morris, and after cunning argument got that official to countermand the order for the arrest of Dot and Dash. Sergeant Morris was also persuaded that Mrs Thomas was an undesirable visitor to Mount Lion, and that her departure by the mail-car which left at ten-thirty that morning would be of service to her.

Chapter Forty-two

Bony—and a Map

BONY HAD ARRIVED at Mount Lion just when Sergeant Morris was about to leave for Windee in Fred Slater's car. He had then informed the official that the arrest of Dot and Dash was of no further importance to his plans, and that he would explain how that came to be in the morning. By no means satisfied, Sergeant Morris had yet given up the prospect of a long night's work with a thankfulness he did not admit openly even to himself.

Bony's explanation, tendered the following morning, was not fully satisfying. He promised, however, to reveal more in the immediate future. He had yet to deal with the inevitable difficulties of disclosing not what really happened, but what was supposed to have happened. Without waiting for Mrs Bumpus to rise and cook breakfast, and declining with thanks Sergeant Morris's hospitality, he left for Windee in Slater's car, arriving at the homestead about eight o'clock.

Here he found one of the four men brought out by Father Ryan temporarily installed as cook. The four men were eating breakfast in the homestead kitchen, and Father Ryan, Marion, and Mrs Poulton were at theirs in the dining-room. The previous evening it had been arranged that Slater should take the four men and Father Ryan out to the scene of the fire.

Breakfast over, the little priest came into the kitchen with Marion Stanton and jovially inquired if everyone was ready.

"You go on, Father. I shall be riding a hack," Bony said.

"All right," nodded Father Ryan, and after au revoirs to the women he and his pressed volunteers were carried off by Slater.

"Now, Miss Marion, if you will give me a few moments, there is something I want to say," Bony stated smilingly.

"Very well. Let us go to the office."

There he said:

"Permit me to be seated at this desk for a minute, will you?" and, Marion consenting, he wrote rapidly some fifty words on a sheet of block paper, folded it, placed with it the paper he had stolen from Mrs Thomas and the jewellers' letter, sealed the papers in an envelope, sealed the envelope with red wax, and wrote on the envelope: *To be opened on the morning Miss Marion Stanton is married. Bony's wedding present.*

Rising to his feet, he approached her and gave the envelope into her hands. For a little while she was silent, reading and re-reading what he had written on it. Then, suddenly looking up, she saw him regarding her with laughter in his eyes.

"Bony—this is not a joke, Bony, is it?" she asked perplexedly.

"Well, no. It is not"—confidentially. "You will remember that recently you asked my advice about a certain trouble which had befallen your father and you. The sooner you become married the quicker will the load of worry be lifted from your father's shoulders, and consequently from your own. The jack that will lift the load is contained in that envelope, but you are not to use it until the day you are to be married."

"It is all very strange. But how am I to get married when my—when Dash is being hunted? Oh, why all this mystery? We seem surrounded by mystery. There is mystery about you, too."

"Well, well, it will not long remain so, Miss Stanton," Bony cried. "I have already lifted the shadow a little. Mrs Thomas is leaving Mount Lion by the mail coach this morning. Sergeant Morris has discovered that, after all, he has no grounds for arresting Dot and Dash. And now I want you to loan me Grey Cloud."

"Loan you Grey Cloud? Why?"

"Because he is the fastest horse in the western district of New South Wales."

"Yes—but why?"

"Because the faster the horse I ride the quicker I shall catch up with Dot and Dash. And the sooner I catch up with Dot and Dash—well, the sooner you will be able to open that envelope."

"Bony, what are you?"

He saw the trouble and the wonder in her steady, cool grey eyes; saw, too, how the corners of her mouth trembled a little. Her breathing was more rapid than normally, and her fingers played about the envelope they held as though she were lost in the darkness and sought for the light. Looking at her, Bony felt no qualms now at the hard path he had chosen to tread, for he knew then, as he had known all along, that she regarded him as of her own colour, and was not that a salve to his bruised soul?

"Bony, what are you?"

At the repetition of her question he chose, wilfully, to misunderstand her. His eyes clouded as ever they did when he remembered or was reminded of what he was.

"Just a poor half-caste, Miss Stanton—a breaker of horses and a builder of stockyards," and, seeing the protest rush into her eyes, he added swiftly: "Have you any news this morning of the progress of the fire?"

"Very little, Bony. Father rang up this morning and said that it looked terrific, and that they all were engaged in burning a break, excepting the riders who are mustering the sheep in all the paddocks near it."

"Have they seen anything of Dot and Dash?"

"Yes. They reached Carr's Tank late last evening and took two of Ned Swallow's horses, saying that Dad had sent them out. Ned Swallow said, too, that they went off south."

"Ah! And what did old Jeff say about Bony?"

"I'd—I'd rather not repeat his words"—and Marion laughed for the first time that day.

"They would be forcible; they certainly would," Bony chuckled. "Now where precisely is this Carr's Tank ? Are there any maps of the country here?"

"Yes. This one on the wall is a large-scale map of the district."

Side by side they stood examining the huge map. Marion pointed out Carr's Tank, and, seeing a box of assorted coloured pins, Bony marked the place with a red one. Just for an instant he re-studied the map, then suddenly he emptied the pins out on a near-by table, and, in a tone of voice she never had heard him use before, he said:

"Pick me out all the red pins—quickly, please."

As fast as she sorted and handed the pins asked for he stuck them here and there over the map, until at last he stopped and stood back.

"Here we have marked all the waters north, west and south of Carr's Tank," he murmured, so softly that the change in his tone was startling. He appeared lost in the maze of a problem of his own making. "Water, Miss Marion, is the source of all life. It is the main element that permits man to live; yes, and horses and sheep and rabbits, even the little wagtail birds. Now, of the two men, Dot is the experienced bushman. He was born in Arizona, a country of wild open spaces. He has spent years in Central Australia. He is an experienced gold-prospector, for the dolly-pot in the blacksmith's shop is his. Probably, nay logically, he has prospected for gold in the Mount Brown district, and he knows the Rufus country, extending westwards from Mount Brown far out into South Australia. Yes. He would know the country. But, it is reported they went south from Carr's Tank. Ah, foolish, foolish Mr Dot! Little mistakes lead to great falls. Had you told Swallow, for doubtless Swallow tells the tale, that you were heading to the north-east towards Mount Brown and the hilly scrub country thereabouts, you would have been wiser. In which case, had you truthfully desired to go there, you would have gone on to Nullawil. Instead, you turned south to Carr's Tank from Range Hut. But from there you will go west—west and then north-west. For southward lies the more settled pastoral country. Well, well, well!"

For five long minutes he was silently engrossed by the map. Marion sought to read his thoughts, but failed. He stood there as a man of stone, but when presently he sighed and turned to her the whole of that vast region of sand and scrub, gibber plain and hill ranges was transferred to his brain like a photographic print.

"That map is of great help, Miss Stanton," he said smoothly. "Permit me now to go out and catch Grey Cloud. In the interim, will you kindly ask Mrs Poulton to put up a little bread and meat, five or six pounds of flour, and small quantities of tea and sugar, into a sugar-sack? Get me also two tins of tobacco and a packet of cigarette papers."

"You are going now?"

"At once. Every delay of a minute means the postponement of the day you open that envelope."

Then he was gone, almost running, and for a little while she stood still, fear that had no foundation writhing in her heart.

Grey Cloud was in a horse-paddock, and it took Bony fully thirty minutes to find and saddle him. Preoccupied, he nodded his thanks for the filled sugar-bag, which he strapped to the pommel of the saddle whilst the gelding fidgeted his surprise at not receiving the usual caresses from the man he had come to trust and love.

A few seconds, and Bony was ready, the embodiment of human resource, dependability, and untiring stamina. Lithe of figure, dressed in white shirt, open-necked and sleeve-rolled, almost skintight grey moleskin trousers, elastic-sided high-heeled riding boots, and wearing on his head nothing but its natural covering, he but increased her wonder at him. And then she saw his dark face light up with his never-to-be-forgotten smile.

"To the west of Windee lies the station owned by Mr Freeman?" he questioned.

"Yes," Marion answered.

"Did your father say if any of Mr Freeman's hands were helping him at the fire?"

"He said he was expecting them. Wondered why they had not turned up, as he had telephoned via Mount Lion telling Mr Freeman about the fire."

"Thank you! I think now I am fully conversant with the situation," he told her gaily. "Do not worry any more. I shall easily catch up to Dot and Dash, and then we shall be able to put the fairy-tale ending to all this hurry and strife and mystery." He seemed to float up into the air and come to rest on the gelding's back with no more shock than a feather. He saw her looking up at him with misty eyes, and laughed down at her with dazzling teeth and gleaming blue orbs. "I saw Runta just now," he cried. "She looked—well, she looked superb in her new yellow frock with the purple spots." And then he was gone, wiped out of her vision by a cloud of red dust.

Chapter Forty-three

Bony Reaches Carr's Tank

EXCEPTING TO DISMOUNT to tie down the wire of a fence with his belt to permit Grey Cloud to step over, horse and rider did not take a "blow" until they stood on the Range Hut track where it began to dip down and round a hill spur to the flat country where lay Carr's Tank. There, in the shade of a stunted mulga tree, Bony dropped the reins on the ground, whereupon the gelding would not move, and, seating himself on a flat stone, smoked a cigarette.

Although the fire lay four miles from him at its nearest point, everything beyond two of those miles lay hidden by the smoke, which seemed only to thin into an even, motionless fog but half a mile from the hills. The sting of it made his eyes smart; the faintly sweet smell of it almost rivalled that of his dwindling cigarette.

Mounted again, he rode at a walking pace down the steep hill track, and continued this slow pace when he reached the plain and skirted the south fence of the horse-paddock, which led in a straight line to the hut. Arrived there, he unsaddled, took the horse to one of the water-troughs near the mill, returned, hobbled the animal, and let him loose in the horse-paddock.

Within the hut he found confusion enthroned. The table was littered with used eating utensils, the fireplace contained a great mound of glowing white ash, with the ruddy gleam of red-hot embers peering through the cracks. A saddle was thrown into one corner, and a man's rolled swag lay in another. Paper littered the earthen floor, and the story plainly to be read there was of the hurried visits of men for a meal and their hurried departure. Such a visitor came whilst Bony ate cold roast mutton and damper, and drank scalding hot tea.

"Cripes! It's you, Bony!" Jack Withers exclaimed, wiping his face with a hairy forearm. "Where the 'ell 'ave you bin? Ole Jeff's callin' yous a double-damned quitter, et cetera, et cetera."

"Very important business detained me," the smiling Bony said in excuse.

For a seemingly long while Withers regarded the half-caste solemnly. Then slowly his left eyelid closed over the eye that looked out through the door, and his mouth widened in a grin. "'Ow's Runta?" he asked.

"She looked stunning in her new dress," replied Bony.

"She'd look stunning 'id be'ind a fig-leaf."

"I believe she would," Bony agreed blandly, inwardly wincing. "How is the fire going?"

"Oh, as well as can be expected, Bony. No worse nor better than other fires. We stopped 'er at the fence wot runs west of the well. Me and the Stormbird and Combo Joe is a-battling with it in the south-west corner, but it's creeping west and north-west against the breeze. Orl the mob an' Jeff is away north of here, burning breaks east of the roar. They tell me the Pardray is boiling the billies and orf-siding to Alf the Nark." Withers cut himself a meal, and with it held in his smoke-grimed hands slid to the floor for a seat and began to eat ravenously. "Me," he added gravely, "I ain't never 'ad no religion, but if Father Ryan ever should lead a rescuin' mob into 'ell, I'll be game to foller 'em."

For a while they ate in silence. Then:

"Dot and Dash get away?" inquired Bony.

Again the slow grin stretched Jack Withers's mouth.

"Nobody ain't put up no argument with 'em yet, and to all appearances nobody ain't goin' to. They left at eight sharp last night, and towards eleven last night the trooper and ole Moon-galliti and Warn shows up. The trooper came in this 'ut for a feed and the nigs 'ad theirs outside. Me and Combo Joe got together—happened to be 'ere for two hours' sleep—and when I finds he never give orl his money to Bumpus, I borrowed two quid orf 'im and a pound of bacco orf Ned Swallow, and give the money and the bacco to the nigs to go along up to Father Ryan and tell 'im they was sent for a pannikin of tea. Out comes the trooper, and there's no black trackers. He's gorn man-hunting all on 'is own. Went south. If 'e keeps goin' 'e'll 'it Broken Hill."

"Perhaps he will find Dot and Dash there."

"He might their shadders, but they'll be sunrise shadders stretching to Broken Hill from Darwin."

"Any of Freeman's men come along to lend a hand?"

"Nope. That is, only one bloke sent with a message to old Jeff saying as 'ow they 'ave got a nice little fire of their own."

"Ah!"

"Yes. Seems to 'ave started beyond their north-west boundary, and orl Freeman's men went out to burn a fire-break along there to save the run. If the wind freshens from the west to-morrow morning, their fire will sweep up against ours at its north end and give us a frontage to fight of fifty miles, maybe a 'undred miles, maybe two 'undred. There ain't been a better year for a fire since nineteen-nine."

"I suppose Dot and Dash didn't say where they were making for?" Bony asked persuasively.

"No, they didn't. Dot 'ud be too fly for that. 'E is a good bush-man, Dot. But I don't envy 'em with these fires about. With a gale of wind to-morrow, starting from the north-west and endin' in the south, they'll be nipped unless mighty careful. What are you goin' to do? Come out and give me an' the Stormbird an' Combo a 'and! Ron left us a tank of water and three bags of chaff."

For a little while Bony was silent. He was acutely conscious of the fact that the partners then had some twenty hours' start. But he had ridden far that day, and, since Grey Cloud would have many more days of hard riding, it was essential he should be rested and fed. A further point that induced Bony to decide to fall in with Withers's suggestion was that there remained but an hour and a half of daylight. He could do nothing for six hours at least. By then it would be very dark, for the smoke would blot out the stars. He could not hope to find the partners' tracks until next day. An hour later he and Withers were riding slowly to join the Stormbird and Combo Joe in the battle with the fire.

Chapter Forty-four

Dante's Undreamed Inferno

To RIDE ALONG THE FENCE that marked the southern extremity of the Windee fire was as though they rode along the outskirts of a great city hidden by the darkness but pointed by its tens of thousands of lights and its flaming sky-signs. Just north of the fence and for some four miles' distance the army of fire-fighters under the leadership of the indomitable Stanton had started little fires which were afterwards beaten out, so that a broad ribbon of grass was burned to ash and presented an impassable barrier to the main fire that a few hours later swept upon it.

Thousands of acres of knee-high grass had vanished, but the burning grass had fired twigs, sticks, and branches fallen from the parent trees during several years, and these, together with dead trees still standing, created a greater heat that fired the pine- and belar trees and scorched and shrivelled the hardy non-resinous mulgas. A hundred million torches, from the great pillars of flame consuming the pine-trees, down to the tiny last flares of dead and fallen branches, turned the steadily rising smoke into lurid horror. From this inferno came an incessant fusillade of reports in all degrees of volume and many qualities of tone. Uprising through the crimson pall, universe after universe of stars rushed into oblivion, as though the gods, stooping to gather handfuls of worlds flung them up in the delirium of their power. Thousands upon thousands, two hundred thousand acres of scrub and wheat-like grass, were disintegrating, turning into those upward-rushing, vanishing universes and the vast low-hanging crimson cloud.

Bony and his companion rode parallel with the fence, but some five hundred yards south of it, so great still was the heat of the fire. When four miles due west of the dam and mill, they came to a right-angle in the fire-break, and, seeing there that the fence was cut, they too made the angle and rode north.

Here the air was comparatively cool, the wind coming from a little north of west, a zephyr breeze that yet smelled of the incense sent up by grass and green leaves. The angle they traversed represented the south-west point where the fire had been stopped. For two miles the break, marked clearly by the edge of the knee-high grass, ran due north, but then it began to curve westward, and Bony saw that at this place the fire had met the fire-fighters, and thenceforward the fire-fighters had been forced slowly back.

So dry was the grass, so dry the air, that the fire moved slowly against the little wind there was. To east and north, seven or eight miles through and beyond the inferno, the main body of firefighters were burning long ribbons of fire-breaks, two men here, three and four north, one or two south, precisely as a battalion of infantry strung out in a long line and ordered to dig in, the isolated parties eventually to link up in one long line of entrenchments.

Under the generalship of old Jeff Stanton, already that line stretched to magical lengths. Truck-loads of men were rushed up and down, widening and lengthening it, striving to the limit of human endurance to make of it a great Hindenburg line, impregnable to the fire advancing on it then as fast as an athlete can run.

Man was forced to become elemental in a battle with the fiercest element. At such moments the soul is glimpsed. Among this small body of men was no thought of wages, of strikes, of go-slowness. There was no thought of saving a vast area of land and many thousands of sheep for the master, even an admired master. Nor was there any thought of striving to preserve their jobs. The dominating motive was to win, to beat back the fire-devil; and they fought in exactly the same spirit that a university eight rows to win, succumbing to nothing short of sheer exhaustion at the end of the race.

We—in Britain and Australia—have been reproached for our love of sport. It was the elemental love of sport which urged on Jeff Stanton's men until they dropped and were picked up by truck-drivers to be rushed to another place, there to work till they dropped once more. It may have been this spirit that made Father Ryan elect to remain in depopulated Mount Lion. Such a spirit may have actuated old Jeff Stanton to pay good wages and yet make a million. In their diverse ways both these men were deep, deep as the ocean, not raw students but experts in the study of human nature.

Knowing men, bushmen in particular, Bony was equally expert with the squatter and the priest. When he and Jack Withers came on the hundred-gallon galvanized tank and the miniature dump of chaff, and, leaving their horses to eat their fill at a bag trough slung between two trees to which they were tied, proceeded along the edge of the fire, he was by no means surprised to see two devils direct from Dante's Inferno running about purposefully with a flaming billet in one hand and an empty sack in the other.

To the uninitiated their actions would have been childish. It was as though they childishly lit little fires in make-believe imitation of the great fire. Then, seemingly afraid of their little fires, they proceeded to beat them out. Yet they worked with systematic thoroughness. Their little fires laid a swath of black ash twenty feet wide and a bare hundred yards from the main fire, there creeping against the wind as an old man may walk.

Now and then one straightened his back and wiped the running sweat from his eyes with fist or forearm. Their clothes were rent and grimed, the legs of their trousers holed by sparks, their boots being slowly burned off their feet. Their bodies were filthy with perspiration and soot, but the living spirit of these two illiterate chunks of humanity was an inextinguishable, indestructible point of brilliant purity.

"Cripes! Where the ruddy hell 'ave yous been?" one of these "chunks", barely recognizable as the Stormbird, demanded of Withers. "Did yous bring the tea and tucker?"

"My oath!" Jack Withers assured the tall, raw-boned and iron-hard man who invariably raised a fight wherever he went. "We left the tea and the billies and the grub on the tank. Better take a spell, an' me an' Bony 'ull carry on."

"'Bout time too," grunted Combo Joe, who was short and broad, and able to lift a ton-truck clear of bog. "Any one 'ud think this 'ere wus a picnic."

"'Oo's yer lady friend, Jack?"

"This 'ere is Bony, friend of mine," Withers grinned. "This 'ere is Mister Stormbird and Mister Combo Joe"; but never could Bony decide which was which, for upon each was directed one of poor Jack Withers's eyes.

The relieved lurched away and the relief took over. Then followed three hours of such work as made it a period of agony. Bony's arms ached excruciatingly. His eyes smarted and wept water. His throat became parched and sulphuric. He was dimly aware of Withers moving with the seeming tirelessness of a machine, and knew not that to his companion he presented a similar picture. Lit by the flames he created, bathed in the lurid light of the main fire, his brain heated to boiling-point, Bony at last came to regard himself as being the one opponent of the creeping monster always pushing him ahead of itself. It became a malignant personality with a million eyes and a thousand fiery arms, with whom he was engaged in a fight to the death. And such a fight, an endless and unequal battle, for his arms and legs were encased in lead.

"Well, 'ow's she going?"

Bony staggered upright and looked into the face of the Storm-bird with glassy eyes. "Tired!" he wheezed.

"Fat-ee-gu-ing kind-er life," the Stormbird remarked, only between each word was an horrific oath. "'Ere, give us yer bag and fire-stick, and let's see yer run like a two-year-old to the tank where we left yous a couple of billies of tea. Come on, Combo! These blank overgrown children ain't done nothink since we bin gorn. Now watch two men 'ave a go!"

He leered like a gargoyle on Notre Dame. Bony forced a smile. In spite of three hours' rest, the Stormbird was a deadly weary man, but the very pride of his manhood compelled him to hide it as much as possible behind his jeers. Whilst Bony had had only one spell of work, the Stormbird and his partner had had three such spells. It was Combo Joe who set the pace, and, hell and damnation, the Stormbird could keep up with him, "blarst im!"

It was two o'clock in the morning when Withers roused Bony from a fitful sleep, and for another three hours they relieved the others on the treadmill of nightmare. They worked without thought, men governed by one idea, driven by it, each muscle whipped by it. But when they were relieved their walk back to the tank and the horses was almost two miles, and in their ears was the Stormbird's injunction to get a spell, for the wind was veering to the south of west and freshening, and the fire there slowed in its march to the toddling of a small child.

●   ●   ●   ●   ●

Withers awoke to daylight, and to find that Bony had vanished and with him Grey Cloud. Bony had left at dawn. He rode back south to the fence, traversed it westward for three miles, and then turned due north. In this way, if Dot and Dash had gone west or north-west from Carr's Tank, he was bound to cross their horses' tracks. Riding at an easy canter, his body crouched over the gelding's neck, Bony searched the ground a good twenty feet beyond Grey Cloud's head, for it is far easier to distinguish a track a little ahead of one than it is to do so at one's feet.

He cut the partners' tracks seven miles north of the fence, just when he saw that the fire, at this distance from the breaks having mushroomed far to the west, lay ahead of him to force him out of his north-bound path. Once on the tracks, he turned north-west, followed them till they struck the Freeman's Run-Nullawil road, followed them on the road to the State Border Fence, thence for a further five miles, and lost them where the road ran, dimly marked across an iron-hard clay-pan.

He was balked for half an hour before he again discovered the tracks, very, very faint, and saw the ruse Dot had adopted to throw off trackers.

Bony understood then that, not meeting with the expected helpers from Freeman's station, Dot had decided at the clay-pan to muffle their horses' hoofs. It had been done at the sacrifice of each man's single blanket. For the four feet of each horse one blanket had been quartered, and each portion tied about a hoof. After that they had ridden over a large area of clay-pans adjoining each other. They had progressed thus but half a mile when the first hoof-tip penetrated its blanket protection and left its tell-tale mark on the clay-pan for Bony's lynx eyes to detect.

Now, in a generally north-western direction, Bony continued, ever following tracks that became more plain, sometimes espying particles of blue-dyed wool, then a worn strip of blue blanket, and finally brought to the place where the pieces of blanket had been discarded and the men had drunk tea made with water from the canvas bags slung from their horses' necks and secured hard against their chests with a strap looped round the saddle-girths.

It was now noon. Bony followed the example of the pursued. Dismounting, he removed Grey Cloud's saddle and the water-bag hanging from his neck. He urged and succeeded in persuading the animal to roll on a patch of loose deep sand, and then left him to graze at will, the bridle still on his head, the bit slipped from his mouth, but the reins dangling because Bony could not afford to risk losing him.

The detective made and drank his tea without sugar, for sugar is a thirst creator in the heat of late December. He ate nothing, but smoked three successive cigarettes, and allowed his aching body to relax for but thirty minutes.

Again in the saddle, he noted that the wind was very much stronger. The air, too, was blue with smoke that came not from the Windee fire.

Chapter Forty-five

Smoke and Flame

BONY CAME TO THE HUT normally occupied by Dot's old friend, situated on the north boundary of Freeman's Station, shortly after noon. The occupant was not at home, and Bony proceeded to water and feed his horse with chaff found in an outhouse and put the absent tenant's billy on the fire he quickly made inside the hut. Whilst it was coming to the boil the half-caste interestedly glanced round to read what was to be read by all-observant eyes.

There were no blankets on the rough wooden stretcher. The ashes in the fireplace had been cold. There were no dogs chained up outside. Within remained the owner's tucker-box and billy-cans; without there were no canvas water-bags. He had left after, and not before, Dot and Dash had called and gone on, for the tracks Bony had been following were obliterated about the hut by the other tracks of horses and men. Dot's friend evidently was interested in sport and bushrangers, for lying on a shelf were several volumes of the late Nat Gould's works, and quite a miniature library of Australian literature featuring Ned Kelly, Starlight, Morgan, and other eminent law-breakers.

After eating, Bony replenished the gelding's feed-box and slept for four hours. Much refreshed, he ate another meal, watered his horse, placed sufficient chaff in a bag for two light "feeds", mounted a fence, set his horse in a wide arc, and picked up the partners' tracks. It was then five o'clock, and he had left himself approximately three hours of daylight.

Now at a gallop, now at an easy canter, he followed after Dot and Dash with the sureness of a bloodhound. Placed at a disadvantage in that he could not follow tracks in the blackness of night, whereas the night would not prevent the quarry from travelling so long as Dot could see the stars, Bony determined to cover as much ground as possible before the daylight waned and vanished. Arrived at the northern boundary of this run he saw where a deep fire-break had been burned along the east-west fence. Ahead of him, to north and west, lay the vast region of "open country", unsettled, unfenced, uninhabited. Into it had gone Dot and Dash in the middle of summer, when there had been no rain for four months, when even the seemingly permanent water-holes might, when reached, be dust-dry.

On this account the detective had no fear, though the country was strange to him. The partners would travel from water-hole to creek pot-hole, and hill range rock-hole. He would reach those watering-places by simply following their horses' tracks. The possibility of the partners' poisoning the water behind them did not occur to him, for that would be a crime no bushman would commit, no matter how great a felon and how hardly pressed.

That evening the sun sank into a bed of crimson down, sank deeper and deeper, whilst its colour changed rapidly from pale yellow to crimson, from dark red to dark amber before it vanished half an hour before it was timed to reach the horizon. Bony watched it disappear, noted the cloud low-hung in the west, noted, too, how the wind came from that quarter. For another hour he pressed on, and when night fell he had not come to a water-hole, and was obliged to tether Grey Cloud to a tree and offer him chaff slightly dampened from the canvas chest-bag, and the ration poured in a heap at the foot of the tree.

Over his little fire Bony boiled his quart pot and made tea, still taking it without sugar. After eating, he sat on the heels of his boots and smoked cigarette after cigarette, pushing together four sticks whilst the tiny fire consumed them. He sat and tended his fire in the way his mother had done—but not his father, who would have built a fire over which it would have been impossible to crouch.

For several hours he sat thus on his heels, his mind working on the rounding-off of this case he was engaged on. He fitted together the few pieces of the jig-saw puzzle given him by the sands of Windee, and added the remaining pieces fashioned by the magic of his imagination. He knew that his work had been good, that once more he had brilliantly succeeded, triumphed as never before had he triumphed; for had he not built a splendid mansion with a few bricks he had made without straw?

And the mansion he had built was never to be seen by men who expected to see it! He was to deny its very existence; further, he was to swear he never had erected it. He was to see men's eyes cloud with cynicism, watch men's lips curl in unuttered gibes, thinking they saw the great Detective-Inspector Napoleon Bonaparte, the favourite of the men on top—the favourite, too, of the fickle god, Luck—brought down to their level by failure. And this was to be because of a woman's beauty, both physical and spiritual, which acted on his scarred soul in a way no white man possibly could understand.

Even so, he did not repent his determination to follow his chosen path. Dereliction of duty, service to justice, was strangely absent from his reflections. He did not think, when he decided to hide his mansion, that he would frustrate the almost universal law of retribution, making himself thereby an accessory to murder, and the accomplice of a murderer.

He was thinking of Marion Stanton, and recalling the inward light that radiated from her, when he sank backward on the ground and fell asleep. The labour of the fire-fighting yet held its effects on his body and, for him, he slept soundly. He did not hear the slow-paced rhythmic thud—thud—thud whilst kangaroos sped by him in tireless twelve-foot jumps. He was unaware of the dingo that came and sniffed at him but a few yards distant, and then faded away in the eastern blackness. Grey Cloud both saw and heard kangaroos, dingo, and several foxes passing eastward, and he fidgeted because his eyes began to smart and his nostrils were tickled by smoke. The awakening fear animating the wild things, instinct making them flee rather than tangible evidence of the thing that reddened the western sky, became transferred to Grey Cloud. Several times he snorted and tested the neck-rope. Why did that man tarry when other living things ran? Why was it this two-legged god lay inert on the ground here in a land where Fear was stepping into its dread kingdom? At last Grey Cloud could bear it no longer: he whinnied long and loud.

Lying on his back, Bony awoke without other movement than opening his eyes. The stars he looked for were invisible, and sleepily he was wondering if this indicated rain, when his horse whinnied again. Bony sat up and, doing so, faced west. He could see the stark outlines of bush and tree, the trunks hidden, the branches forming a silhouette of domes and towers, spires and masts, and the filigree-work of giants, held against a background of vivid scarlet that gradually faded towards the zenith of the sky. The smoke-laden air was the colour of old port.

And the wind blew on his face direct from the west, a steady wind, stronger than it had been for many days.

Now on his feet, Bony examined the conflagration that he knew was sweeping towards him as fast as a horse could gallop. To his credit, he weighed his chances of escape whilst he drank the remainder of the tea in the quart pot and with long flexible fingers rolled a cigarette.

A probable twenty-five miles lay between him and the hut tenanted by Dot's friend. There lay safety, for about the hut the land was free from grass, as to a greater extent it was free about the wells and tanks of Windee. It was quite possible for the fire to cut him off before he could reach it, and drive him eastward, where he would surely meet the slowly westward-creeping Windee fire.

On the other hand, somewhere north of him—indicated by the map in Jeff Stanton's office—lay a great gibber-stone plain where the sparse grasses and stunted bush would not feed the advancing fire. How far north was that plain he did not precisely know, for when he examined the map he memorized chiefly the station watering-places. Anyway, Dot and Dash were riding north of him, and he had promised Marion Stanton to bring back Dash.

Two minutes later he was astride Grey Cloud, headed into the trackless, uncharted north lands. The fire-reflecting sky revealed the earth as though seen through dark-red tinted spectacles; it showed, too, the fleeing forms of many animals and sometimes the upright figure of a rabbit observing all this disturbance with wondering eyes which reflected the scarlet glow.

Unable now to follow the partners' tracks, Bony rode a little east of north, rode at an easy loping canter, as though he were giving Grey Cloud gentle exercise. Even when the sting of the smoke noticeably increased he refrained from urging the horse to greater speed. Once they crossed a clay-pan measuring an acre in extent, and he was tempted for a moment to dismount on that area of bare ground and await the coming and the passage of the fire-demon. On foot he would gladly have availed himself of this slender chance; but the fiery onslaught, he was sure, would prove too much for Grey Cloud, who would become unmanageable, would bolt away and meet his doom.

When the dawn penetrated the smoke pall, paled its terrifying colour and painted it warship grey, Bony now and then could see between the trees the tips of high-flung flame in the far distance. The horse was going like a machine, but his breathing was taxed and the steady pace was beginning to tell at last.

Direction was no more ascertainable now than it had been in the starless darkness of early morning. Bony trusted implicitly to his bushman's sixth sense, and when finally the sun penetrated the smoke pall, appearing in colour as it had done when last he had seen it, he found he was heading only a degree or two west of north.

He kept Grey Cloud's head pointing in that direction, riding for a further half-hour, when the outward appearance of the gelding and the inward hint of sluggishness decided him on a "blow". Pulling up his animal, he removed the saddle, rubbed the horse down with the saddle-cloth, and took a mouthful of water from the bag, at which Grey Cloud looked pertinently.

Within the bag was a little more than a gallon of water, and, observing how the horse regarded it and him, Bony hesitated, regretting he had not brought with him a hat. However, his shirt of stout calico served. Removing it, he first scooped out a hole in the ground, and, pushing the shirt over and into the hole, covering it, he emptied therein half the contents of the bag. It was barely sufficient to moisten Grey Cloud's mouth, and Grey Cloud wanted more, but was refused.

Not now on the partners' tracks, horse and man in strange unsettled country, the scarlet sun threatening to make the day unbearably hot, and a vast bush-fire racing on them, the unthinking might say that Bony did a very foolish thing, and the animal-worshipper pronounce it a noble deed. Bony was neither fool nor sentimentalist. He realized that he was in a most dangerous position, with the odds against him of getting out of it. His single hope of winning through lay in the stamina and speed of Grey Cloud. Of not lesser importance than the "blow", taken whilst precious minutes went by, was the little drop of water given a horse that had not drunk its fill for more than eleven hours at a time of year when Central Australia is at its worst.

Man and horse delayed no longer than fifteen minutes. When again in the saddle, Bony could see on his left hand columns of smoke whirling upward against a background of dark grey. He started then to ride east of north, a slow loping gallop, and, whilst thus riding, numberless kangaroos, with an occasional fox, and, at lesser intervals, a dingo, raced across his path headed east, knowing not, as he did, that most probably the Windee fire spreading north awaited them.

The wind, fortunately, did not increase when the sun rose, changing in colour from crimson to deep yellow, yet in less than thirty minutes the oncoming fury compelled Bony to turn several degrees eastward. Anxiously he sought to peer through the drifting, stinging fog for some fortunate haven of refuge that might be presented in the form of broken clay-pan country or the gibber plain. After another twenty minutes he again was forced to alter his course farther to the east, with the racing fire less than a mile distant.

Bony rode now with but two regrets in his heart. His hope of salvation was vanishing quickly. He regretted that he would fail to take Dash back to Marion Stanton, and he regretted that he had not brought a revolver, for when the end drew very near a revolver bullet would be far more merciful than fire. He thought of his wife, so understanding of his dual nature, and of his sons, especially of Charles, who would so easily slip into his shoes and honourably carry on his father's successes.

He and the horse suddenly swept on a mob of kangaroos halted in frightened perplexity. The grey and the red and the chocolate coloured forms, some with white chests, hardly moved when Grey Cloud dashed through them. They were stupid with fear and dazed by the smoke. A fox on a rabbit-burrow was digging furiously, and not two yards from it a rabbit sat at an entrance-hole calmly cleaning its face as does a cat. The fear of natural enemies was swamped by the greater fear of the advancing universal destroyer.

The minutes passed, three all told, when Bony saw the barrier that had turned back the kangaroos. The smoke ahead rapidly thickened. Then within it he saw first a faint pink glow that deepened with his progress. As from a photographic plate in a developing bath the opaqueness began to break up. There appeared blots of crimson that magically brightened into glittering flames, magically increased in number, isolated flames and chains of flame, flames that remained stationary, and lines of running darting flame which clung low to the earth.

There burned a section of the Windee fire, creeping slowly as a man may walk against the wind. Bony knew it was the beginning of the end, for he was now in a fiery corridor less than a mile in width, a corridor whose walls of fire were rushing on him together.

He was forced northward. For the first time he dug his heels into Grey Cloud's flanks, determined to ride until the horse dropped or became mad and ungovernable with the swelling terror. That would be the exact end for both horse and man.

The reality of life became an horrific phantasmagoria. To them gathered a racing escort. Before, beside, and behind them fully a thousand creatures of the wild fled in their company, seeing in Grey Cloud a leader, a living thing that still moved with purpose. Excepting on their right, where lay the Windee fire, the racing horse and its rider became hedged in by bounding kangaroos, galloping foxes and dogs, bellies to ground, tongues lolling, tails horizontally stiff. Rabbits scurried or crouched, dazed by the flying forms and pounding feet of the larger animals. Snakes writhed and struck in impotent fury: goannas glared down malevolently from the topmost branches of the trees, hate and anger incarnate in reptilian beauty.

Rapidly the temperature rose. The corridor now had shrunk to a quarter of a mile in width. The multitude of terror-impelled animals so increased that many were swept against the trees and left struggling with broken legs. A flock of half a hundred emus—the ostriches of Australia—rushed into the escort, joined it. and pounded along with it.

No longer did Bony attempt to guide his horse. Panic governed Grey Cloud as it governed the wild host about them. The man's eyes burned, great circles of pain bathed in gushing tears. He was aware now of individual incidents that excluded the grand total effect of this inferno undreamed of by Dante. He saw flames, blue and yellow, lick upward about a giant sandalwood tree. He saw another such tree more firmly gripped by fire, and with a flash of his old interest in natural phenomena saw how the fire was forcing the oil of the tree to the leaves and causing it to drop from their points, splashing into little founts of fire on the ground.

He saw a thirty-foot pine-tree split open in a gush of fire with the report of a gun. He saw rabbits running aimlessly, lost from the scattered burrows, not pausing even when they raced into the line of scarlet creeping with a hiss through the grass. He heard their screams between the sharp reports of bursting trees, the thudding of falling branches, the roar of flame, and the upward rush of heated air.

The smoke shut out the sun. The daylight waned, and was replaced by a crimson glare that lit the scene of a vast stampeding mob of animals, in whose centre sped a grey horse bearing a hunched rider. A grand drive by the hunter, Death!

Quite suddenly the passing trees vanished. The ground rose gently. To Bony came the sound of pebbles being struck by hoofs, and then he knew and would have screamed his triumph, and the triumph of all those animals and birds who had followed his leading, had not the smoke so choked him. As through the narrow end of a funnel, horse and man, kangaroos, emus, foxes, and dingoes poured out on the blessed gibber-stone plain where the fire could not pursue.

Chapter Forty-six

Bony—and a Prisoner

THE SUN AT ITS ZENITH laid the shadow of Bony's head about the toes of his boots. It beat down on him and the horse he was leading with a more pitiless heat than that of the roaring, crackling fire from which they had escaped, almost by seconds, early that morning. It heated the smooth gibber-stones to a temperature that would have fired a match held against any one of them.

Slowly horse and man were moving over a vast treeless expanse, a plain so gently undulating that it appeared deceptively flat, yet which gave effect to the mirage that offered delusive glimmering sheets of water in every direction. Here and there low, stunted bushes, greenish blue in colour, defied the scorching sun long after the tussock-grass had died. Tiny lizards, brown, grey, and green fled into the shelter given them by the bushes. An goanna, four feet long, with yellow-marked green body, snakish head and long tapering tail, slid with astonishing rapidity into its hole. Of other ground life there was none. Two thousand feet above the earth three eagles circled as so many manoeuvring aeroplanes. Little larger than pinheads, they swerved and circled with never a beat of a wing, waiting and watching, watching and waiting.

The man's head was covered with a blue silk handkerchief, knotted at the corners. He walked at his normal pace, head bent downward, eyes following the tracks made by two horses. The gelding, which he led, followed with sagging head and lack lustre eyes. It was Grey Cloud, but he appeared to possess the chameleon power of changing colour, for now he was the colour of old brickwork, and his hair was matted and caked hard with the dust a thousand animals had raised in their race for life.

Grey Cloud then could neither gallop, nor canter, nor trot. His big heart was almost broken, and if he could not drink before night fell he would lie down never more to rise. Bony's supply of water would not have filled a pint pannikin, and if he did not reach water by nightfall, then shortly after the dawn of the next day he would lose his reason, gradually discard his boots and his clothes, stagger a little way naked, and fall down on his face never again to rise and walk.

Yet still he possessed hope. He had circled in a great arc, and so had cut the partners' tracks. Then he had followed them across the gibber-littered plain, where for long distances the tracks were invisible to a white man's eyes, where the only indication of the passing of the men he sought was a freshly disturbed stone moved by a horse's hoof. Those tracks must lead him to water eventually, for the horses ridden by Dot and Dash could not exist without a drink at least once in the twenty-four hours.

Bony's head ached. His eyes felt like twin balls of simmering fire. It was far too agonizing to raise his head and look out over the plain that jazzed in the heated air. The silence of the world was that of the King's Chamber in the Pyramid of Cheops, and when Grey Cloud plaintively whinnied the low musical cry startled the half-caste and caused him to stumble. Even then he dared not subject his tortured eyes to the glare of the plain. A whistling breath fanned his neck, and he became aware that Grey Cloud was very close behind him and was suddenly excited.

Then it was he forced himself to look up, and between blinking eyelids he saw a scattered clump of dwarfed scrub-trees a hundred yards ahead, and the forms of two horses tethered each to a tree. Grey Cloud tried to whinny again, but it was an imitation of water being sucked out of a sink. Now he was level with his master, now he pulled on the reins, now he was attempting to run forward; for among the trees lay a wide slab of rock, at whose foot aboriginals had laboriously widened a long crack in the rock that supported the slab.

Whilst partly controlling his horse, Bony untied one end of the long neck-rope brought for the purpose to tether him to a tree, and during the last frantic dash the animal made towards the rock-hole, Bony managed to whip his end of the rope round a tree and secure him.

"So they sent you, Bony?"

Bony in a dazed way heard Dash speaking. He saw Dash as though he looked at him through slightly frosted glass. He tried to speak, but his tongue stuck to the roof of his mouth, and, knowing he would be unable to speak unless aided by water, he struggled with the frantic gelding till he loosed the canvas bag, whereupon he drank some of the contents and spat out the remainder.

"Give horse a drink, Dash," he managed to force through cracked and bleeding lips. "In your hat. Two hatfuls only."

"Righto! But mind how you tread. The place is alive with snakes. Dot was bitten."

"Dot was bitten! Dot was bitten!" The phrase kept repeating, the consonants striking his brain with hammer blows. As through the frosted glass he saw a tree just out of reach of Grey Cloud's hoofs, and, lurching to it, sat down with his back to the trunk; and only by long practice, for he could not see what he was doing, he rolled a cigarette. Slowly he smoked, his head resting against the tree, his eyes closed. Two minutes later Dash gave him a pannikin of cold tea, slightly sweetened. He managed a smile.

"You and Dot are my prisoners," he said.

"I may be, but Dot has escaped you," Dash said with his chin out-thrust. "We got here early this morning. It was just as dawn was breaking. Dot trod on a tiny snake not more than six inches in length. It struck him above his boot, and he died in less than ten minutes. I did all I could, but he went out."

When Bony again spoke his voice was nearly normal, but Dash thought he was delirious.

"I am glad of that, Dash. It was best for him and for me, although it was not a nice death. If the law had taken its course he would have been hanged, and in other circumstances you would be hanged also."

"I think not. Dot would have spoken," Dash rejoined harshly.

"Well, well! We'll talk of it later," Bony murmured. "I'm all in. Bring me a little more tea, and give Grey Cloud another hatful of water. No more." And, when the tea had been brought him: "Don't run away, Dash, my dear man! I'd only have to run after you, and I'm leg-weary."

•   •   •   •   •

Four days later, when the sun was westering, Bony and his prisoner arrived at Carr's Tank Hut. There was no one in occupation. The two men dismounted, and, after tying the horses to the hitching-posts close by, Bony with his head invited Dash to follow him inside.

There Dash proceeded to make a fire, and was aware that Bony went at once to the telephone and gave one long ring, which was the call for the Windee office. The prisoner knew that to get through to Mount Lion police-station, Bony would first have to ring up Windee. Then Bony was speaking.

"Yes, this is Bony. Yes, I have him here with me. Oh no, he has given no trouble. Does there happen to be a car or a truck available?"

A long pause. Then: "Oh, then please send him out for us, will you? You'll come too? Very well. All right. Yes, everything is all right."

Dash watched Bony replace the receiver. Then he heard: "Quick! Off-saddle! We must wash and shave and get into something clean. Miss Stanton is coming to claim my—yes, my dear Dash—you!"

Chapter Forty-seven

The Infallible Bony

ON BEHALF of several politicians and more than one general it has been claimed that each was solely responsible for winning the Great War. All of which argument, of course, is absurd. The generals played their part equally and no more thoroughly than the privates in the trenches and the nurses in the hospitals. If any people did not win the war it was the politicians. Not because of, but in spite of the politicians, was the war won for the Allies.

Father Ryan's part in the war with the Fire Demon was equal to that of every individual man who wielded a bag and a fire-stick. Victory found him no less exhausted than any of them, and it was with a sigh of contentment that he sank into an easy-chair in his study after a hot bath and an excellent dinner provided by Mrs Morris.

In the little priest's world everything was well. Jeff Stanton was giving all his hands a holiday and a dinner the following day which would be talked about for many a year. The good Father had found on his return to Windee homestead that which delighted and astonished and perplexed him, for Sergeant Morris could be induced to make no explanation. Not only had he seen Marion regard her lover with shining eyes, but he had been informed by her that she was to be married to Dash as soon as a special licence could be procured. And lastly, to his infinite relief, Sergeant Morris had informed him that he had "moved on" Mrs Thomas.

Whilst he sat and smoked a cigar, seated in the great armchair facing the window, with the red-shaded standard lamp behind and the excitable moths trying to come into the room and frustrated by the wire gauze screen, Father Ryan felt the luxury of eased limbs as well as that of an easy mind after a period of doubt and worry. On the table lay a few letters and several bundles of newspapers and magazines, but he was far too comfortable, physically and mentally, to deal with them just then. He heard someone, a man, talking with Sergeant Morris in the policeman's office farther along the veranda, but this called for no remark, since the sergeant was often busy late into the night. The voice came to him in a low murmur for quite a little time. Then suddenly it ceased. The office door was closed, steps sounded on the veranda. His study door, which opened on the same veranda, was opened quietly, and as quietly closed, and when he lazily turned his head he beheld Mr Napoleon Bonaparte.

"Good evening, Father Ryan!" Bony said in greeting. "I have called because I am in trouble, mental trouble. Will you render me help?"

On his feet at once, the little priest smiled benevolently, and indicated a chair. He remained standing until Bony had seated himself.

"Try one of my cigars," he said in his clear voice. "They are a fine medicine for trouble."

"Thank you, but cigarettes of my own make are not so strong. Permit me to be busy for a moment." Then, when the cigarette had been lit and Bony had inhaled deeply: "Whilst not of your particular faith, Father, the practice of confession interests me. I want to confess certain matters to you, and hope to receive from you absolution for what I have done. I am a weak man and a vain man, but I wish you to judge if my weakness was a sin or a virtue. You are not too tired?"

"I am never too tired to receive confidences or confessions. Nor am I ever too tired to help a distressed soul. Speak on, my son! Francis Bacon has it that 'the light that a man receiveth by counsel from another is drier and purer than that which cometh from his own understanding and judgment'."

Bony did not speak for a little while, and Father Ryan surveyed him with interest, noting his grey lounge suit, the dark grey tie beneath a spotless collar, and the black shoes. He wondered at Bony's taste in clothes and the absence of striking colours. There seemed nothing odd, therefore, when the half-caste produced a card and, leaning forward, placed it in the little priest's hand. For fully a minute Father Ryan read and re-read what was printed on this card. Then with knit brows he said:

"You surprise me, Mr Bonaparte. I was not aware that you are a detective-inspector of the Queensland Police."

"It is part of my confession, Father. Only the police of Mount Lion are aware of my position other than now yourself. Before I come to the personal question I should like to tell you about an affair that happened many years ago."

"Proceed!" Father Ryan settled himself deeper into his chair.

In concise terms Bony told him the full story of the stolen bride, and because the priest remembered odd details of the affair he found himself becoming deeply interested. Yet he wondered why he was being told all this in Bony's low clear voice and somewhat flamboyant language. His words came without hesitation or fumbling in their selection, and then quite suddenly Father Ryan was jerked upright by the calm statement that:

"The stolen bride is Mrs Thomas, lately a visitor at Mount Lion; and the abductor, Joseph North, is Jeffrey Stanton, of Windee."

"Are you sure?"

"Quite sure," he said, his voice lowered, his eyes for a second resting on the open window behind the priest. "There is nothing I shall say to-night of which I am not sure. The legacy that the affair of the stolen bride left was in the form of a document purporting to be a confession of the man to whom North took the girl for shelter. It was obtained by or for the girl's mother, and was given to Mrs Thomas, as she was and remained legally, and a clever copy came into the possession of her brother, Luke Green, alias Marks.

"For a while we will follow this Luke Marks. As a young man he joined the New South Wales Police, resigned to join the A.I.F., was granted a commission, and was wounded in the head. After the war he became a member of the Licensing Branch of the police and, using the power invested in him, gathered together quite a little sum. A subsidiary source of income was blackmail, and one of his victims was Joseph North, alias Jeffrey Stanton.

"Both these sources of illicit income naturally would have an end. Marks was compelled to run from an investigating commission which, as is the way of commissions, would invariably punish a guilty man of low rank and whitewash as guilty a man of high rank. He determined to get out of the country, and approached Jeffrey Stanton for the sale outright of the forged copy of the document.

"The interview took place in the Windee dining-room, and the conversation was partly overheard by the book-keeper in the office. Roberts did not deliberately eavesdrop. There happened to be a crack in the wooden wall and his desk was close to it. Young Jeff was with him, and when the nature of the visitor's errand became plain to Roberts he invited young Jeff to—er—'listen in'.

"The price asked for the document was fifty thousand pounds, Father Ryan. An astonishing figure, and one which Stanton declined to pay. He offered ten thousand, but this was refused, and Marks left Windee threatening to make public the fact that Joseph North and Jeffrey Stanton were the same man, as well as to publish the document.

"By a coincidence the same morning that all this occurred Miss Stanton lost one of the sapphires from her ring. Young Jeff picked it up from the floor of the office immediately before his attention was attracted by Roberts at the wall crack. He placed it in a pocket of his drill shirt and forgot all about it. It was still in his shirt pocket when he hid himself in the tonneau of Marks's car beneath a rug.

"Unaware of his passenger, Marks drove off on his way to Broken Hill, and when the car reached the junction of that road with the Windee-Mount Lion track, young Jeff made himself known by demanding the document. Marks refused to give it up. He also refused to stop the car, and when he attempted to accelerate young Jeff threw his arms about the fellow's neck, the car swerved into the bush, and finally was stopped by a low ridge of sand.

"The fight in the car was witnessed by two men: Ludbi, the son of Moongalliti, and Dot, the American. It was observed by Ludbi that young Jeff was quickly getting the better of it. Marks at last realized this, and with a final effort forced young Jeff across the back of the front seat and produced a very efficient knife with which to commit murder.

"At that precise moment Dot, unobserved by Ludbi, fired from a distance of approximately one hundred yards. The weapon he used was a .22 Savage owned by Dash. It was not a weapon with which he was familiar. With his own rifle, a .44 Winchester, he was an expert shot, and when he fired at Marks, intending to disable him, he did not allow for the heightened trajectory of a bullet fired by a much stronger explosive than the gun-powder used in his own rifle. The bullet smashed Marks's head, killing him instantaneously.

"Ludbi fled when he saw Dot run towards the car. Dot, who considered his action justifiable, naturally wanted to know what the struggle was all about, and when he saw young Jeff obtain the fatal document and burn it he was minded to concoct a story to fit the tragedy, a plan that young Jeff, still controlled by emotion, agreed to. But it was then that Dash arrived with Dot's .44 Winchester rifle.

"The temporary exchange of these rifles was the result of friendly rivalry between these two men as to the number of skins each procured. On an average shoot Dash obtained the greater number. He claimed his success to be due to his rifle, and induced Dot several times—that day was one of them—to exchange rifles to prove his contention.

"With the plan Dot devised to explain the shooting Dash would have nothing to do. Possessing a higher intelligence than Dot, he could see that there was far more behind the document than what it actually disclosed. He knew also that the Australian police could not be so easily hoodwinked as Dot seemed to think the police of his own country could. Another thing that counted with him, when he had learned all young Jeff knew about Marks, was that, no matter how cleverly the affair was arranged, Jeff Stanton, senior, would be dragged into it, and, most important of all, his daughter too.

"Dash sent young Jeff to their camp to change clothes and put his own bloodstained garments into a sack, then to return to the homestead, keep his mouth shut, and behave normally. Dot and Dash then sat down and between them evolved a perfect method of destroying the body of Marks without leaving a trace. I complimented Dash on the result of the conference, but he told me that to his partner was due the chief point of the method.

"Between them they carried the body some few hundred yards away, and there burned it very efficiently, as also the sack holding young Jeff's stained suit. Afterwards they examined the car and, also with high efficiency, obliterated all traces of the struggle. Knowing that there was no stock in that particular paddock, they went back to their own camp, where Dot admitted that he had taken from the car the treasury notes and securities which Marks had in a brown leather bag, the bag that had held the document of contention as well as others having nothing to do with this case. He was commanded by Dash to burn the money, and Dot nodded agreement. Even so, Dot's love of money overcame his scruples and his loyalty to his partner, and only at the point of their parting on the eve of Dash's return to his former social status did he clear his conscience by confession.

"The day after the killing of Marks they proceeded to the scene of the fire, near where Dot shot three kangaroos, and, after the ashes had been thoroughly sifted for bones and metal, over the spot were burned the carcasses of the kangaroos. Thus was hidden the spot where the body of Marks had been destroyed, for in the same locality these men had burned all the kangaroos they shot so as to leave no breeding-grounds for the blow-fly.

"The metal salvage they dissolved in nitric acid, purloined by Dot from the station workshop. The burned bones were very carefully pounded to dust in a gold-prospector's dolly-pot and scattered to the winds.

"Thus was accomplished what is almost the perfect murder," Bony continued after a pause for rolling and lighting a fresh cigarette. "The body of Marks was destroyed beyond identification by human intelligence. These men were aware that, with no body or identifiable portions of it in existence, the likelihood of their being charged with murder was nil. For my part, as a criminologist, I doff my hat to them, Father Ryan. To them are due my sincerest thanks for the entertainment the problem they set up has afforded me. As a minister of God you may not believe in luck, yet in this case luck played a momentous part. Perhaps I should say more definitely bad luck, for it was very bad luck for everyone concerned that I, Bony, became interested in it."

Chapter Forty-eight

Bony's Choice

THE FACE OF THE PRIEST, absorbed in Bony's narrative, was indicative of astonishment, but at the oral evidence of Bony's stupendous vanity he was compelled to smile in his benignant way.

"Wait one moment before you continue," he said tersely, and set about producing a bottle of wine and two glasses. With these filled he selected another cigar, and, having lit it to his satisfaction, he again seated himself opposite to his visitor, saying: "Well, go on, man. You've made me impatient for the rest."

Bony then related how he had seen the official report of Marks's disappearance and what he discovered in Sergeant Morris's snapshot of the abandoned car. He described his arrival at Windee, his finding the sapphire, the silver disk, and the boot-sprig.

"It was only recently that I cleared up the mystery of the sapphire, which Miss Stanton lost from her ring at the homestead of Windee, and which I found being used by ants to keep their eggs warm," the half-caste went on. "I found a letter from an Adelaide firm of jewellers, addressed to Jeffrey Stanton, junior, and in effect saying that they did not think the sapphire they had set in the ring would be in any way inferior to the accompanying stones, but if the stone which Mr Stanton had found and had lost should be found again they would be pleased to replace their own stone with it at a nominal charge, or to buy it at a fair market price.

"I knew then, of course, that it was young Jeff whom Ludbi had seen fighting with Marks in the car. This fact had eluded me always, because Ludbi died before I could question him, and when, through a North Queensland aboriginal chief, I had Moongalliti—er, well, hypnotized, I found that Ludbi had not told his father the name of this man. I suspected Roberts on account of events that occurred, notably Roberts warning Miss Stanton, who warned Dot and Dash, that the police were there to arrest them, and afterwards prompting the men to put up a strike in order that no driver should be found to man a pursuing car. I was mystified by Moongalliti's stupidity when asked to track about Marks's car, and the reason why he threatened the pointing-bone to any of his tribe who talked about what Ludbi had seen. Whilst Ludbi had not seen Dot, Dot had seen him and saw the danger in that quarter. It was Roberts who bribed Moongalliti to silence with tobacco and food. This I discovered through Illawalli. When I found that someone had ridden a horse about the scene of the crime I thought it was Roberts, but it was young Jeff. And I thought Roberts was in love with Marion Stanton. As a matter of fact, he was merely loyal to the Stanton family."

"Maybe," interjected Father Ryan, adding dryly: "Nevertheless, Roberts proposed to Marion a year ago."

"Ah, then love did prompt loyalty, Father. Anyway, that aspect was cleared up. The other mystery that held my attention was the little silver disk I found in the fork of a tree. I could not understand for what purpose it had been made until I received Marks's dossier from Sydney, which informed me that when on active service he had received a head wound. Knowing—who does not?—the war services of the great Sir Alfred Worthington, who probably was concerned in all the trepanning operations—not too many—required by the Australians in France, I sent him the disk, believing it possible to have come from the head of Marks. I gave Sir Alfred the date of Captain Green's, alias Marks's, head wound.

"Sir Alfred Worthington replied in a letter that according to his war diary he inserted a plate like the one submitted in the skull of Captain Green the day after he received the wound. He stated further that, in his opinion, it was most unlikely it would fall accidentally from Captain Green's head, and that without it fixed thereto he would at the least suffer from excruciating headaches.

"The agreement of name and date settled that matter for me. In that small disk, Father, I had proof that Marks no longer lived. The otherwise perfect murder was marred by one flaw. One oversight was committed by the killer, yet no one could blame either Dot or Dash for not knowing that Sir Alfred Worthington had carried out a trepanning operation on Green. The clue was given by Dot when he fired at Marks with Dash's rifle, for the bullet from the high-powered cartridge smashed the man's head and carried away the plate in it. It was just that little trick of Fate which ruined a perfect crime."

"Maybe the clue which actually spoiled it—may I be forgiven for saying so?—was not the silver disk, but Ludbi's sign revealed to you by Morris's photo," objected the little man with twinkling eyes.

Bony laughed at the gentle reproof of his vanity. Then he went on to explain how he had learned of the stolen bride case, and how he had despoiled Mrs Thomas of the potent paper she held—an incident over which the priest chuckled heartily. Bony had doubts of the validity of this document, obtained by intimidating a sick man, but it was in safe hands now, and Mrs Thomas could do nothing without it. He went on to describe his adventures when pursuing Dash, and the final revelation of Dot's death by snake-bite.

"It seemed, by what Dash was persuaded to tell me," he said, "that when Dot learned from Miss Stanton that Sergeant Morris was at Windee to arrest them, he wanted to take the whole thing on his own shoulders and face it out by flat denial. Dash would not consent, because I was suspect, as Ned Swallow remembered seeing me in Queensland, and, too, because of the danger of Jeff Stanton, junior, being brought in. Although of opposite temperaments, in spite of wide diversity of education and social upbringing, these two men were cemented by a bond of friendship exceedingly rare and, therefore, a beautiful thing.

"Even now I am inclined to the belief that, had Dot prevailed on his companion to allow him to face it out alone, no judge or jury would have convicted him—especially in these days, when wholly circumstantial evidence is discredited. We could have charged Dot with theft of Marks's money, which he would have explained by saying he picked it up while hunting kangaroos where, obviously, Marks had thrown it down or lost it during his search for the car. For that he might have received one year's imprisonment, possibly three. Recent Australian criminal history records a case where a murderer has got off with eighteen months' imprisonment. It is possible to commit a crime against humanity with impunity, but any crime against capital is invariably dealt with severely."

Bony suddenly ceased speaking. After waiting a few moments for him to go on, Father Ryan said gently:

"Although you have interested me exceedingly, you have not explained why Dash is not arrested as an accomplice, and young Jeff with him. Behind this question, I fancy, lies your trouble. My son, have no fear of an ould priest wid the love of God in his heart."

For the first time that evening Father Ryan had fallen into the brogue of his country. He saw the effect his words had in the expression of Bony's blue eyes, he saw the look of hurt perplexity, and at once his great heart went out in sympathy.

So Bony slowly told of his meetings with Marion Stanton and of the conversation between them in Marion's sitting-room. He explained his upbringing, and attempted to explain the duality of race constantly in turmoil within his soul.

"I do not believe I suffer from an inferiority complex," he said, with his head bent to the task of cigarette-making. "I am a proud man, and take pride in my accomplishments and my civilized state. I loathe the dirty, the bestial, the ugly things of human life, and adore the beautiful. In the art gallery in Sydney there is a painting of a dead knight who lies on a bier in full armour, and beside the bier is a great dog looking up at its dead master. Every time I am in Sydney I spend two hours looking at that picture and marvelling at the expression on the dog's face and the calm majesty of the mask laid on the dead man.

"In Miss Stanton I found beauty of a different order which affected me as does that picture. She represents my ideal of womanly beauty. Sex has nothing to do with my ideal. I do not love Miss Stanton as I love my wife. Not knowing that she and Dash were in love, I ordered the arrest of Dash, who I knew was implicated, in the hope of bringing the whole truth to light. Miss Stanton was surrounded by her relatives and her friends, yet it was to me she turned. Father, I am not a callow youth, I am not a fatuous man seeking a woman's favours, but when she made her appeal I could not—simply, I could not refuse.

"I suspected strongly that the killing of Marks was not done with forethought and malice. I knew he was that most loathsome of all creatures, a blackmailer. And I saw in the moment of her appeal that inevitably she would suffer by the revelation I was there to make and was being paid to make by the State. Even my sympathies were with Joseph North in the affair of the stolen bride, which was the precursor of Marks's death and the tangle which I have unravelled.

"There remain now two courses, one of which I must adopt. I can render my report wholly based on lies which will place the blame of Marks's death on the shoulders of Dot, and attribute to him as motive the passion to gain money, thereby blackening his character as he would have done himself had he lived and had Dash permitted him. Or I can return to Sydney and admit failure to find evidence of murder. I have not told Morris everything, and what I have told him is consistent with Dot's concealing Marks's money, which is proved, and is all that can be proved. Dash need not be implicated, and Dot's death would finalize the case.

"One moment!" he said hastily, when Father Ryan was about to speak. "I have been a member of the Queensland Police for sixteen years, and I have not once failed to complete a case successfully. I am a man without a failure against him. They have given me cases on which other men have failed. They now send me out on a case believing without a shadow of doubt that I shall bring to justice the criminal.

"My superiors believe me to be infallible. I know I am infallible. Arrived here, I found myself faced by a crime carried out by clever men, having at their disposal plenty of time. It was, I say, almost the perfect murder, and I did not start my investigations until two months had elapsed and all traces about the scene of it had been wiped out by wind and sand.

"And I won, Father—I won the greatest case that any detective ever had given him. Now I can only create a fabrication of lies, calumniate a dead man who was lovable and honourable, or else admit that I, the infallible Bony, have at last met my Waterloo.

"You see, Father, do you not, the quandary I am in? You see the cup that is offered me? Can I set it aside and, now that a snake has placed not beyond reach of human justice, can I raise my structure of lies and save my reputation?"

Father Ryan beheld Bony's appealing expression with a sad heart. The look in the blue eyes of the man, torn between vanity and honour, weighed him down with the knowledge that here was no ordinary problem. Without a word he rose and brought a volume from one of his shelves, and in a moment had found a page and a paragraph he needed. Softly yet clearly he read:

"'Methuselah lived nine hundred, sixty and nine years and begat sons and daughters—and what then? *And then he died.'* That is what Daniel Defoe wrote on the occasion of the death of the Duke of Marlborough. Again of him Defoe wrote this, Bony: 'All his victories, all his glories, his great projected schemes of war, his uninterrupted series of conquests, which are called his, as if he alone had fought and conquered by his arm what so many men obtained for him with their blood—all is ended, where other men, and, indeed, where all men ended: *he is dead!*

"It appears, Bony, that you are confronted with the choice of telling lies about another man or telling lies about yourself. Without my advice I know precisely which choice you will make. Remembering all the circumstances, knowing that the innocent will suffer more than will the guilty, knowing that the killing of Marks was legally justifiable to prevent his committing murder, I must concur in your choice."

"Father Ryan, it will be a hard path to tread," pleaded Bony.

"A lesser man than you, Bony, could not tread it."

"It *is* hard. Can you not think of a third way?"

"There are only the two, my son. Let us again refer to Defoe, who in effect so aptly says: 'Men remarkable for all the virtues and all the vices, famous men and infamous men, they are but mortal clay.' Death is the end of them, although I know it is not the end of their souls. What is a man's reputation? Merely a manifestation of vanity. Pride is vanity. Vanity is the spur of success. Next to love the greatest human virtue is— sacrifice. But it takes a big man to make a big sacrifice—the bigger the sacrifice, the bigger the man. I believe you are a big man, my son."

The little priest held out his hands and, rising, Bony took them with tears in his eyes.

"I will try to be big, Father," he said with a tremor in his voice.

"You *are* big. Also you have won your case, and a little old foolish priest in Mount Lion knows you won it."

Bony sighed. Father Ryan smiled and gripped his hands the more tightly.

EPILOGUE

Colonel Spender, Chief Commissioner of the Queensland Police, looked up at the entrance of his secretary.

"Detective-Sergeant Wills has reported from Toowoomba, sir. He states that the money and securities stolen from the bank have been recovered in the cashier's garden, and the cashier arrested."

"Good! It is about time that matter was finalized," growled Colonel Spender. The secretary then made a further announcement:

"Ex-Detective-Inspector Napoleon Bonaparte has called to see you sir."

Very deliberately Colonel Spender laid down his pen, his face becoming ominously red.

"I will see him—at once," he snapped.

When Bony entered, the police chief was writing rapidly, and when Bony stood before his desk, he continued to write.

"You appear, sir, to be very busy this morning," Bony murmured. "Shall I call again?"

The pen scratched horribly. Ink spattered over the document. The pen was flung down on the desk. A fist crashed after it.

"What the devil do you want?" Colonel Spender roared, lifting up his well-nourished body and with it the chair. The chair banged on the floor. Colonel Spender glared.

"I have to apologize for not reporting sooner," Bony explained gently. "I was detained."

"Well, as you like New South Wales, you had better get back there quick. There is nothing for you to do here."

"I was not detained in New South Wales, but in Toowoomba, which, as you know, is in Queensland. You see, sir, as Toowoomba lay in my way, I thought it as well to stay there a day or two and clear up the little difficulty of that bank robbery."

"But Sergeant Wills——"

"An excellent man, sir," Bony cut in; "methodical and sure. However, he lacks imagination. His methods plus my imagination achieved results. I took over the case two days ago—last Wednesday. I presume that my reinstatement will date from Wednesday morning, sir?"

Bony was smiling. His blue eyes beamed benevolently on the red-faced colonel. Again Colonel Spender bumped his chair. He tried to snort, but failed. He could only glare.

"The New South Wales Commissioner will doubtless report to you my failure in the Far West case," Bony went on. "Paradoxically, I succeeded, yet failed. I have admitted failure in Sydney. I shall admit failure to my colleagues in Queensland."

"Fail! You fail!" gasped the astounded chief.

"Yes, Mr Chief Commissioner, I have failed for the first time in my career."

"Damn you! I don't believe you, Bony."

"Officially, sir, that is my report."

"And unofficially?"

"Sir, we have known each other for many years," Bony said gravely. "Will you permit us now to meet as private individuals? I have lost or shall lose the respect of my colleagues, but I want badly to retain yours. I owe it to you and to myself."

"I knew there was something behind your insubordination," Colonel Spender said more calmly. "Lock the cursed door and tell me the yarn."

Bony told "the yarn". He told Colonel Spender what he had told Father Ryan. He explained that the death of Marks was not really murder, but justifiable homicide. He described how he had found Dot, the American, dead of snake-bite, and how he found he could not drag out from the past all that was best left buried there because a white woman had been kind to him.

And when he ceased there sat in the Chief Commissioner's chair a very kindly looking white-haired, white-moustached old gentleman who at that moment felt humbled by the gentle soul of the half-caste within whom warred the impulses and complexities of two races.

"You see how it is," Bony concluded. "This case turned out to be the perfect murder. It would have remained unsolved had it not been for a wholly extraneous incident in the victim's past—that head wound received in the war which necessitated a trepanning operation. Dot and Dash in combination were very clever men, clever because they were calm, calm because their consciences were clear. Marks was a bad man, and the world certainly is no poorer by his exit."

"And you will suffer the stigma of failure to protect that girl's happiness?"

Bony inclined his head.

"She is a great woman, sir. I—I am only Bony, after all."

Colonel Spender cleared his throat violently. Once more he was Chief Commissioner of the Queensland Police.

"As from last Wednesday you are reinstated without loss of rank or privileges," he said. "As a subordinate you are a damned nuisance, yet I can't do without you. Go up to Longreach and find the murderer of that station-hand. And don't come back here and admit failure because of a pair of eyes."

"Very good, sir," consented Bony, smiling in his old frank way. "I shall take Marie, my wife, and little Ed. and Bob, who is so restless, and we'll go there on a walkabout. My wife's eyes are grey. I shall see no others. Good-bye, sir!"

The door closed.

"Well, I'm—well, I'm——" Colonel Spender snorted. He blinked his eyes and banged the desk bell for his secretary. "Thank God, he's a policeman and not a scoundrel!"

CPSIA information can be obtained
at www.ICGtesting.com
Printed in the USA
BVHW03s0708160218
508099BV00003B/170/P